TRACKS ALONG THE CLEAR FORK: STORIES FROM SHACKELFORD AND THROCKMORTON COUNTIES

Edited by
Lawrence Clayton
Joan Halford Farmer

TEXAS A&M UNIVERSITY PRESS • COLLEGE STATION

Tracks along the Clear Fork
Stories from Shackelford and Throckmorton Counties
Edited by Lawrence Clayton and Joan Halford Farmer
Texas A&M University Press
College Station

Copyright © 2012 by Texas A&M University Press
Manufactured in the United States of America
All rights reserved
First Texas A&M University Press edition
Previously published in 2000
by McWhiney Foundation Press, Abilene, Texas
This paper meets the requirements
of ANSI/NISO Z39.48ñ1992 (Permanence of Paper).
Binding materials have been chosen for durability.

Library of Congress Cataloging-in-Publication Data

Tracks along the Clear Fork : stories from Shackelford and Throckmorton
counties / edited by Lawrence Clayton and Joan Halford Farmer.
— 1st Texas A&M University Press ed.
p. cm.
Originally published: Abilene, Tex. : McWhiney Foundation Press,
McMurry University, 2000.
Includes bibliographical references and index.
ISBN 978-1-60344-785-0 (cloth : alk. paper) —
ISBN 1-60344-785-7 (cloth : alk. paper) —
ISBN 978-1-60344-784-3 (pbk. : alk. paper) —
ISBN 1-60344-784-9 (pbk. : alk. paper) —
ISBN 978-1-60344-788-1 (e-book) —
ISBN 1-60344-788-1 (e-book)
1. Shackelford County (Tex.)—History.
2. Throckmorton County (Tex.)—History.
I. Clayton, Lawrence, 1938–2000. II. Farmer, Joan.
F392.S46T73 2012
976.4'734—dc23
2012003944

TABLE OF CONTENTS

PREFACE v

ACKNOWLEDGMENTS viii

INTRODUCTION ix

FORT GRIFFIN
by Carl C. Rister 1

THE COMANCHE RESERVATION IN TEXAS
by Rupert N. Richardson 17

CAMP COOPER AND FORT GRIFFIN, TEXAS
by Col. M. L. Crimmins 48

LEE'S "TEXAS HOME"
by Carl C. Rister 67

NOTES TAKEN WITH MARCY LOCATING THE TEXAS INDIAN RESERVATIONS
by W. B. Parker 84

LIFE IN THE TOWN OF FORT GRIFFIN
by Ben O. Grant 106

EXPLORERS AND EARLY SETTLERS OF SHACKELFORD COUNTY
by Ben O. Grant 125

THE FRONTIER ADVENTURES OF JOHN CHADBOURNE IRWIN
by J.R. Webb 156

ON THE CATTLE TRAIL AND BUFFALO RANGE
by Joe S. McCombs
Contributed by Ben O. Grant and J. R. Webb 172

FORTING UP ON THE TEXAS FRONTIER DURING THE CIVIL WAR
by Marilynne Howsley 185

SANDSTONE SENTINELS
by Joan Farmer 195

JOHN CALVIN LEDBETTER/S. W. WESLEY:
ONE INDIAN CAPTIVITY NARRATIVE OR TWO?
by Lawrence Clayton and Morris Ledbetter 214

THE FRONTIER LIFE OF PHIN W. REYNOLDS
by J.R. Webb 226

LETTER TO HARRY E. CRAIN FROM W.D. REYNOLDS 263

AN ACCOUNT OF THE DEATH OF GLENN REYNOLDS
by Jess G. Hayes 268

THE HUNT FOR THE FUGITIVES AND
RECOVERY OF THE GOLD WATCH AND PISTOL
by Bob Green 292

LETTERS RELATED TO REYNOLDS' WATCH AND PISTOL 294

CONTEMPORARY BIOGRAPHIES OF PRINCIPAL FIGURES
Sec. I: from *Historical and Biographical Records* 300

GEORGE T. REYNOLDS 300

W. D. REYNOLDS 312

J.B. MATTHEWS 315

Sec. II: from *Prose and Poetry of The Livestock Industry* 319

WILLIAM D. REYNOLDS 319

GEORGE T. REYNOLDS 330

A PARTING WORD 350

FURTHER READING 350

PREFACE

The genesis of this book was a request in 1993 by Cliff Teinert to have Lawrence Clayton write a thin volume to highlight the centennial celebration of the founding of the Long X Ranch at Kent, Texas. The purpose was to honor the contribution of the Reynolds brothers, especially George and W. D., to the cattle business and ranching. Along the way other elements were added to the proposed volume. Completion of that volume, which came to include some parts of the present volume, was delayed for a number of reasons, and just before Christmas of 1998, Teinert approached the current editors to produce a book with a different focus while still keeping the Reynolds brothers an important part of the volume. The editors feel we have honored that charge, particularly with the information dealing with Phin, Glenn, George, and W. D. Reynolds and J. B. Matthews. The funding was provided by Prairieland' Foundation of Albany, Texas.

This volume contains details of people and events from the previous century from along the Clear Fork of the Brazos River in what are today northern Shackelford and southern Throckmorton counties of Texas. The authorship of the materials is diverse and the contents varied. The principal focus is the military fort and the town called Griffin as well as the pre-Civil War military post named Camp Cooper, also located on the Clear Fork. Two of the writers are Carl Coke Rister and Rupert N. Richardson, two of Texas's premier historians from an earlier day. In addition, Richardson edited the account of W. B. Parker, who accompanied Capt. R. B. Marcy through the area. Col. M. L. Crimmins left an important legacy in his research as well.

A second focus centers on the adventures of civilians who came to the area to establish their lives. John Chadbourne Irwin, Joe S. McCombs, Johnny Ledbetter, and others are the center of stories that reveal the life of the people in the region. Authorship of these owes much to J. R. Webb, Ben O. Grant, Marilynne Howsley, Joan Farmer, Morris Ledbetter, and Lawrence Clayton, all individuals with intense interest in the region.

A collection of pieces intended to stand alone has some overlap in subject matter. We have made no effort to eliminate these repetitious passages. Touching a familiar subject more than once will, we hope, be like hearing a familiar chord in a piece of music. We have added Editor's Notes where appropriate to explain varied interpretations by the different writers.

The purpose of the editors has been to select materials both interesting and informative. When possible, we chose stories used to make up segments of the *Fort Griffin Fandangle*, Albany's remarkable effort to dramatize the story of the region that this book helps interpret. All of the material has not been readily available to readers in a long time, and we are pleased to present it to a new generation of readers.

Lawrence Clayton
Joan Halford Farmer

This new Texas A&M University Press
edition of *Tracks along the Clear Fork*
is dedicated to the people of Albany, Fort Griffin,
and the Clear Fork Country.

CLIFF TEINERT
January 2012

ACKNOWLEDGEMENTS

The editors want to thank Cliff and Lynne Teinert for making the volume possible. Lynne's mother, Marilynne Howsley, wrote one of the chapters. We are especially grateful to Bob Green for his perceptive introduction to the volume. Few if any have his grasp of the history of the area under examination as well as what we hope to accomplish with this and any subsequent volumes.

We also want to thank Dr. B. W. Aston, long-time editor of the *West Texas Historical Association Year Book*, and Dr. Paul Carlson, the current editor, for permission to reprint articles from the Year Books. We thank the University of Oklahoma Press for permission to reprint passages from Rister's *Robert E. Lee in Texas*. We appreciate the encouragement of Sam Webb to use the materials of J. R. Webb.

Further thanks go to the staff of the Old Jail Art Center, especially Diana Wilfong, for assistance from the Robert Nail Archives, especially for photographs for the book.

The assistance of Peggi Gooch in data entry and layout is here acknowledged, as is the design work of Dr. Randy Armstrong and editorial assistance by Winifred Waller. The English IV AP class of Albany High School provided assistance in proofreading:

Camille Jones	Justin Lenamon
Becky Loeschen	Chris McCarthy
Shawn McCauley	Tim Miler
Jessica Morrow	Michael Prince
Scott Riley	Erin Woods

INTRODUCTION

We who have grown up in the Albany area have long wished to see a published work that to our eyes, at least, presents an accurate, true, and reliable account of the exploits of some of our more notable pioneers while living on our West Texas frontier. There have been several new books published recently concerning Fort Griffin and its environs. These new books were written by outsiders with little background of our area who presented the big historical picture of frontier days according to the more revisionist interpretation of their research. Their modern accounts of our frontier are filled with dates, facts, and figures but do little to transfer to a reader the nitty-gritty feel of how life really was as experienced by the individuals who were actually coping with it on the frontier.

For many years we have enjoyed Sallie Reynolds Matthews' book *Interwoven*, now considered to be a classic. *Interwoven* tells of her life growing up on the West Texas frontier. It is a valuable account, but its scope is somewhat narrowed down to her family's frontier experiences. Being viewed through her gentle eyes perhaps softened her interpretations of the rougher edges of frontier life.

We have also been fortunate in having the published works of regional writers like Rupert Richardson, Ben Grant, and Carl Coke Rister, all trained historians. In the past they have astutely chronicled the main events of our frontier. Some of their writings are included in this work, a work that makes it possible for us to gain a better insight into the actual, often roisterous day-to-day life that actually took place here in the frontier days. With this new book we can now read the accounts of such pioneer figures as John Chadbourne Irwin, Joe McCombs, the Reynolds brothers, and J.R. Matthews. Some of their exploits have been used by fiction writers of the American West in the plots of their novels, movies, and TV miniseries. For us who enjoy having the opportunity to read about the real thing, not hyped make-believe, we must thank such Albany lay people as J.R. Webb, Bob Nail and Joan Farmer. They were the ones who early on recognized the value of the personal reminiscences of the old pioneer settlers, and strove mightily to get so many of their stories written down while they were still alive. Even as important, they zealously protected and preserved these accounts for posterity.

Now for the first time we have many of these accounts gathered together in one book, compiled under the careful, critical eye of Hardin-Simmons University dean and historical writer Dr. Lawrence Clayton, and the loving, caring eye of the area's archivist, Joan Farmer, long a keeper of Albany's historical flame. The two of them have made a good team in selecting and compiling these primary sources of our local history.

Mark Twain was supposed to have said, "History is just a bunch of lies that have been agreed on." But even old cynical Mark Twain, if he could read these stories, would have to admit that there is embodied in these personal essays the clear, unvarnished ring of truth. In this book the reader will discover more than dates or documented facts, but voices that once again tell us what it was really like to have lived in those rough and tumble days on our Texas frontier.

Bob Green

FORT GRIFFIN

BY CARL C. RISTER

Dr. Rister presents one of the earliest efforts to tell the story of the post-Civil War fort on the Clear Fork. He later expanded this view in Fort Griffin on the Texas Frontier.

When the United States acquired Texas in 1845, the people of the new state thought that they could return to their homes in peace and take up their occupations without any fear of hostile invasions again being directed against them such as those formerly sent from across the Rio Grande; but little did they count on the power of the wild savage races on their western frontier. For these Indians to feel that they were bound by treaty agreements was exceedingly difficult. They had been accustomed to the free, open life of the plains and naturally regarded the efforts of settlers to restrict their freedom on their former hunting grounds with jealousy and suspicion. More and more they found themselves circumscribed in their hunting grounds; and faced with an ever narrowing circle of advancing people from Kansas and the Platte on the north, and from Texas on the south, a war of extinction faced them.[1] Thus the period of depredations and border forays which followed was largely the consequence of this state of affairs.[2]

Since it was recognized by the federal government that this would lead to a prolonged struggle, a line of defense was thrown out in advance of the frontier to protect the exposed settlements in the western part of the state. This chain began with Eagle Pass on the Rio Grande, running northward to Preston on the Red River. The line of defense was composed of the following forts: Duncan, Clark, Territt, McKavett, Chadbourne, Phantom Hill or "Post on the Clear Fork of the Brazos,"[3] and the supply post at Preston.[i]

During the period of the Civil War the frontier posts were abandoned by the federal government and the frontier was occupied by state troops; but with the close of the war in 1865, it was necessary for the state forces to abandon the frontier, leaving the frontier settlers to the mercy of the marauding Indians.

When the dawn of peace came following the close of the Civil War, the frontier presented a pitiable spectacle. Homes were in ashes; horses and cattle were gone; fields were filled with weeds and grass; fences were down; and along the entire border were evidences of desolation. The frontier had been pushed in for a distance of 150 to 200 miles, and where civilization once held sway, now wild beasts and savages roamed at will.[4] The "Waco Register" of April 21, 1866, carried an account of a visit made to the frontier by some of its citizens in the following words: "The Indians seemed to swarm all through the country—mostly Comanches. Not more than one fifth of the old ranches are occupied. The inhabitants remaining, for the most part, have run together and forted up for self preservation.[5] A great many people have left and others are leaving, and the whole country seems to be in a desperate condition indeed." One of these observers gave it as his opinion that one reason why the Indians were so numerous on the frontier was that the buffalo range extended sixty miles east of Camp Cooper and Phantom Hill, and that the Indians naturally followed their game.[6]

The white people taking up the unoccupied lands on

the frontier at this time were dismayed to find that the federal government was slow in sending adequate forces to the frontier after the Civil War. Here was to be found a far-flung frontier of 1300 miles, open to depredations of the Indians and white outlaws. The border people were helpless to prevent the constant incursions directed against them.⁷ Unaccustomed as they were to border warfare and savage cunning, their half-hearted attempts to defend themselves were pitifully futile. Usually when news spread through the country that the savages were pillaging, before a posse could be organized to follow them up, the Indians would be well out of reach of any such punitive expedition. The blow from the marauders would fall suddenly, and without a moment's loss of time, the stolen stock would be hastily driven from the country. The quickness with which this was done was due to the fact that the Indians were usually mounted on swift, agile ponies, and to the additional fact that they knew every hill, valley, and plain intervening between their camping grounds and the settlements. Knowing the character of the country over which they had to drive their stolen stock gave them every advantage in out-distancing their pursuers. Under these conditions even the soldiers, trained in border warfare, were no match for the savages when it came to pitting their skill against that of the latter. Much less then could the settlers be expected to protect themselves against such raids.

With the increased depredations from the Indians it became necessary that the old frontier posts be occupied and new ones built. This policy was soon put into operation with the result that there was a frontier line of defense beginning with Ft. Richardson on the north, and passing through Fort Griffin; the picket posts of Belknap, Phantom Hill, and Chadbourne; Fort Concho; Fort McKavett; then almost to the west of Fort McKavett, in the "Big Bend" country, were the four posts of Stockton, Davis, Quitman, and Bliss. Then from Fort McKavett was another line composed of Forts Clark, Duncan, McIntosh, and Brown, which followed the Rio Grande.

It was the line of posts from Fort Richardson to the Rio Grande, including the four posts of the "Big Bend" District, which played the more important role in the defense against the hostile Indians. Of these posts none was more important than Fort Griffin. This post was established on the afternoon of July 31, 1867, by Brevet Colonel Sturgis, Lieutenant Colonel of the Sixth United States Cavalry. The forces under his command consisted of four companies of the Sixth Cavalry, which formerly had been stationed at Fort Belknap. The latter place was found to be unsuited for a military post, due to the fact that the water was insufficient for the use of the garrison stationed there.[8]

When the military authorities decided upon the giving up of Fort Belknap, a surveying board was sent out to locate a site for a new post. After carefully going over the surrounding country, a site was finally located on the Clear Fork of the Brazos River, thirty-seven miles above Fort Belknap. The post was first designated Camp Wilson in honor of Lieutenant Wilson, son of a United States Senator from Massachusetts. The name was subsequently changed to Fort Griffin by the officer commanding the post in honor of General Griffin, a commander of the department after the Civil War.

It was proposed to construct the permanent buildings of stone, and every preparation to that end was made. Steam saw mills, window sashes, door frames, tools, etc., were provided for and a number of mechanics were sent out by Brevet Colonel J. B. C. Lee, Depot Quartermaster at San Antonio, Texas. As it was supposed to take years to complete the permanent structures, temporary quarters for the officers and men were erected.⁹ Small wooden houses were built for the privates and non-commissioned officers, and a line of officers' quarters were put up, consisting of one room and kitchen each. Two buildings of two rooms and a hall each were hauled in from deserted ranches nearby, one of which was to be used for commissary quarters and the other for a hospital. A sufficient number of huts could not be erected at this time with the result that six men were compelled to sleep in one of these huts, fourteen by eight feet, and five feet and ten inches to the roof.¹⁰

During the early period there were no stables built with the result that the horses suffered severely,¹¹ many of them dying from pneumonia. The hospital, commissary, and Quartermaster's storeroom were originally made of logs; but additions made from time to time, as the necessary lumber could be secured from the sawmills, partially satisfied these needs. Much of the lumber, however, was sawed from the timber in the vicinity and put up before it had dried out sufficiently with the result that the winter winds and the summer showers made it uncomfortable for the men while inside the huts. When the lumber began to dry out much it would warp, leaving great cracks in the buildings. Due to the fact that the frontier moved on westward, the more permanent buildings were never erected; however, inexpensive buildings were added from time to time, as was the case in the history of a majority of the posts, when there was an imperative need for such additions.

The experiences of the men stationed at this post were monotonous enough to them, but to those who read of their activities, colorful and romantic. Arduous were the duties of these frontier soldiers. Patrols were constantly out on the frontier, escorting government mails, surveying parties, cattle drivers, and following up and punishing bands of depredating Indians. The arduous nature of many of these expeditions is typified in the following order issued by the post commander at Fort Griffin on June 19, 1873: "First Lieutenant U. Kelly, Tenth United States Cavalry (Negro troops) with two non-commissioned officers and ten privates, will leave the post at once and proceed to Matthews' ranch, there take the trail of a party of Indians supposed to have stolen stock from the latter place, and endeavor to overtake and punish them. He will not merely follow on until it is lost, but will continue on until every effort and stratagem is exhausted, sparing neither men nor horses."[12]

It is needless to say that the majority of these expeditions sent out did not succeed in overtaking the savages, but some of them did with the result that the Indians were punished. Even where success was met with in such enterprises, the post commanders were meager in their details of them, as is illustrated by the following account: " A party was sent out from Fort Griffin, Texas, commanded by Captain A. R. Chaffer, Sixth Cavalry, composed of troops from companies F and I, Sixth Cavalry, consisting of four officers and sixty-two enlisted men, and seven Indians. Departed March 5, 1868; returned March 9, 1868. Passed through Haskell and Jones counties. Traveled a distance of 130 miles to operate against the Comanche Indians. Indians killed, seven; property captured, two horses, two ponies, one mule, with bows and arrows, and all the saddle equipment of the party; enlisted men wounded, three; Privates Ryan, Company F, Hoffman, Company I, and Butler, Company I, Sixth Cavalry, were wounded."[13] Another account of this same engagement is as follows: "Company F, Sixth United States Cavalry, left Fort Griffin, Texas, March 4, 1868, and marched to Ledbetter's ranch, from thence (marching in the night) to Deadman's Creek, and camped on the night of March 5th or March 6th at Paint Creek. Attacked a camp of Comanche Indians and

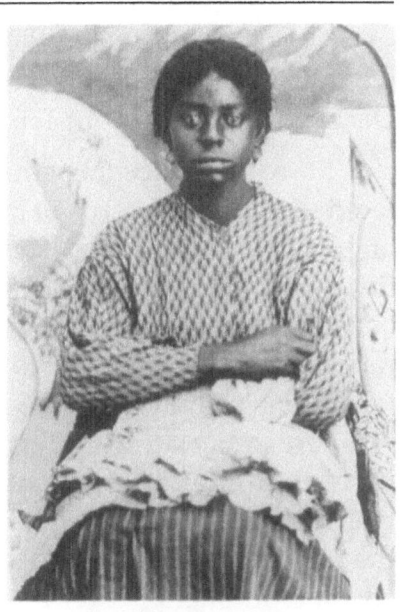

Russell Young Gilbert, first government scout out of Fort Griffin. (James Gilbert Collection)

Mahalia Cook, laundress at Fort Griffin.

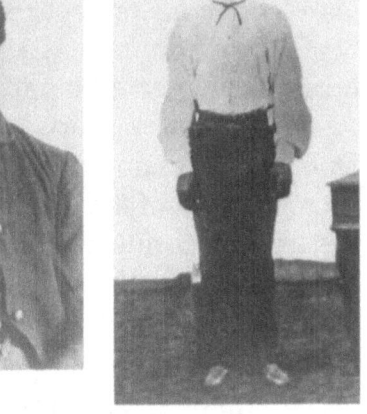

Buffalo Soldier at Fort Griffin. (Cotton Collection)

Buffalo Soldiers at Fort Griffin.

succeeded in killing seven. Privates Hoffman and Butler wounded. Returned to Fort Griffin on the 9th of March, 1868. Distance marched about 150 miles."[14]

More than once the work of pursuing troops was interfered with by vast herds of buffaloes. As an instance of this on July 8, 1870, a scouting party was sent out from Fort Griffin westward in pursuit of Indians, (consisting of thirty-seven enlisted men and ten Tonkaway Indian scouts). The marauders were overtaken and a sharp encounter followed in which one Indian was killed and a captured herd of cattle was turned back toward the range from which it was being driven. In the melee the Indians managed to escape and were again followed, but the trail was finally lost because of the fact that herds of buffaloes passed between the pursued and the pursuers. After having traveled a distance of 324 miles, the scouting party returned to Fort Griffin on July 22, 1870.[15]

One engagement in which a band of Comanches was severely punished is told of in the following brief account: "11th of February, 1874—Lieutenant Colonel Buell and command reported on last return as absent operating against hostile Indians, rejoined post having marched about 220 miles, and defeated a party of hostile Indians encountered on the fifth of February, 1874, at a point in the valley of the Double Mountain Fork of the Brazos River, about twenty-six miles west of the Double Mountains, killing eleven Indians and capturing twenty-six head of stock.[16] Aside from those killed in this engagement, a large number were wounded and taken from the field by their brother warriors.

Many of the depredations in the vicinity of Fort Griffin were committed by white outlaws and not by Indians. As an instance of the culpability of these white desperadoes the following is a type: "May 5, 1873, 1st Lieutenant R. H. Pratt,

Tenth Cavalry, with detachment from Company D, Tenth Cavalry and three Tonkaway scouts, scouted through Jones and Throckmorton counties in an effort to find the Indians who had stolen horses from Kennedy's ranch, eighteen miles distant, but upon arrival, Kennedy informed Colonel Buell that the thieves were white men and not Indians as first supposed."[17] He stated that he had followed the trail for five or six miles and had exchanged shots with them at long range. The command arrived on the ground eighteen hours after the thieves had left and in the meantime it rained and obliterated the trail, so the command returned to the post on April 18. On the next day, however, another expedition was sent out from the post toward the north after horse thieves and followed their trail for seventy miles but did not succeed in overtaking them.

The harboring place for these desperadoes was a settlement of whites and Tonkaway Indians called "The Flats" near Fort Griffin. Here gathered the most desperate and lawless gangs of thieves and desperadoes in the entire west. The post surgeon at Fort Griffin in May, 1872, said that a short distance from the post in the valley of the Clear Fork was "a camp of Tonkaways and a settlement of 66 squatters." Prominent among the latter was a saloonkeeper called "Tol Bowers," a noted desperado, who killed a citizen named Cockerall without being tried by military authorities. He stated that such a state of lawlessness existed in this settlement as to make it unsafe for one to go there unless well armed. Tonkaway Indians intoxicated were so dangerous as to keep the settlement in constant terror. He said that "It becomes a frequent sight to see Indians with men and women in a state of beastly intoxication."[18] So turbulent were the lawless characters in this notorious settlement that robbery was frequently perpetrated in open day light, and at night. "The Flats" was an inferno of ribaldry, lewd women, drunken gamblers, and designing thieves. The soldiers of the fort had very little to do with the inhabitants of "The Flats" save when they were off duty and came to the settlement saloons for liquor. On these occasions many tribulations were brought to those in authority at the post by reason of the many excesses in drink. It was because of this condition that the post commander on one occasion wrote: "Fully one-half of the surgical cases occurring in times of peace are produced through whiskey supplied to the troops."[19]

The environment of the post together with the loneliness of frontier life probably caused many of the troops to desert. On April 6, 1873, the "Post Returns" records: "One Sergeant and six privates of calvary left the post in pursuit of deserters. Returned April 24 with one deserter....Several small detachments have been sent in pursuit of deserters during the month." To the young recruit from the East, Fort Griffin was a lonely place indeed. The only means of communication with any town or nearest railway station (which was Calvert, Texas) were government trains. These trains consisted of a number of wagons drawn by horses, mules and oxen; sometimes as many as ten wagons tied in one train. These trains were often, during the rainy season, obliged to camp on the banks of rivers for some days before they were able to cross.

Four mails per week were received at the post, viz: from the East via St. Louis and Fort Smith, Sundays and Thursdays; from the west via San Antonio and Fort Concho, Mondays and Thursdays. The mails were often delayed by floods and freshets that occurred during the rainy season, and occasionally were captured by the Indians. Eight days were required for a letter to reach department headquarters and twelve days to reach Washington. The arrival of the stage coach was an event of considerable interest to the shut in soldiers. It was then that they received news from the outside world.

Then again, another cause for desertions might have been the kinds of food which the soldiers had to eat. Rations consisted of the following articles: pork, bacon, fresh beef, flour, hardbread, cornmeal, beans, peas, rice, hominy, coffee, tea, sugar, vinegar, candies, soap, salt and pepper. Concerning the diet of the troops on duty, the Post Surgeon of Ft. Griffin wrote: "When the troops are on escort duty, they are furnished with an abundant supply of fresh meat, by killing buffaloes, large herds of which are found in northern Texas. . . .When the troops are absent on escort duty or scouting expeditions, they are furnished with flour and bake their own bread in Dutch ovens. A large amount of baking soda is used in its preparation, and the bread is of a most unwholesome character. There is no doubt that many cases of diarrhea and diseases of the digestive system are produced by the bad quality of the bread."[20]

Since vegetables could not be raised in sufficient quantities in the post garden, and since they would decay before the freighters could bring them to the post, the soldiers suffered greatly from the lack of vegetables in their diet. To make up partially for this deficiency, canned vegetables were used, but even this did not wholly meet the need.

The frontier developed so rapidly that Fort Griffin soon found itself within the line of settlements. However, the settlers still desired the government to retain forces there. On August 2, 1873, having heard of a proposed abandonment of Fort Griffin, the citizens of Shackelford, Throckmorton, Young, Stephens, and Palo Pinto counties sent a petition to the Secretary of War asking that the post not be abandoned, giving as their reason for the petition the frequency of Indian raids. The petition called attention to the fact that the abandonment of the post would make it necessary for the people to vacate the country.[21] In transmitting the petition of the people to the Secretary of War, Colonel Buell gave it as his opinion that the abandonment of the post would result in the depopulation of the country.

In the following year the Commander of the Department of Texas made a tour of the frontier line of defense and in his report, concerning the conditions at Fort Griffin, said: "At most of the posts they are comfortably quartered. (Speaking of the men). Fort Griffin is an exception to this rule. It may be made to answer this coming winter, but no longer, and if troops are to be kept there another year, new barracks must be built for them. There is nothing there on which repairs can be made. The buildings are mostly huts. One building alone at the post is possibly worth intrinsically one hundred dollars. This post is a very important one, in my opinion, and should be retained. I respectfully recommend that $80,000 be asked for to build suitable quarters there for six companies, four companies of Cavalry and two of Infantry."[22] The recommendation of the Colonel was never carried out as it became more and more evident that the post must be abandoned.

The coming of railways and the remarkable growth in population along the frontier made the Indian frontier posts unnecessary. General Augur, commander of the Department of Texas, in his annual report of 1881, said that Forts Concho, McKavett, and Stockton were thus rendered unnecessary, and that Fort Griffin, ceasing to serve a useful purpose, was abandoned in May of that year. Thus the history of one of the most colorful forts on the Texas frontier comes to a close.

Texas Frontier Forts

	Occupied	Abandoned
Fort Belknap	1850	1861
Fort Chadbourne	1852	1861
Fort Phantom Hill	1851	1854
Fort Bliss	1848	1860
Fort Davis	1854	1861
Fort Clark	1852	1861
Fort McIntosh	1847	1861
Fort McKavett	1852	1860
Fort Quitman	1858	1861
Fort Griffin	1867	1882
Fort Richardson	1868	1878
Fort Concho	1867	1889
Fort Stockton	1858	1861

	Reoccupied	Abandoned
Fort Belknap		
Fort Chadbourne		
Fort Phantom Hill		
Fort Bliss	1867	
Fort Davis	1867	1891
Fort Clark	1866	
Fort McIntosh	1868	
Fort McKavett	1868	1883
Fort Quitman	1868	1877
Fort Griffin		
Fort Richardson		
Fort Concho		
Fort Stockton	1867	1886

NOTES

[1] Agent Wm. Bent, in *Annual Report of Commissioner of*

Indian Affairs for 1850, pp. 137-139, gives this as a cause for Indian depredations.

[2] The departmental reports of the frontier officers from 1850 to 1854 dwell at some length upon the growing hostility of the Indians. As a type of such an attitude see *Annual Reports of the Departments of Texas, 1854*, on file in Old Records Section, Adjutant General's Office. War Department.

[3] Designated as such by War Department Reports.

[4] "Record of Engagements with Hostile Indians," p. 16, compiled from official records, Headquarters Division of Missouri, 1882, has this to say of Indian forays: "So boldly has this system of murder and robbery been carried out that since June, 1862, not less than 800 persons (1868) have been murdered, — the Indians escaping from the troops by traveling at night when the trail could not be followed, thus giving enough distance and time to render pursuit, in most cases, fruitless." Another writer has this to say: "The whole of the frontier line of counties of the state west of Grayson County has been, for the past four years, subject to the inroads of the Indians during the fall of each year. Prior to the war the population of Jack County was about four fold of what it is now; the settlements have been deserted during the war, owing to increased dangers from the Indians, at a time when fighting material was engaged elsewhere." Circular No. 4, S.G.O. Washington, D. C., Dec. 5, 1870.

[5] A custom of several families of one of the frontier settlements seeking protection from Indian forays by choosing one of the stronger houses of the community as a defense position.

[6] The "Flakes Daily Bulletin" (Galveston) of April 27, 1866, called attention to the fact that the Indians were depredating in the vicinity of Austin.

[7] The general impression that the frontier people were acquainted with all phases of Indian warfare does not seem to be well authenticated by documentary evidence.

[8] Besides a well at the post, which was almost dry during dry summers, the nearest supply was a stream about six miles distant. *Med. Record of Post,* Vol 51, pp. 1-3.

[9] One writer complained that the soldiers were being used to erect comfortable quarters for the officers rather than defending the frontier. Cf. "San Antonio Daily Express," March 3, 1871.

[10] For details connected with the building of the posts, number of houses, etc., cf. *Medical Record of Fort Griffin,* Vol. 51, pp, 1-3.

[11] Ibid. All the frontier posts to the north of Fort McKavett were built on very much the same plan.

[12] *Special Orders, Fort Griffin, Texas,* Vol. 1, p. 222.

[13] *Messages and Documents. War Department,* Part I, 1868-1869, pp. 713-714.

[14] "Return of the Sixth Regiment of United States Cavalry," March, 1868.

[15] "Expeditions and Scouts," Department of Texas, 1870.

[16] "Post Returns," Fort Griffin, Texas, February, 1874. A brief account is also found in *Med. Hist.,* Vol. 52, p. 14.

[17] "Tabular Statement of Scouts and Expeditions. Department of Texas, 1873."

[18] *Fort Griffin, Med. Hist. of Post,* Vol. 51, p. 266

[19] Ibid.

[20] *Med. Record, Fort Griffin, 1875,* Vol. 52, pp. 37-39.

[21] *House Ex. Docs.,* No. 284, 43 Congress, 1st Session, Vol. XVII, p. 38.

[22] *Messages and Documents, War Dept.*, Part I, 1874-1875, p. 43.

EDITOR'S NOTE

[i] Rister omits mention of Camp Cooper, probably because its principal purpose was to oversee the Comanche reservation located adjacent to the post.

THE COMANCHE RESERVATION IN TEXAS

by Rupert N. Richardson

D*r. Richardson's book* The Comanche Barrier To South Plains Settlement *was among the earliest scholarly work on the tribe and is still considered a classic in the field. In the following material Richardson discusses the Indian reservation that gave Camp Cooper its reason to exist prior to the Civil War.*

On the Clear Fork of the Brazos, about twenty miles north of Albany, Texas, may be seen the crumbling ruins of Old Camp Cooper, a federal outpost of the late 1850s. One of the buildings has been kept in repair and even yet serves as a residence; the very building which, of course, tradition has fixed as the headquarters of Robert E. Lee when he was in command of that post. The old post is often mentioned by writers of frontier history, but the reason for its location at that point is apt to be forgotten. In May, 1855, the Comanche Indian reservation was established, the agency of which was located about two and one-half miles down the river from the point where the post was located about eight months later. The observer of our own times can find nothing of the remains of this agency but a few foundation stones, some cedar posts or pickets and a depression in the ground which seems to mark the site of an old cellar. However, the Indian home established here is a matter of more than local historical interest for it represented the first efforts of the United States government to apply the reservation system to nomadic Indians of the plains. My purpose here is to give a review of this experiment and to take some notice of its significance in the frontier history of this region.

The reservation system had recently been tried with the Indians in California and was reported to be working successfully.[1] The plan was to confine the Indians within a comparatively small area and give them every advantage possible in the way of schooling and instruction by paid agents and employees of the government. It was expected that at first the Indian Department would be obliged to sustain them almost wholly but that after a few years they could be made largely self supporting. In adopting this policy to solve the Comanche problem in Texas, the United States Government failed to take into consideration many difficulties peculiar to the Texas Indian situation as well as the inherent characteristics of the plains tribes not found in the Indians of other regions.

Establishing the Reservation

The question of a permanent home for the Indians of Texas was often raised during the decade following annexation; but the problem was difficult to solve, especially since the state maintained that neither the Indians nor the United States had any property rights in the Texas public domain. Under the terms of annexation the state had shifted to the federal government the responsibility of managing the Indians but had retained her public lands. Thus, the savages were regarded as tenants at will, and in its effort to keep them pacified the United States Indian service had to contend with the steady encroachment of the settlers.

Naturally the misery and poverty of the savages increased from year to year, and the problem of restraining them grew proportionately greater. The following words are given as those of Ka-tem-e-see, a Southern Comanche chief:

Over this vast country, where for centuries our ancestors roamed in undisputed possession, free and happy, what have we left? The game, our main dependence, is killed and driven off, and we are forced into the most sterile and barren portions of it to starve. We see nothing but extermination left us, and we await the result with stolid indifference. Give us a country we can call our own, where we may bury our people in quiet.[2]

East of the Comanches, along the Valleys of the Upper Brazos and Trinity rivers, were Caddo, Anadarko, Kichai, Haini, Tawakoni, and other Indians whose condition was quite as desperate as that of the Comanches. Finally after one or more "location" bills had failed, the Legislature of Texas by an act of February 6, 1854, authorized the federal government to select not more than twelve leagues of land to be used for Indian reservations.[3] Captain Randolph B. Marcy of the United States Army, and Robert S. Neighbors, representing the Indian Department, were appointed to locate and survey the reservations and, after an extensive reconnaissance, two tracts, one of four leagues on the Clear Fork of the Brazos and the other of eight leagues on the main Brazos, were located. The site of the Clear Fork or Comanche reservation is on the line of Shackelford and Throckmorton counties and that of the Brazos reservation, used by the sedentary tribes, is in Young county.

Thus did the Indian Department prepare to confine more than a thousand nomadic savages on a reserve of a little more than eighteen thousand acres. Today this land is the home of a few stock farmers and ranchmen and probably not as many as fifty people live on it. Compared with the vast stretches the Comanches has considered as their home this was indeed a parsimonious grant; but the state contended that the Indian problem should be entirely a federal burden, the cession was regarded as a gift, and Texas was not in a liberal humor. Yet, since the cardinal idea underlying the reservation system was not simply to feed and care for the Indians but to teach them to become self sustaining, it is strange that the federal government undertook the project at such an obvious disadvantage. It was to be expected that a nomadic people would take more interest in stock-raising than in farming; but herds could not be maintained on so small a tract and white men soon came and laid claim to the adjoining range. Furthermore, only a small part of the reservation lands were arable. Naturally the wild Comanches were loathe to accept such a cramped environment.

However, some of the Indians were in such desperate straits that they awaited with eagerness the establishing of the reservation. Chief Ka-tem-e-see went far out onto the prairies to meet Marcy and Neighbors on their return from the reconnaissance in order to assure them that his followers were ready and anxious to occupy the home they were expecting. Also, it may be observed in passing that the chief was not at all reticent in talking Comanche politics and describing the different factions that prevailed among the Penatekas (Honey-eaters) or Southern Comanche bands. But soon Chief Sanaco appeared before the commission to inform them that Ka-tem-e-see was an imposter and that he, Sanaco, was the real head of the Comanches.[4] Years of warfare with white men and savages and the struggle for existence incident to this confusion had demoralized the savages and weakened their tribal organization. There was not, in fact, any head chief and there had not been for several years. But these jealousies added substantially to the many difficulties the United States was destined to encounter in its efforts to point these people towards peace and civilization. Pride and independence were virtues these Indians no longer could boast of. Even Ka-tem-e-see begged of the commission corn and meat from their private stock of goods.

When Agent Neighbors returned in November, 1854, to establish the reservation, he found on the Clear Fork large parties of Wacoes, Caddoes, Tawakonies, and other smaller bands together with "the whole Southern band" of Comanches, the number of the latter being, according to his estimate, between one thousand and twelve hundred souls. Another council was held, and the Indians urged that the government hurry the preparations for the reservation since they were in a starving condition.[5] But notwithstanding the general eagerness on the part of the Indians about two-thirds of them were not located on the reservation at the time and perhaps half of them never accepted life there because of an unfortunate circumstance which must be charged largely to a blunder of the United States military forces. While some of chief Sanaco's people were at Fort Chadburne, about sixty miles to the southwest, on a friendly trading expedition, they were told by a certain Leyendecker, an Indian trader, that the white people were making plans to attack them and kill them all. "If you want anything more," said Leyendecker to the Indians, "trade quickly, mount your horses, go to Sanaco's camp, and tell him the white people are collecting together to kill him and his people. I see it on this paper. Tell him if he wishes to live to go north as quickly as possible—do not eat, sleep or rest, until you give him this talk from his friend."[6]

On the very day that the chief received this message he had been out with an army officer and a citizen in an effort to help them locate some horses which the Indians were accused of stealing. Whatever may have been his sins of the past, the chief was then trying to preserve peace and control his people. But when this message came the Indian did not wait to investigate. The savage in him asserted itself. The information had come from a friend and, the fact is, it contained a great measure of truth! Orders for such a campaign had actually been received at Fort Chadburne, and a few weeks later the expedition left under the command of Captain Calhoun. The orders called for a campaign against all Comanches, Northern and Southern alike, wherever they might be found. It is true that the officer did not propose actually to go on the reservation and attack the Indians there, but all Comanches met with outside of that vicinity were to be chastised.[7] The whole affair illustrates perfectly the lamentable lack of cooperation between the military and Indian forces so often in evidence along the frontier. It was unfortunate indeed that of all the times the army might have sent an expedition to punish the savages, they chose to go at this critical time. News on the frontier was carried with the swiftness of a breeze, and this report set the Indians wild. Sanaco fled with several hundred of his people, and the sensible Ka-tem-e-see found it difficult to hold his own followers and prevent their joining in the stampede.

As soon as a measure of quiet was restored, runners were sent to induce the renegades to return; but the band had scattered and only a few of these Comanches were ever reached and persuaded to return. Because of this confusion, the Comanches were first located on the Brazos reservation, but they were taken to their home on the Clear Fork about the first of May, 1855. By June 10, they numbered 249 with others reported to be coming in.[8]

Rivalry of the Chiefs; the Wild Bands

Thus the Comanche reservation was inaugurated by a stampede. If Neighbor's estimate of a thousand or twelve hundred souls be accepted as the approximate population of the Southern Comanches, it is evident that not more than a fourth of these Indians were at the reservation when it was established. The two most influential chiefs, Buffalo Hump, a chronic disturber, and Sanaco, destined to become quite as great a rogue, were still at large. Other Indians came in at different times, so that on one occasion there were 557 souls; but 350 or 400 would represent a fair average for the whole period.[9] Evidently many Indians came and left very much at will, in spite of the efforts of the agents to hold them.

It would have been much better if the renegades had stayed away altogether, for their chiefs were jealous of Ka-tem-e-see and frequently connived to supersede him. During the winter of 1855-1856, Sanaco came in, gave up some horses his people had stolen in the country west of San Antonio, and returned to the prairies to bring in his band. He brought in his people according to promise, but soon left because, as he alleged, troops were arriving at Camp Cooper and he felt that this would mean that his braves could get whiskey. However, he must have known that his men could get whiskey while running at large even more easily than at the reservation. A more plausible reason for his leaving is that given by the agent, John R. Baylor, namely, that he found he could not supersede his rival, Ka-tem-e-see. His band became even more lawless and was charged with a number of robberies and murders. Once, in jocular mood, the chief sent word by an Indian runner that he would bring his people in if Major Neighbors would furnish him and his People with all the whiskey they could drink. And they would stay, he said, as long as the whiskey lasted!

Buffalo Hump was even more troublesome than Sanaco. He would come in and make many promises stating that he had reformed and was determined to live the life of a good, honest Indian henceforth. But, if the spirit was willing, the flesh was weak in the case of Buffalo Hump; and as soon as the agent had made him presents in consideration for his profession of good intentions he would steal away to the prairies to plunder and rob and live in his old savage way. Then, when his blankets were worn out and game became scarce and stealing unprofitable, he would return to repeat the process.[10] On one occasion this chief almost started a war between the Comanches and the Indians on the Brazos reservation. With Ka-tem-e-see and about seventy-five warriors, he went to that reservation and approached the Anadarko village in a threatening manner. The women and children of this and neighboring villages fled, and panic seized the entire Indian community. Fortunately the veteran Anadarko chief, Jose Maria, was looking for trouble, had his men armed and prepared for action, and informed the intruders that he was ready either for a "fight" or a "talk." The Comanches chose to talk, and through the efforts of the Brazos agent, S. P. Ross, and his interpreter, Jim Shaw, violence was avoided. When called upon to explain their extraordinary conduct, the Comanches, evidently much embarrassed at the turn the affair had taken, said that all was well, they were satisfied, but they wished to ask just one question: "Were the Caddoes going to continue to act as guides for the troops?"

This question explains the whole affair. No doubt Buffalo Hump, using the milder Ka-tem-e-see as a tool, had hoped to frighten the smaller bands into discontinuing the valuable aid they had been rendering the troops as scouts and guides. It may be that Buffalo Hump himself had suffered because of the skill and faithfulness of these scouts. It is certain that in the years that followed the wiley old renegade was much annoyed by these scouts, for as a leader of the wild Comanche bands he was often trailed and surprised by these very Indians. Although these Comanches were wards of the government and living off of its bounty, their sympathy for their wild, marauding kinsmen was stronger than that for any agent or soldier and they resented the fact that these more civilized Indians were taking such an active part in the interest of law and order.

In addition to these run-away Southern Comanches, other wild Indians made the work of the agents difficult and caused the life of the reservation Indians to be haunted by many fears. There were several distinct Comanche bands that had never had any intimate relations with the Penatekas or Southern bands. Along the Red River and the Canadian were the Tanimas, Nokonies, and Kotsotekas, to the north were the Yamarikas, and in the plains region were the fierce Kwaharies. Associated with these northern bands were the Kiowas, fierce and powerful. Parties from these different bands frequently visited the reservation, coming as friends or lurking near as enemies as best suited their purposes. Naturally the going and coming of these wild kinsmen and their occasional presence at or near the reservation made it very difficult for the agents to control their wards. Furthermore, in their raids against the Texas settlements and the north Mexican states, these parties often passed near the reservation. This, according to Agent Leeper, was done both to steal additional horses from the reserve Indians and to direct the attention of the pursuers to those Indians in order that they might be charged to the innocent while the guilty made their escape. Indeed the Indians of the reservation frequently suffered severe losses of horses at the hands of these marauders.[11] During the last years of the reservation there developed an estrangement between its inhabitants and their wild kinsmen and at times the wards felt that their lives were insecure, although the agency was near by and the military post but two miles away. In May, 1858, Ka-tem-e-see took his boys out of school in order to keep them near him and better protect them from the wrath of the marauders of the north. By this time the chief had lost his enthusiasm for the wild Indians and on one occasion said that he did not care if the troops killed them all.[12]

On at least one occasion a lawless visitor came near causing a general revolt. One Santa Anna, a notoriously bad Indian, came and put up in Ka-tem-e-see's cabin. Since this was the only cabin on the reservation, perhaps the insolent fellow felt that lodging accommodations were poor enough and he proposed to take the best. It was even rumored that he planned to supersede Ka-tem-e-see and make himself chief of the reservation. The chief ordered this Indian and his companion, a Nokoni Comanche, to leave; but they informed him that they were resting from their arduous journey and did not propose to leave until it suited their convenience. When this was reported to Agent Leeper, he called on the detail of troops stationed at Camp Cooper (only twenty men) to come at once. The lieutenant, Van Camp, came at once and surrounded the building. But to his chagrin and alarm, fifty or sixty warriors, armed with bows and guns, together with about thirty women and boys, armed with sticks and clubs, closed in around the cabin and took the side of the visitors so positively that Van Camp saw that a fight was ahead if he forced the issue. He ordered his men to prepare for action, and a battle would have followed but for the fact that he discovered that his men had but one round of ammunition. They had used up nearly all their ammunition the day before in target practice. Thus, since it was impossible to apply force, all that was left for the lieutenant to do was to use persuasion. An agreement was patched up whereby the intruders were permitted to leave, and this they did at once.

On the following day the Indians who had taken an active part in protecting the visitors came to Leeper and explained that they had offered resistance to the troops because they thought when they saw the soldiers approaching that all Indians on the reservation were going to be attacked and slain and they were determined to die fighting. Obviously they thought no such thing. Their bad faith in the whole matter was made more in evidence by their telling Leeper that they expected him to say that their "talk" was "good." In case he should not assent and say that their "talk" was "good," they would kill him and his family and leave the reservation.[13]

Naturally the army officers and the Indian agents as well were sorely vexed with the Indians because of this affair. About all that can be said in defense of the savages is that they regarded the intruders as visitors and felt that to abandon them to the soldiers while they were guests at the reservation would be treachery. Some of the older men and women tearfully begged Ka-tem-e-see not to force the issue, just let the man escape and he would not bother them any more.

Inadequate Protection

The lack of proper protection by the troops was largely the cause of the fear and uncertainty that clouded the lives of the reservation wards. During most of the year 1855 there were no troops closer than Fort Belknap, about fifty miles away, and none but infantry there. However, early in January, 1856, Camp Cooper was established on the reservation and for a time the Indians enjoyed a sense of security.[14] But after a few months, ill feeling developed between the army officers and the Indian agents, each side charging that the other would not cooperate. Both the army and the Indian records are well supplied with documents containing charges, denials and counter charges, but it would not be expedient or profitable to follow the quarrel in detail. No doubt the agents were prone to do much complaining and fault finding while the army men responded with a patronizing attitude and cynical remarks about the "beef eating" policy of the Indian Department. Once Captain Stoneman at Camp Cooper took it upon himself to count the Indians or to attempt to count them and, according to the agent, almost caused a panic by proceeding without the assent and knowledge of the agents. The Indians were ever shy in the presence of soldiers and army officers. Naturally Leeper and Neighbors regarded Stoneman's conduct as an insult for it implied that their reports were not correct and that supplies were being fraudulently drawn. Most of the army officers naturally sided with their fellow officer, and the breach widened.[15]

In the spring of 1858, the army forces decided to remove Camp Cooper from its old location near the agency and Indian camps to a point some six or eight miles away from the agency. Leeper intimated that this was for the purpose of locating the post near a ranch owned by Captain Givens of the Second Dragoons.[16] However, it seems more plausible to conclude that the change was made as an act of spite and in retaliation against the charges made by the agents that the soldiers were not properly disciplined and were spending too much time among the Indians. When the agent protested at this move, complaining that he and his wards were left in a defenseless condition, the department commander of the army advised him that if he felt insecure he could move the agency to a point nearer the new site. Thus for a while no troops were stationed nearer than eight miles from the agency. Now, when the troops moved out of Old Camp Cooper the Indians moved in and stored their grain and hay there. But soon a detachment of troops was ordered back to the old post and the Indians had to move out.[17] It seems that thereafter some troops were stationed continuously at the old post, but later the agent complained that the force consisted of but fifteen or twenty men, not enough to be of much aid in an emergency. During the crisis in June, 1859, when the frontier citizens were threatening to attack the reservation, an adequate cavalry force was stationed there and maintained until the Indians were removed.[18] However, it must be said that during much of the four years of the reservation's history, the United States Army did not give the protection which even its limited means might have permitted. The several hundred nomadic savages just taken from the prairies and confined to a reservation of a few square miles were too numerous to be adequately described. Sometimes the conduct and practices of the savages were enough to have exhausted the patience of a saint, and that they were dealt with so successfully is a credit to the white men in charge.

Savage lawlessness and lack of self restraint naturally provoked clashes between individuals of a tribe where freedom of action had so recently been limited by this new environment. In a fit of anger one of the head men stabbed his wife, and her brothers vowed to avenge her. The husband's friends came to his side, and a general fight seemed dangerously near. But, much to the surprise and relief of the agent, the guilty Indian came to him in a penitent mood and offered to receive any punishment that might be imposed. The agent left the matter to the other chiefs, and quite naturally nothing was done. The woman recovered and her brothers apparently became reconciled.[19]

The health of the Indians was not always good. Venereal diseases were virulent and common, and there was not sufficient medicines and doctors. Typhoid pneumonia is mentioned among the diseases reported by the doctor who occasionally attended the patients.[20]

The reservation farmer had his troubles also. The Indians would turn their horses into the corn field, or turn them loose where it was evident that they would get in the field. They would pull melons no larger than an egg and were want to consume all their corn before it had grown to good roasting-ears. In the spring of the second year they refused for some time to plant their crops until they had been given presents, but finally the agent persuaded them to go to work without the presents.

Sometimes there was violence unto death. A chief engaged in intrigue with another man's wife and, according to custom, the injured man demanded that the chief compensate him to the amount of a horse. When the chief refused or hesitated to do this, he was slain at once by the sons of the injured man. Then the father and his sons together with their women and children fled from the reservation and were not overtaken, although a scouting party followed them for a hundred and fifty miles.[21]

And yet, notwithstanding these evidences of savage crudeness, it must be said that at least some of the Indians were making progress toward a more civilized existence. Under the direction of the reservation farmer they worked and occasionally made fairly good crops, but the amount of land in cultivation was small. In 1857, they made but 50 bushels of wheat off of the 20 acres sown, and 500 bushels of corn was produced on the remainder of their land in cultivation. For awhile the Indians were prone to rely too much on their prisoners to do the work, but after these were freed and returned to their people in Mexico, that abuse was corrected. In 1858, the reserve farmer reported a better yield. In the spring of that year he had divided the community fields into six divisions in order that each of the prominent clans might have a parcel of ground suited to its numbers. He thought that they would have made enough grain (principally corn) that year to do them but for the fact that the fear of the white frontiersmen and wild Indians forced them to keep up their horses and feed them much of the time.[22] This partial elimination of the communist system had a wholesome effect, but it would have been impossible to carry it much farther because of the scarcity of arable land. A division of land so that each family head would have had a parcel separate and apart from the others would have become utterly impossible after a generation or two. Thus the cramped conditions on the small reservation would have acted as a barrier to progress, even if the Indians had been permitted to remain there.

Many of the citizens of Texas complained that the reservation Indians were treacherous and dangerous and yet some of those persons living near the reserve vouched for the honesty of the Indians and stated that they regarded them as friends rather than enemies.[23] The settlement and development of the country in the vicinity of the reservation indicates that the white people generally had confidence in the peaceful disposition of the savages. It is significant that the most serious complaints did not come from those persons living near the reservation but from settlements a hundred or more miles away.

Some of the children made good progress in school. In 1858, it was reported that ten boys were in school and, in a later account, they were reported to be learning remarkably fast. Thomas T. Hawkins, special agent, who was sent to investigate the reservation in 1858, wrote of the Comanches: "I regard them as superior in natural sense and intelligence to any of our full-blooded native tribes—and I have seen many specimens in Washington, in the west and upon my journey hither."[24]

At times the Indians manifested some disposition to exercise tribal government sufficient to restrain unruly members. Once when a certain Indian, named Jack Porter, and two or three followers returned from a raid to Mexico with twelve stolen horses, a council of chiefs was called to consider the matter, and the culprits were informed that if they repeated the act they all would be shot.[25] However, it must be said that the exercise of authority generally stopped with admonition, and an influential warrior had little to fear from a council composed of his fellow warriors. Chief Ka-tem-e-see was given the use of a cabin and was paid thirty dollars per month to act as head chief. From all accounts he took his position quite seriously and worked faithfully to lead his people aright. In one report it is stated that several females had recently deserted the reservation because of punishment he had inflicted upon them. Apparently the braves were dealt with more tactfully.

Breaking Up the Reservation

Naturally the people of Texas had expected that the establishment of the reservations whereby the Indians were given the opportunity to maintain a comfortable existence under government supervision would improve frontier Indian conditions. But this hope proved to be in vain. The various bands of Southern Comanches who refused to settle, together with parties of their northern kinsmen and the Lipans and small parties of other tribes, continued to harass the settlements to such an extent as to call forth protests from many sources. Conditions not only did not improve but, according to the accounts of that day, grew worse from year to year, especially after 1856.

From the very beginning, and for good reasons, some of the frontier citizens had come to regard the reservations as a source of trouble. It is true that the agents did their best to control their Indians, and they certainly never tolerated theft when they could prevent it. However, with Indians coming and going in such promiscuous fashion it was utterly impossible for the agents to know just what their wards were doing. Although some of the frontiersmen made allegations to the contrary, there is overwhelming evidence to the effect that ranchmen who came to hunt their lost or stolen stock were extended every aid and courtesy by the agents and Ka-tem-e-see. They rarely ever found their property there, but when they did it was readily given up.[26] But no agent, however tactful, could long avoid a clash with the frontiersmen on this point. They naturally gave little consideration to the rights of the Indians, expected the word of the white man to be accepted over the denial of any number of Indians, and misunderstandings and disputes over property soon arose. The agents all the while stoutly maintained that their Indians were innocent and, although we may have some doubts to their contentions, they were just as sincere in laying much of their trouble to the wards of the agents, and as affairs progressed each side became more determined and emphatic. When the citizens failed to find their stock at the reservation, they concluded that the marauders had left the reservation, had stolen the horses from the settlements, and then had made their way to join their wild friends to the north; and the large number of desertions from the reservation evidenced by the census returns furnish considerable foundation for this point of view. There was no means left for them whereby they could secure their property. Other complaints were made, one being that signed by twenty-seven men addressed to Agent Leeper, informing him that they would not henceforth honor his passports to Indians but that they proposed to attack any and all Indians found off the reservation except where they were accompanied by responsible white persons. Their reasons for this threat appears to have been the report they had received that certain Indians whom they had pursued had since made threats against them. Furthermore, they would have Leeper inform the Indians that if there should be "a man killed on this river and there is the least proof that it was done by the Indians from the reserve... We will attack the reserve with a sufficient force to break it up regardless of consequences."[27]

In January, 1858, a select committee of the state senate criticized severely the United States Indian policy in the state, referring to the fact that only a fraction of the Comanche Indians were located on the reservation and that friendly Indians were in the habit of passing and repassing into the settlements. Thus, they contended, wild Indians were mistaken for friendly ones and the white people were thus placed at the mercy of marauding bands. In addition to their recommendations for better military protection, the committee stated that the agents should not permit the Indians to leave the reservations.[28]

If these charges should be accepted at their face value, they would represent within themselves rather convincing proof against the reservation Indians, but the records show that the whole issue was so completely shot through with bias and personal animosity that one is unable to know what to accept or reject. Reference has already been made to the ill feeling that prevailed between Robert S. Neighbors, the Superintendent of Indian Affairs in Texas, and some of the army officers. Furthermore, John R. Baylor, who seems to have been dismissed from the Indian service through Neighbor's influence, led in much of the agitation.

But regardless of the merits or injustice of the charges brought against the reservation Indians, feeling against them became so widespread and bitter that in February, 1858, Neighbors asked that special instructions be given the military to protect the reserve Indians from attacks by citizens. In May he made a trip to Washington to place the matter before the officials there, alleging that the soldiers could not be depended upon to protect the Indians because of the indifference of their officers.[29] In October, the sheriff of Young County, armed with a writ issued by the county court, set forth from Belknap with a posse of about forty citizens to arrest a reservation Indian charged with committing an attack on a young man named Johnson some months before. On hearing of the approach of the party, Neighbors called on Captain Palmer at Camp Cooper for an escort, advanced with the escort, and met the sheriff's party some distance from the reservation and finally persuaded the party to give up their purpose. Whether the sheriff desisted because of the law in the case or by fear of the United States soldiers was a matter of doubt in the minds of observers.[30]

The complaints against the agents and the reservation Indians led to the sending of a special agent to investigate the administration of affairs. This agent, Thomas T. Hawkins, stayed at Camp Cooper for five weeks and every opportunity was given the complainants to make their appearance and testify as to their charges; but few of them did so and nothing of consequence was submitted. Hawkins' report commended the agents and the administration of both reservations very highly. The critics alleged that the investigation was ex parte and that it was intended from the beginning to "whitewash" the record of the Indian administration in Texas; but we should have more sympathy with them if they had gone through with their part of the program and submitted whatever evidence they had.

Perhaps the strongest testimony in favor of the Comanches is that of John S. Ford and E. N. Burleson of the Ranger forces. They came with their command to the vicinity of the reservation in the spring of 1858 when they and their officers were practically unanimous in the belief that the reservation Indians were committing depredations. These men were seasoned frontiersmen, had the frontiersmen's natural hatred and distrust of all Indians, and were determined to secure evidence against the savages that could not be refuted. However, although they stayed for some time and sent out many scouts, they found that they could not secure any evidence against the Indians. Captain Allison Nelson, one of the foremost critics of Neighbors, suggested to him that it would be very easy to make a trail leading into the reservation, but Ford would not hear of this. Nelson reported that the people in the vicinity of the reservation did not want it broken up, and it was decided to abandon the idea. Ford quoted Nelson as stating that Neighbors had always escaped from the attacks of his enemies, but that men were after him now who were going to get his job.[31]

Naturally so much excitement and ill will inspired cruelty. In May, 1858, an inoffensive old Comanche was slain by a party of white men who wanted to get his horses and took advantage of the fact that he was away from the reservation without an escort or pass.[32] Late in December, a little party of friendly Indians from the Brazos reservation, known as Choctaw Tom's party, was attacked in their camp at night near Palo Pinto, whither they had gone by the consent of their agent and where they were regarded by the people of the immediate community as friendly and dependable. In fact, Choctaw Tom, the leader of the party, had returned to the reservation, but some of his people had remained near Palo Pinto in order to accept an invitation of some citizens of the community to stay a little longer and hunt bear with them.[33] The party that attacked the Indians was composed of citizens of Erath and neighboring counties further down the Brazos valley. They alleged that these Indians had been committing depredations, but there is very little foundation for this contention.

The killing of these Indians created general excitement along the frontier because of the fear that their tribesmen would retaliate. The men who made the unwarranted attack on Choctaw Tom's party were never arrested, although the governor by special proclamation called for their arrest. The grand jury of Palo Pinto county refused to indict the men but instead indicted Jose Maria, the Anadarko chief, for horse stealing and in their report stated that the reservations were nuisances and that the people ought to take up arms against the Indians.[34] "Gatherings" of frontiersmen began to take place and many white men who had up to this time maintained a neutral or indifferent attitude began to join in the clamor against the savages. No doubt many of these men felt that the party from Erath county had made a mistake in attacking the peaceful Indians, but they believed that the kinsmen of these Indians as well as the Comanches would retaliate and that there could be no peace on the frontier until both reservations were broken up. The agitators took advantage of this state of mind and never lost an opportunity to appeal to the fears and prejudices of the frontier people. It must not be understood that these men were "the very worst frontier characters" as the Indians agents sometimes charged. Among their leaders were John R. Baylor, former Indian agent; Peter Garland, of Erath county; R. W. Pollard, of Palo Pinto county; J. B. (Buck) Barry, of Bosque county, all prominent citizens in their communities and highly regarded by most of their neighbors. The years of bitter struggle with the Indians had hardened the hearts of the frontier people. As one of the more conservative of them has written in his memoirs, the frontier people were "always crazed at the sight of Indians and determined to kill,"[35] and when the safety of their families was involved they were wont to act first and investigate afterwards.

However, notwithstanding these "gatherings" of frontiersmen with all their fear and frenzy, no drastic action was taken during the winter of 1858-1859, which is to be accounted for in part, at least, by the firm attitude maintained by the army officers who were guarding the reservations. The immediate objective of these threatening movements had been the "lower" or Brazos reservation. This was not because the white men regarded these Indians as the more culpable but rather because they felt that both the Brazos and Comanche reservations must be broken up and the Brazos Indians being the more numerous and powerful were regarded as the chief obstacle to be overcome.

Long before this crisis came the agents had felt that the Indians should be moved from Texas and as early as the summer of 1857 Neighbors had recommended that they be taken to the Indian Territory.[36] But the authorities in Washington did not give any consideration to the proposal, and it was dropped for the time. Then came the demonstrations against the Indians during the winter and spring of 1859, and Neighbors again insisted that if the Indians were not removed, they would be driven away by the mad settlers. The government at Washington was slow to appreciate the gravity of the situation, and the agents became frantic in their effort to secure authority to do what they knew was essential to save their wards from destruction. Finally, on March 30, the Commissioner of Indian Affairs wrote that the Indians would be moved in the fall or winter following. But this announcement did not satisfy the white people, and Neighbors continued his efforts to secure authority to remove his wards at once.[37] Neighbors said that he and his associates had "stood their ground" so far but that they wanted their superiors to share with them the responsibility for determining what should be done when the next crisis came, as it certainly would come. A little later came a resolution signed by a hundred and fifty men demanding that Neighbors and the resident agents, Ross and Leeper, resign.[38]

The situation was already critical enough when an army officer by an imprudent act provoked a disturbance that removed the last ray of hope for peace on the frontier until the Indians were removed. A Brazos reservation Indian named Fox had been killed by a party of Jack County Rangers in brutal fashion. This officer led a party of reservation Indians in search of Fox's slayers and caused great consternation by escorting them into the town of Jacksboro one night. This incident gave the radical party an excellent torch, and they now set the whole frontier aflame with excitement.[39] The citizens at once organized themselves into "ranger companies and surrounded both reservations, threatening the Indians and their agents day and night and preventing the savages from gathering up their stock."[40] On May 23, John R. Baylor at the head of about 250 men came onto the Brazos reservation; but the soldiers stood their ground and the citizens withdrew, not, however, until they had picked a fight with some of the Indians. The Indians pursued them for some distance and considerable fighting took place.[41] The settlers declared that they would raise a thousand men and take both reservations by storm. But sufficient forces were not forthcoming, and the "Army of Defense," as the frontiersmen had called themselves, disbanded for a time. Their fury was allayed somewhat by the act of the governor in appointing a board of commissioners to visit the camp of the citizens and endeavor to work out a peaceful method of attaining their ends. The commission visited the frontier communities, heard the complaints of the angry citizens and in their report of findings quite naturally declared the Indians guilty of the offenses charged.[42] But Baylor and other frontier leaders kept up the agitation and, in order to prevent another gathering, G. B. Erath, one of the governor's commissioners, called out a special force of one hundred militiamen from McLennan and Bell counties in order to assure the citizens that the Indians were being watched.[43] However, from all accounts it seems that the frontiersmen did not propose to leave to others the matter of watching the Indians and during the last few weeks preceding the removal the Indians of both reservations were harassed on every hand and dared not leave their agencies to gather up their animals, many of which were out on the range. On one occasion a fight occurred near the Comanche reservation in which both the Indians and citizens suffered some injuries.

Authority for the immediate removal of the Indians was finally granted on June 11 and on July 31, the Indians from both reservations, escorted by United States soldiers, started on their journey to the valley of the Washita in Indian Territory.

The census made at the time the journey was begun showed that 1112 Indians left the Brazos reservation and 384 Comanches left the upper reservation. It was estimated that the Comanches took away with them livestock worth $9,550, and that they lost, or were forced to leave behind, livestock worth in the aggregate of $14,922.50.[44] The cost of both reservations to the United States government had ranged between $61,655.25, for 1857, and $91,707.50, for 1856.[45] Probably about one-third of these sums were expended on the Comanches. During the last year preceding the establishment of the reservations the United States had spent $129,820 on the Texas Indians.

A sequel to the bitter controversy over the removal of the Indians was the killing of Robert S. Neighbors on the streets of Belknap by a man he scarcely knew, if indeed he had ever seen him before or knew the man had aught against him. Neighbors had seen the Indians safely located in the Leased District in Indian Territory, had turned them over to their agent there, and was returning home to make his final report to the Indian Office. He stopped at Belknap on matters of business and was killed as he was preparing to proceed on his way to his home in San Antonio.[46]

Perhaps in their zeal to protect their wards from the wrath of the white people, Neighbors and his associates were blind to the faults of the savages, but their courage and devotion to duty in protecting the Indians against what they regarded as the prejudice and avarice of the white men is one of the finest examples of public service to be found in the annals of the American frontier. They were confronted with great odds with their former friends and neighbors aligned against them. At times they had to fight almost single handed, but they stood at their post and were never lacking in either physical or moral courage.

Thus ended the Texas reservation experiment. It may well be doubted that even without the hostile attitude of the white frontiersmen, the Comanche reservation could have been made successful. Many of the Southern Comanches never did live on the reserve, and of those who came there, large numbers refused to remain. The experience of the agents was prophetic of the difficulties the federal government was destined to have two decades later when the plan was tried for all the nomadic tribes of the plains under circumstances far more favorable. As long as vast stretches of uninhabited prairies and herds of fat deer, antelope, and buffaloes invited them, the savages were loathe to accept the monotonous life of farming on the reservation. The old and decrepit might gladly stay, but the spirited young warriors would hide away, taking with them when they could their families and friends. But the record made by these reservation Comanches proved that the nomadic tribes were amendable to progress and the equals intellectually of their more sedate kinsmen of the progressive agricultural tribes.

NOTES

[1] Lena Clara Koch, "The Federal Indian Policy In Texas, 1845-1860," in the *Southwestern Historical Quarterly*, XXIX, 98. Miss Koch's chapter, entitled "The Reservation System and Its Results," contains much information on both the Comanche and the Brazos reservations. The Brazos reservation was established for the sedentary Indians of Texas about fifty miles to the east.

[2] Horace Capron, United States Indian Agent in Texas, to Howard, September 30, 1858. Ms., in the University of Texas Library, photostat copies of papers in the United States Indian Office.

[3] H.P.N. Gammel, *Laws of Texas*, III, 1495-1496.

[4] R. B. Marcy, *Thirty Years of Army Life On the Border*, (New York. 1866), p.204. See also W.B. Parker, *Notes Taken Through Unexplored Texas*, 1854 (Philadelphia, 1856), p. 180.

[5] Neighbors to Manypenny, Commissioner of Indians Affairs, January S. 1865. Ms. University of Texas, photostat copy.

⁶ Hill to Neighbors, August 31, 1855, gives an account of these happenings of January preceding. Thirty-fourth Congress, First Session, Sen. Doc. No.1, Part 1, 502.

⁷ Hill to Neighbors, January 11, 1855. Ms. University of Texas photostat copy. The affair produced quite a tilt between the army officers and the Indian agents. The army men never did deny the broad scope of the order they were to act under, but they did contend that the troops were not the cause of the run-away since the Indians fled long before the troops arrived in their vicinity.

⁸ Neighbors to Manypenny, June 10, 1855. Ms. University of Texas photostat copy.

⁹ The different reports of the agents show numbers as follows: January 1, 1856, 460; September 8, 1856, 557; September, 1857, 424, January 17, 1858, 381; September 16, 1858, 371; October 30, 1858, 341; July, 1859, 382.

¹⁰ See Anna Heloise Abel, *The American Indian as Slaveholder and Secessionist*, p. 315, for a letter from M. Leeper, once Comanche agent in Texas, to Elias Rector, December 12, 1861. In this letter Leeper gives a short biography of Buffalo Hump and pronounces an anathema to his memory.

¹¹ Leeper's Report. December 31, 1857. Ms. University of Texas photostat copy.

¹² J. Shirley, employee of Barnard's trading house at the reservation, to C. E. Barnard, May 6, 1858. Ms. University of Texas Photostat copy. Also, Leeper to Neighbors, February 5, 1858, Ibid.

¹³ Leeper to Neighbors, August 31, 1858. Ms. University of Texas photostat copy.

¹⁴ Baylor's report, September 12, 1856, Thirty-fourth Congress, Third Session, House Exec. Doc. No. 1, 728. See

also, George F. Price, *Across the Continent with the Fifth Cavalry*, (New York, 1885), p. 4.

[15] George Stoneman, Captain Second Cavalry, Camp Cooper, to Neighbors, September 5, 1857. Ms. University of Texas photostat copy. Also, Leeper to Neighbors, December 5, 1857, Ibid.

[16] Leeper to Neighbors, March 29, 1868. Ms. University of Texas photostat copy.

[17] T. T. Hawkins, special agent to investigate conditions on the reservation, to Charles E. Mix, October 30, 1858. Ms. University of Texas photostat copy.

[18] Neighbors to Greenwood, June 10, 1859. Thirty-sixth Congress, First Session, Sen. Exec. Doc. No. 2, p 636.

[19] Baylor to Neighbors, June 8. 1856. Ms. University of Texas photostat copy.

[20] J. Shirley, bill for medical services, March 29, 1858. Ms. University Of Texas photostat copy. Neighbors to Manypenny, March 7, 1856. Ibid.

[21] Leeper to Neighbors, April 9, 1858, Ibid.

[22] Neighbor's report, September 16, 1857. Thirty-fifth Congress, First Session, Sen. Exec. Doc. No. 11, Vol. 11. Also, Neighbors to Manypenny, May 14, 1856, and H. P. Jones, reservation farmer, to M. Leeper, October 29, 1858, University of Texas photostat copies.

[23] Thomas Lambshead (a citizen) to Manypenny, May 1, 1856. Ms. University of Texas Photostat copy. Also, Hawkins to Mix, October 30, 1858, Ibid.

[24] Hawkins to Mix, October 30, 1858. Ms. University of Texas photostat copy.

[25] Neighbor's report, September 16, 1858, Thirty-fifth

Congress, Second Session, Sen. Exec. Doc. No. 1. Vol. I, p. 524.

[26] On this moot point see J. B. (Buck) Barry to Hawkins, November 8, 1858. Ms. University of Texas photostat copy. Barry, who in his "Reminiscences" (Manuscript, University of Texas Archives), bitterly assails the reservation Indians, said this letter of 1858, that Major Neighbors treated him in a "clever and gentle-manly manner" in the matter of his efforts to recover stolen horses.

[27] W.G. Preston and others to M. Leeper, February 1, 1858. Ms. University of Texas photostat copy. John R. Baylor, Comanche agent until he was dismissed in May, 1857, is among the signers of this letter to Leeper.

[28] "Report of Select Committee on Indian Affairs," *State Gazette*, Austin, March 27, 1858. George B. Erath, Henry E. McCulloch, Forbes Brittin, J. W. Throckmorton, and E. B. Scarborough composed the committee.

[29] Neighbors to Mix, written at Washington, D. C., May 18, 1858. Neighbors complained that Major Paul at Fort Belknap, Captain Stoneman at Camp Cooper, and Captain Givens, who owned a ranch about six miles from the reservation, had opposed him all along and had tried to incite the citizens against the Indians.

[30] See the letter of a correspondent to the *New York Herald*, November 15, 1858.

[31] Affidavit of John S. Ford and E. N. Burleson, November 22, 1858. University of Texas photostat copy.

[32] Shirley to Barnard, May 6, 1858; Evans to Leeper, May 2, 1858. Ms. University of Texas photostat copies.

[33] J. J. Sturm, farmer at the Brazos agency, to Ross, December 28, 1858. Thirty-sixth Congress, First Session, Sen.

Exec. Doc. No. 2, Vol. 1, p. 588. See also, the statement of Daniel Thornton, Peter Garland, and others who attacked the Indians, made at Palo Pinto, January 4, 1859, Ibid, p. 606.

[34] A copy of the report of the Grand Jury may be found in the Runnels Papers, Texas State Archives.

[35] "Memoirs of George B. Erath," in the *Southwestern Historical Quarterly*, XXVII, 15.

[36] Neighbors to Mix, August 5, 1857. Ms. University of Texas photostat copy.

[37] Mix to Neighbors, March 30, 1859, Thirtieth Congress, First Session. Sen. Doc. No. 2, p. 631. Neighbors to Mix, April 11, 1859. Ms, University of Texas photostat copy.

[38] "Resolutions," April 25, 1859. Ms. University of Texas photostat copy.

[39] J. R. Worrall of Jacksboro, June 1, 1859, to the Editor, *The Dallas Herald*, June 15, 1859.

[40] Neighbors to Mix, May 12, 1859, and Ross to Neighbors, May 12, 1859. Ms. University of Texas photostat copies.

[41] Report of Chaplain J. B. Plummer of the United States Army. Thirty-sixth Congress, First Session, Sen. Exec. Doc. No. 2, p. 644.

[42] Report of John Henry Brown, G. B. Erath, J. M. Steiner, J. M. Smith and Richard Coke, to Governor Runnels, Waco, June 27, 1859. Thirty-sixth Congress, Second Session, Sen. Exec. Doc. No. 2, pp. 665-671.

[43] Erath to Ross and Neighbors, June 20, 1859. Thirty-sixth Congress, First Session Sen. Exec. Doc., No. 2, p. 663.

[44] Neighbors' Memorandum, no date. Ms. University of Texas photostat copy.

[45] Clara Lena Koch, "The Federal Indian Policy in Texas," in the *Quarterly*, XXIX, 110.

[46] Leeper to the Commissioner of Indian Affairs, September 15, 1869. Thirty-sixth Congress, First Session, Sen. Exec. Doc. No 2, p. 701. On their return from Indian Territory, Neighbors and Leeper, who were traveling together, were attacked by wild Indians, and Leeper was seriously wounded.

CAMP COOPER AND FORT GRIFFIN, TEXAS

by Col. M.L. Crimmins

The explanation given here details the purpose and activities associated with the two early posts on the Clear Fork.

Following the annexation of Texas by the United States in 1846, the question of the control of hostile Indians was imminent, and Robert S. Neighbors was appointed superintendent of Indian affairs. However, the Mexican War was then occupying the attention of the federal government, so nothing much was done for several years. Then a chain of army posts was stretched across Texas from the northeast corner to the southwest, with the line crossing the center, from north central Texas south to the Rio Grande. By 1856, Camp Cooper became part of the east and west and north and south chain, which crossed near this point. It was in addition a point of observation adjacent to the Upper Indian Reservation where the restless Comanches might be watched. It was established on the Clear Fork of the Brazos about seven miles above what later became Fort Griffin. The first garrison in that vicinity was comprised of companies A, F, and H of the Fifth Infantry, who had left Fort Washita, July 8, 1851, under the command of Captain John A. Whitall. They first marched to Camp Belknap, arriving there July 23, 1851, and then arrived at the site of future Camp Cooper on July 29,

1851. It was then occupied by the Caddo Indians. It was not, however, until January 2, 1856, that Camp Cooper was officially established, five miles east of the mouth of Otey's Creek.

On April 9, 1856, Col. Robert E. Lee, Second United States Cavalry, arrived there. It became the first United States Army Post which he commanded, and he was stationed there longer than at any other post in Texas. He wrote in his diary that it was about two miles above the Indian Agency, that the lodges of the Indians were on the left bank (looking down stream) of the Clear Fork of the Brazos, and that Catumseh[i] was the Chief of the Comanche Reserve. Colonel Lee relieved Major William T. Hardee, who arrived in Camp Cooper January 3, 1856. This distinguished officer was brevetted for great gallantry during the war with Mexico and eventually became a Lieutenant General of the Confederate Army. Camp Cooper was named in honor of the Adjutant General of our army, Samuel Cooper. Colonel Lee found four companies of the Second United States Cavalry at Camp Cooper, divided into two squadrons, as the custom was then. The officers were Captain Earl Van Dorn, commanding Company A, who later was a Major General in the Confederate Army; Captain George Stoneman, commanding Co. E, who later was brevetted Brigadier General for meritorious service in the capture of Charlotte, North Carolina; Captain Theodore O'Hara, the author of the famous poem "The Bivoauc of the Dead," commanding Company F; and Captain Charles J. Whiting, commanding Company K. Whiting was of that distinguished army family that has given us outstanding officers since 1808; was a member of the United States-Mexican Boundary Survey from 1849 until its termination; then he became Surveyor General of California prior to joining the Second United States Cavalry in 1855.

Colonel Lee wrote to his family from Camp Cooper April 12, 1856, that the government was attempting to humanize Catumseh's band of Comanches. He had a talk with Catumseh, which was tedious on his part and very sententious on Lee's. Lee hailed him and his tribe as friends as long as they behaved themselves but he would meet them with force if they misbehaved. He wrote that one thousand of the hostile Comanches lived to the north. He visited Catumseh the following day and found he had six wives. Of them he wrote: "Their paint and ornaments rendered them more hideous than nature made them."

The troops lived in tents during that winter, which was one of the most severe ever experienced in that section of high winds. Northers followed one after another, and the horses of the Cavalry were frequently covered with frozen sleet, as they had no stables to protect them. An attempt was made to erect a shelter for the animals, but the proper material was lacking. Two picket lines were located under the shelter of high banks of the creek, and two on benches on the mountainside nearby. Many of the horses died of the exposure although, strange as it seems, none died until good weather came, when they were attacked by blind staggers. The excellent hunting in the vicinity of the camp made it popular with sportsmen.

The Comanches went on the war path and companies A and F marched from Camp Cooper and B and G from Fort Mason, on June 12, 1856. They joined at Fort Chadbourne June 18, under the command of Lieutenant Colonel Robert E. Lee.[1] They proceeded to the headwaters of the Brazos and Colorado rivers where Captain Earl Van Dorn and his company after a tedious pursuit surprised a party of Comanches on July 1, and killed two warriors and captured one, as well as twelve animals and other property. They returned to Camp Cooper on July 23, the columns having covered sixteen hundred miles, according to Colonel Lee. They also visited the Double Mountains and all the branches of Double Mountain Fork and in five separate columns swept down the valleys of the Concho, the Colorado, and Red Fork of the Brazos to the San Saba country and Pecan Bayou. The Indians had set fire to the high grass which covered their retreat and made it difficult to feed the horses of their pursuers. He wrote: "The weather was intensely hot and as they had no tents, they had no shade. The men, however, were healthy though the water was scarce and bad, sweet, salt, bitter, or brakish." He wrote that he spent the Fourth of July on the Brazos after a march of thirty miles in the hot sun. He put blankets upon four upright sticks in order to get some shade "for the air was like the blast from a hot-air furnace, the water salt, still my feelings for my country were as ardent, my faith in her future as true and my hopes for her advancement were as unabated as if called forth under more propitious circumstances."

Colonel J. K. F. Mansfield inspected Camp Cooper from July 1, to August 3, 1856, inclusive while Colonel Lee was in command. The troops were Company E, Second Cavalry, under Captain George Stoneman, Company K, Second Cavalry, under C. J. Whiting, Company A, First Infantry, under Captain J. N. Caldwell, and Company I, First Infantry, under Captain J. H. King, aggregate of eight officers and 174 men. He reported that the hay cost $20 a ton and corn $2.50 a bushel and that the season was so dry that no more hay might be furnished, as the Indians herds had ruined grazing. The supplies came from San Antonio and fresh beef cost 6 7/10 cents a pound and the flour, which was excellent, came from Texas via Fort Belknap. He wrote: "The post is very well commanded by Colonel Lee and in good discipline." The following ammunition was at hand at the post: 900 Sharps carbine, 1,000 Halls carbine, 8,150 rifle musketoons, and 11,060 rifles, 18,970 Colts pistol cartridges. The Cavalry was armed with sabers, Colts revolvers, and musketoons or rifled carbines. The infantry had muskets with Maynard primers, which did not always discharge at the first blow of the hammer. There was a civilian guide who was paid $40 a month and ration for man and horse, and six teamsters, four expressman, six wagons, sixty mules, and one spring wagon. Captain J. R. Baylor was the Indian Agent at that time. Colonel Lee left Camp Cooper September 1, 1856, on court-martial duty on the Rio Grande, and he wrote on April 19, 1857, from Camp Cooper: "After an absence of over seven months I have returned to my Texas home." He reports that while he heard of Indians, he had not met any and felt as safe in the wilderness as in a crowded city. He wrote on July 9 that the great heat at Camp Cooper had produced much sickness and that a little child died and the parents asked him to perform the burial rites, as there were no clergymen there. As he read the beautiful funeral service of the Episcopal Church, he undoubtedly thought of his own dear children at Arlington and tears of sympathy ran down his cheeks. This gave rise to the story that it was his child, as he was seen to cry at the burial. There were four officers named Lee in Texas, and stories connected with the others have been attached to Robert E. Lee. Then again on June 22, he wrote of the death of a baby boy of a sergeant. The father came to him with tears flowing down his cheeks, begged him to read the funeral service for his little son and he complied, knowing how the father felt.

On July 23, an express came form San Antonio with news that Colonel Albert Sidney Johnston was ordered to Washington and Lee was to telieve him at San antonio where he arrived July 27, 1857, and assumed command of the post per

Special Order one hundred.

In 1858, it was decided that the Indian reservation at Camp Cooper was too small for the Indians. They were restless and dissatisfied, and the citizens blamed the Indians for losses of stock, the officers thought, unjustly. The citizens threatened to organize and attack the Indians, so it was planned to move them into Indian Territory. Maj. George H. Thomas reported in May, 1859, that 250 armed men under an ex-Indian agent had marched toward the Brazos Agency near Camp Cooper intending to attack the village. But they stopped and killed an Indian and then withdrew to William Martin's Ranch, where they were followed by the Indians and six white men, and three Indians were killed or wounded. The Indians were moved to Camp Cobb, Indian Territory, in August, 1859, by Major George H. Thomas with Company G and H of the Second Cavalry as escort.

Headquarters of the Second United States Cavalry were established at Camp Cooper by Major George H. Thomas, later known to fame as the "Rock of Chicamauga" with companies C, D, F, G, and H. On October 1, 1857, he started on the "Cimarron Expedition" to the headwaters of the Red and Canadian rivers. They marched to a point thirty miles west of 100' west longitude and then north and west until near the Cimarron River, having followed the Indian trail until a herd of buffalo obliterated it. They then put in at the Supply Camp on the Canadian a month after they started. After a rest of five days they marched southwest to the headwaters of the Wichita, thence along the eastern boundary of New Mexico and south to Sweetwater Creek. They got to Camp Cooper November 2, after being out fifty-three days.

On July 23, 1860, Major Thomas, Lieutenant William W. Lowe, and thirteen men of the Second United States Cavalry set out from Camp Cooper for the headwaters of the

Concho and Colorado. They were joined on the 27th by Second Lieutenant Fitzhugh Lee with Co. B Cavalry, on the Colorado River, and by Captain Richard Johnson and Lieutenant A. Parker Porter, with Company A on Kiowa Creek. On August 25, they followed an Indian trail discovered twenty-five miles east of Mountain Pass, and the next day they ran into the Indians on the Salt Fork of the Brazos. After a hot pursuit the Indians abandoned their horses consisting of twenty-eight head and escaped, except one who dismounted and, before he died, wounded Major Thomas twice and also five enlisted men.

First Sergeant John W. Spangler of Company H of the Second Cavalry started with a detachment of his company and some state troops in December and encountered a war party of the Comanches on the Pease River, a tributary of the Red River, on December 19, when they killed fourteen warriors, wounded some, and captured three warriors and forty-five animals without loss. Sergeant Spangler joined Captain L. S. Ross, Texas Ranger, afterwards governor of Texas, on Elm Creek, December 6, 1860, and with his forty men brought the party up to one hundred and thirty-six. On December 19, the Indian camp was discovered, and Spangler's men concealed themselves near the mouth of the creek northwest of where the Indians were encamped. When Captain "Sul" Ross charged them with his Texas Rangers, they ran into Spangler who personally killed six warriors. Cynthia Ann Parker was riding a pony, was covered with a buffalo robe, and looked like a man, and when Ross raised his rifle to shoot her, she held up her baby. She was taken to Camp Cooper with her baby, and her uncle Isaac Parker was sent for. She cried most of the time at first, but later she told her story through a Mexican interpreter to her uncle and A. B. Mason. She was only nine years of age when she was captured by the Indians on May 19, 1836, so she was thirty-three years old at this time. She had evidently forgotten the English language and that she was a white woman. She sat despondently on a box with her chin on her hands and with her elbows on her knees, and when she heard English spoken by her uncle, she seemed as though she had heard it before, so it was repeated. He said, "If this is my niece, her name is Cynthia Ann." Then she arose, her despondency vanished, and she patted herself on her breast and said, "Me! Me! Cynthia Ann." Through the interpreter she reported what had happened at Parker's Fort, but had difficulty remembering names and only recalled her brother, John. She gave the time she was captured twenty-four years before with surprising accuracy and only missed it by four moons or months. She told them that she once had a pale-faced mother and father.

In obedience to orders of Brevet Major General David E. Twiggs dated February 18, 1861, Camp Cooper was officially abandoned February 21, 1861, and Captain Innes N. Palmer and Company D and Company H United States Cavalry marched to Green Lake, about thirty miles from Indianola, Texas, where Companies B, D, E, G, H, and I, Second United States Cavalry assembled. They then marched to Indianola, where they embarked on the steamship Coatzacoalcos, March 31, and proceeded to New York via Key West, Florida, and Havana, Cuba. They arrived at their destination April 11th. Companies D and H from Camp Cooper were ordered to Washington for duty and arrived there April 17th.

Camp Cooper with its supplies, less the trains and other supplies needed by the troops evacuating the post, was turned over February 25, 1861, to Col. W. C. Dalrymple of the State troops by Captain Stephen D. Carpenter, First

United States Infantry, who commanded Company I, First United States Infantry, at Camp Cooper. Captain Edmond K. Smith, Second United States Cavalry, later known as Lieutenant General E. Kirby Smith, Confederate States of America, was at Camps Cooper and Colorado until March 20, 1861, and did not accompany his regiment when it left Texas. He said he was awaiting the action of his state, Florida, and when Florida seceded, he resigned April 6, 1861. He openly expressed his sympathy for the Southern States and H. E. McCulloch "Com'r. and Col. Comdg. N. W. frontier of Texas" states, on Feb. 25, 1861, that he was in command of Camp Cooper and that his negotiations with him "were of the most kind and agreeable character," and he made more beneficial arrangements with him than General Twiggs had made with the Commissioners at San Antonio. McCulloch's account is recorded in the Journal of the Texas Secession Convention, 1861.

And so ends my story of Camp Cooper, the Texas home of Lieutenant Colonel Robert E. Lee, where the lessons he learned in handling troops in the field led to his selection to the highest rank in the Confederate Army, and enabled him to become the grand salient central figure of the War between the States.

Fort Griffin, Texas

During the Civil War and for some years afterwards, the depredations of Indians and outlaws drove back our western frontier in Texas from fifty to one hundred miles. To re-establish law and order our government first used our army, as being the best available body of trained men. A line of forts stretched across our western frontier from Jacksboro to El Paso, starting with Fort Richardson, on the east, and

Military Fort Griffin on Government Hill above the town.

including Forts Griffin, Concho, Stockton, Davis, Quitman, and Bliss.

Fort Griffin was established July 31, 1867, and was first called Camp Wilson. It was situated at latitude 33' 58' and longitude 99' 10' on the Clear Fork of the Brazos River, 73 miles west-south-west of Fort Richardson at Jacksboro; 150 miles west of Dallas, which was the nearest railway station, and 305 miles north of San Antonio. After a careful survey of the surrounding country, the site for the fort was selected on Maxwell's Ranch, on a plateau 100 feet above the Clear Fork, so as to be well above high water, with a well-wooded valley half a mile to the east.

The fort was called after Major General Charles Griffin, who commanded the District and who died September 15, 1867, after twenty-five years of honorable and distinguished service, from the Mexican War period to the Civil War. During the latter, he was brevetted for gallantry at Bull Run, the Wilderness, Welden, and Five Forks with ranks from major to major general.

It was originally intended to build the fort in the form of a square and to have permanent stone buildings. Steam saw mills, window sashes, door frames and the necessary mechanics were brought all the way from San Antonio, and it was estimated that it would take a year to complete the buildings as planned. In the meantime wooden shelters were built to protect the troops from the northers. A line of officers quarters, consisting of one room and one kitchen, was erected. The commanding officers quarters were made from an old log house hauled from a deserted ranch and consisted of two rooms. A similar building was used for a hospital. For some unknown reason, the original plans were never carried out, and the fort was abandoned in 1881. Probably the extinction of the buffalo had something to do with the change of plans, for when first occupied the village which grew up nearby was the headquarters of the buffalo hunters, and for about ten years was the wildest town in the wild West. As many as 200,000 hides of buffalo were brought to Fort Griffin for trade in one year. With the year 1877, hide hunting was at an end, and the garrison at the fort was reduced.

The buildings consisted of quarters for six companies and a band, eleven sets of officers quarters, an adjutant's office, hospital, guardhouse, five storehouses, forage houses, bakery, four stable sheds, workshops, and laundresses quarters. The supplies were shipped from the depots at St. Louis, New Orleans, and San Antonio. The route from St. Louis was via the Missouri, Kansas & Texas Railway to Denison and by wagon train to the post, a distance of 756 miles.

A drawing of the fort and the town of Griffin.

All drinking water was furnished by wagons which drew it from the Clear Fork of the Brazos. During the summer this water had a bad taste and was unfit for drinking. No bathing facilities were furnished, and during the summer the men bathed in Collins Creek and the Clear Fork. There were no gardens at the post, as there were no means to irrigate them and the rainfall was insufficient. Fresh potatoes were obtained at Jacksboro and Weatherford at a cost of from $3 to $5 a bushel and a dollar more for delivery. The only means of transportation was by horse, mule, or ox-wagon. Four mails a week were received at the post as follows: from the east, via St. Louis and Fort Smith on Sundays and Thursdays; from the west, via San Antonio and Fort

Concho, on Mondays and Thursdays. The Indians and floods sometimes interfered with the schedule. It took eight days for mail to reach department headquarters at Austin and twelve days to reach Washington.

Among the distinguished officers who were stationed at this post may be mentioned Adna R. Chaffee. He had a very gallant career during the Civil War and was one of our leading heroes at Santiago during the Spanish-American War and at Peking, during the China Relief Expedition. He was appointed Lieutenant General January 1, 1904, and served as Chief of Staff of the United States Army until he retired February 2, 1908. He died November 11, 1914.

He was assigned to a troop of the Sixth Cavalry at Fort Griffin in February, 1868. It was at a period following the War, when conditions were deplorable. Bands of outlaws under Lee and others ravaged the country and did as much harm as the Indians. He had only been at the post a few days when a band of Quahada Comanches attacked a wagon train hauling wood from the saw-mill thirty miles from the post, and all the mules were stolen. These Comanches were reinforced by mulatto and Mexican outlaws, and they had lain in wait for a wagon train with a weak escort. The report of the attack was received at 7:30 a. m., March 5, 1868, and within an hour Captain Chaffee with a detachment of Troops F, I, and K, Sixth Cavalry and Tonkawa Indian Scouts were in pursuit. They proceeded via Ledbetter's Ranch, nine miles south of Albany, and Dead Man's Creek during the night, crossed the Clear Fork of the Brazos twelve miles below Phantom Hill, struck the Indian trail next morning and followed it all day. The trail split, those with the stolen mules having taken one trail and the warriors the other. Captain Chaffee was in for a fight and followed the warriors. Early the next morning the Tonkawa scouts sighted the Comanche camp and reported to Captain Chaffee. He immediately sent the Tonkawa scouts around their camp to cut off their retreat and with his men armed only with revolvers, he charged the Comanches and killed seven. The following order was published concerning this affair:

Headquarters, Fort Griffin, Texas, March 10, 1868.

General Order No. 19.

The Commanding Officer takes pleasure in openly announcing to the troops of this command the complete success of the detachment that left this post on the 6th, instant, under command of A. R. Chaffee, 6th U. S. Cavalry. This short and decisive campaign has resulted in the killing of five Indians and one Mexican and one mulatto (both of whom were leaders). The capture of five horses, together with a large number of shields, bows and arrows, etc., and the total breaking up of an Indian camp, which had for a long time been a scourge to the people of the frontier.

The casualties on our side were three men wounded, viz.: Privates John F. Butler and Charles Hoffman of I Troop and Private James Regan of F Troop. With the exception of the wounds of these men, the result is extremely gratifying, as was also the soldierly manner in which the troops bore their deprivations throughout the pursuit, suffering from want of water and the want of shelter from the cold storm that raged throughout the entire march without a murmur of discontent.

In all campaigns where important results are achieved and especially against Indians, where the nature of the country is not well known, troops must expect to undergo hardships and deprivations, which cannot be foreseen or obviated; yet it is only the true soldiers who accept these inconveniences as necessary and unavoidable and who, like men, maintain their spirit in spite of these.

(Signed)   S. D. STURGIS,

Lieut. Colonel, 6th Cavalry, Commanding.

The most horrible massacre that ever took place in the vicinity of Fort Griffin was when the teamsters of Captain Henry Warren, the government contractor at Fort Griffin, were killed by about one hundred Indians on May 18, 1871. It was on Salt Creek Prairie between Fort Griffin and Fort Richardson. Captain Robert G. Carter told me this story, so I will repeat it in his own words.[2]

"The report proved not to have been exaggerated in the least and in a perfect deluge of rain, such as had scarcely ever been known in Texas before, flooding the parade of Fort Richardson to the depth of several inches, General Mackenzie with four companies (A, B, E and F) arrived on the scene. It was supposed that this war party of Ki-o-was[ii] under Sa-tan-ta, their principal war chief, hearing that General Sherman was coming that way had planned to intercept that and to capture him, and then hold him as a hostage for a heavy ransom, but this story he (Sa-tan-ta) always most strenuously denied to us in broken Spanish during the period—June until November—that he was held a prisoner at Fort Richardson.

"There could be nothing more appalling, heart rending, or sickening to the human senses than the spectacle which was witnessed when our command reached the scene of the Salt Creek Prairie massacre. The poor victims were stripped, scalped, and horribly mutilated; several were beheaded and their brains scooped out. Their fingers, toes, and private parts had been cut off and stuck in their mouths, and their bodies, now lying in several inches of water and swollen, bloated beyond chance of recognition, were filled full of ar-

Marker of murdered teamsters between Jacksboro and Fort Griffin at the site of the Warren Wagon Train massacre.

rows which made them resemble porcupines. Their bowels had been gashed with knives, and carefully heaped upon each exposed abdomen had been placed a mass of live coals, now of course, extinguished by the deluge of water which was still coming down with a torrential power almost indescribable.

"One wretched man, Samuel Elliott, who, fighting hard to the last, had evidently been wounded, was found chained between two wagon wheels and, a fire having been made from the wagon pole, he had been slowly roasted to death—"burnt to a crisp." That he was still alive when the fiendish torture was begun was shown by his limbs being drawn up and contracted. The grain sacks had also all been cut open and contents dumped upon the ground, where it was found, littered and scattered in every direction. Some distance from the wagons, dead mules, piles of corn soaking in the water, harnesses, and other evidences of the fearful struggle were to be seen. Here and there a hat, an Indian gew-gaw, and a plentiful supply of arrows and other debris of the fight were spread about the rain-soaked ground. There were seven men killed . . . S. Long, N. J. Baxter, Samuel Elliott, James Bowman, James Elliott, James Williams, and John Mullen. Forty-one mules had been cut loose from the wagons and run off by the retreating Indians—the others had been killed. The balance of the men, some of them wounded, escaped into the timber, and later came into Fort Richardson. Taking the trail, Mackenzie attempted to follow it. It was but an attempt, for the powerful rains that fell daily in quick succession pounded every vestige and obliterated every sign until there was no trace remaining, and rendered it impossible to more than taking the general direction which led through the Wichita swamps and across the Big and Little Wichita Rivers and Red River toward Fort Sill."

And so ends the second part of my story—Fort Griffin—where Captain Adna R. Chaffee learned lessons in fighting Indians and in handling troops in the field, like his predecessor Lieutenant Colonel Robert E. Lee, that led to his elevation to the highest rank in the United States Army, Lieutenant General and Chief of Staff.

NOTES

[1] In this connection see "Robert E. Lee's Expedition in the Upper Brazos and Colorado Country," by R. C. Crane, *Year Book*, 1937, pp. 53-64.

[2] Captain Carter told me this story about January, 1926, and showed me his manuscript started forty years before.

EDITOR'S NOTES

[i] This is a variant and more popular spelling of *Ka-tem-e-see*.

[ii] Commonly spelled *Kiowas*

Bibliography

Captain George F. Price, *Across the Continent with the Fifth Cavalry*. New York: D. Van Nostrand, 1883.

"Circular 4," Surgeon General's Office, December 5, 1870, Washington, D. C.

Emily V. Mason, *Popular Life of General Robert Edward Lee.* Baltimore: John Murphy and Company, 1872.

Joseph Carroll McConnell, *The West Texas Frontier*, 2 vols. Jacksboro, Texas: Gazette Printing Company, 1933; Palo Pinto, Texas; Legal Bank and Book Company, 1939.

Thomas H. S. Hamersly, *Complete Regular Army Register, 1779-1879* (Washington, 1880).

"Colonel J. K. F. Mansfield's Inspection Report of the Department of Texas, 1856," M. L. Crimmins ed., *Southwestern Historical Quarterly*, XLII, 369-373.

Robert G. Carter, *On the Border with MacKenzie* (Washington, D.C.: Eynon Printing Company, Inc.; n.d.

Lee's Texas Home
by Carl C. Rister

This narrative is from Carl Coke Rister's Robert E. Lee In Texas, *published in 1946 by the University of Oklahoma Press. Rister details the general events of life for Lee at Camp Cooper.*

This was Lee's first field command—four companies of the Second Cavalry! He was on a raw frontier amid homespun men. His situation gave him anxious concern. Army officers on the border, far away from the amenities of civilization, were inclined to be a rough lot; drinking, gambling, and carousing were common, in the absence of other forms of social activities and entertainment. But Lee was known as the "gentleman soldier," the "best-read man in the army," a "puritan," and he was as much at home in the drawing room as on the drill field. Could he, with this background, hold the respect of his brother officers, of his enlisted men? Certainly his splendid Mexican War record and his West Point superintendency were to his advantage.

He spent the morning following his arrival at Camp Cooper in conferring with Hardee and other officers of the post, most of whom he had known at Jefferson Barracks or elsewhere. Then Katumse came, greasy and filthy, undoubtedly embracing Lee, as was his custom. Agent John R. Baylor had probably sent him. Lee received him unceremoniously. Katumse assured him "volubly and tediously" that the Comanches were the white men's friends and had accepted their customs. But Lee, "very sententious," retorted that he would regard him as such only as long as he deserved his friendship, and that he would meet him "as an enemy the first moment he failed to keep his word." This warning was not what Katumse had expected to hear, and he went away perplexed.

The next day Lee returned Katumse's call, and what he saw and heard must have given him, for the first time, a realistic conception of his new task. In the past his engineering problems had been concrete and physical and had required the application of well-known mathematical formulas and rules; but here must be solved human equations, involving intangible cultural factors, for which there were no known rules.

Katumse's village was typically Comanche. Wolflike dogs, lean and snarling, snapped at the visitor's heels; and the air was filled with a bedlam of noises. The village, comprising about one hundred lodges, whose irregular spacing was wholly unlike that of the tents in Lee's army camp, sprawled for a great distance along the river. Only Katumse's teepee, standing conspicuously apart and decorated with red and yellow pictographs, differed from the others. The whole scene bespoke primitiveness and poverty. That these were buffalo Indians was indicated by their skin lodges, meagerly furnished—a skin mat on the dirt floor, robes for bedding piled in one corner, parfleche bags, thongs, ropes, and other belongings. In front of each family lodge or in an adjacent, smaller lodge was a smoke-blackened meat pot suspended from a tripod over a fire, and near by thin strips of buffalo or deer meat hung from a scaffold, drying in the sun. Lee found a total lack of order—bones carelessly strewn, camp refuse, and swarms of flies.

Unkempt children, evidencing malnutrition, quite unlike the Virginia children Lee knew, peered from lodges or played near the village. Indian men and women, stolid and indifferent, were engaged with domestic tasks or lounged about, watching him curiously. His visit was short and unpromising. Katumse greeted him as before and expected Lee to observe a ceremonial rite of disrobing, but he removed only his necktie.

Katumse had six wives, some of whom were riding in and out of camp. They did not impress the visitor favorably. He wrote Mary that their paint and ornaments rendered them "more hideous than nature made them." Indeed, he found the whole tribe "extremely uninteresting," far more so than he had ever conceived and returned to his camp with a feeling that the government's experiment was ill advised.

On the morning of April 13, Lee assisted Major Hardee in checking out prior to his departure for Fort Mason on the following Monday. Many other duties awaited him, the most immediate of which was inspection. Before the morning was far gone, therefore, he stepped from his tent to meet the two squadrons of the Second Cavalry (12 commissioned officers and 226 enlisted men) drawn up on the small parade ground. For Lee this was an important occasion, and he was meticulously and correctly groomed. His soldiers would be as interested in the man who was to lead them through fair and foul weather and stress and strife, as he was in studying their qualities.

It is reasonable to suppose that he did not disappoint them, for he was a man of striking military bearing. He was five feet, eleven inches tall and weighed 175 pounds. His brown eyes, set in a broadly rounded face, with prominent brows and wide temples, normally beamed with gentleness and benevolence. He had black hair streaked with gray, and he was clean shaven except for a black mustache which covered his thin upper lip and extended half an inch beyond the corners of his mouth. He had fine teeth, vision, and hearing, and a voice of lower middle register, rich and resonant. His massive torso rose from narrow hips; his hands were large, but his feet were unusually small; and his legs were flat—well suited for a cavalryman. His hair was parted low on the right side and fluffed above the right ear, and from the part it swept to the left across his forehead and turned up, curling above his left ear.

This morning's inspection was more than routine, and Lee went about it carefully and appraisingly. As he looked at the bronzed border-seasoned men before him, he was pleased. Amidst a primitive wildness, here was military pageantry unsurpassed, and he must have gazed on it pridefully. Other than their shoes, his troopers' attire was as showy as the dragoons', the only difference being trimmings of yellow instead of orange. Even the cavalry horses, no one of which had cost less than $150, fitted into this colorful setting. Those ridden by troopers of Company A were grays; those of E, sorrels; those of F, bays; and those of K, roans—all well curried and in good fettle.

Lee next inspected his men and their equipment. His four company captains were all distinguished soldiers. Three—Earl Van Dorn, George Stoneman, and Charles J. Whiting—were West Pointers. Van Dorn had been cited for valor in four Mexican War battles and had been secretary of the Louisiana Pascagoula Military Academy when he was called to the Second Cavalry. Whiting had served in the Florida Seminole War and as an assistant engineer on the American-Mexican boundary survey of 1849. Stoneman was also a Mexican War veteran, having marched with the Mormon Battalion to California and later having acted as aide-de-camp to Wool. Theodore O'Hara had not attended West

Point, but he was a ripe scholar, a modest gentleman, a Mexican War veteran, and author of "The Bivouac of the Dead" and other poems. Assisting each of these were competent junior officers.

The enlisted personnel came from several states and sections of the country, some even from Mexican battle fields. For the most part, those of Company A were recruited in Alabama ("Alabama Grays"); those of Company E, in Missouri; of Company F, in Kentucky; and of Company K, in Ohio. Already they had become acquainted with routine duties—guarding supply and emigrant trains and mail coaches and scouting. Each man was furnished a brass-mounted Campbell saddle with wooden stirrups, or Grimbsby equipment; a spring, movable stock, or Perry carbine; a Colt navy revolver and dragoon saber, carried by saber belt and carbine sling; a gutta-percha cartridge box; and a cape or talma, with loose sleeves extending to the knees. He wore pale blue trousers, a close-fitting dark blue jacket trimmed with yellow braid, a silken sash, a black hat with looped "eagle at the right side" with trailing ostrich plumes on the left. On his shoulders he had brass scales to turn saber strokes of the enemy. He wore no boots or gauntlets.

Lee must have been pleased by his inspection. And after he had completed it, he could then turn with confidence to other daily tasks.

Before joining with other border commanders in patrol work, Lee set to work to study the defense system of Texas. The immense task of the Second Cavalry in helping to defend the frontier appalled him. The state had an area of 237,000 square miles, or about 150,000,000 acres. Across it, from the Red River to the Rio Grande, stretched an irregular border line of settlements, with arms of occupation here and there reaching up fertile river valleys still farther west. Well in front of the border stood isolated army posts, like lonely sentinels. The map showed why it was possible for Comanche and Kiowa marauders to slip past cavalry patrols undetected. At points, the distance from one post to another was two hundred miles; and numerous hills, canyons, waterless badlands, and dense forests afforded the Indians many approaches.

Lee found three systems of Texas forts. The federal government had established the first system to keep its annexation promise to Texas. These posts—Mason, Croghan, Graham, Worth, and Gates—stood now well among the westernmost settlements, so rapid had been the occupation of the state's domain. But west of these, and beyond the frontier, were newer posts—Belknap, Camp Cooper, Phantom Hill, Chadbourne, Camp Colorado, and McKavett. Farther south, to guard the Rio Grande frontier from Brownsville to El Paso, were Forts Brown, Ringgold Barracks, McIntosh, Davis, and others.

It was apparent now why he, the regiment's second ranking officer, had been sent to Camp Cooper. Cavalry units here not only shared in reconnaissances and patrol work but also saw that the government's "humanizing" experiment with the wild Comanches was given a fair trial. No doubt General Scott had ordered this.

At Camp Cooper, Lee must so lose himself in his work that his sense of loneliness would be smothered. His deep love for his family, his longing for Virginia and army friends, and his great interest in national affairs, all caused him to feel his border isolation most keenly. But at least he could be with this family in spirit and could glean from the Alexandria Gazette the trend of state and national events. He would hide occasional heartache and loneliness in letter writing.

Lee's task was understandable to him only in terms of the federal government's attempts to solve the longstanding Comanche raiding problem, including Captain R. B. Marcy's and Supervising Agent R. S. Neighbors's work in locating the Comanche reservation on the Clear Fork.

He could well appreciate why Comanche hostility had risen in proportion to the westward advance of the settlements, for that advance had been at Indian expense. Surveyors had claimed the Comanches' choicest hunting grounds for future homesites, and white hunters had killed their game. Lee learned, too, why the Comanches were gravely alarmed because of the disappearance of wild game: their families were entirely dependent on the buffalo, elk, and deer.

For example, as early as 1852, Horace Capron had come to Katumse's and Sanaco's Penateka (Southern Comanche) village near Camp Johnson on the Concho River and had found the Indians starving. The chiefs had complained to him bitterly. "What encouragement have we," one had asked, "to attempt the cultivation of the soil, or raising of cattle, so long as we have no permanent home? In every attempt we have ever made to raise crops, we have been driven from them by the encroachment of the white man before they could mature.

"Over this vast country, where for centuries our ancestors roamed in undisputed possession, free and happy, what have we left? The game, our main dependence, is killed and driven off, and we are forced into the most sterile and barren portions of it to starve. We see nothing but extermination left for us, and we await the result with stolid indifference. Give us a country we can call our own, where we may bury our people in quiet."

Undoubtedly this had a touching appeal to the Texans

of that time, as it had later for Lee. The Indians had been the victims of the white man's land hunger. But the federal government could not step in to help the Indians, for upon entering the Union in 1845 Texas had reserved all its public land. More than once Indian officials had asked the Texans to relieve the federal government's embarrassment by appropriating land for reservations; and at last on February 6, 1854, the state legislature had set aside for this purpose twelve leagues, to be located in not more than three tracts.

When Marcy and Neighbors, preparing to survey the reservation sites, procured a map from the Texas Land Office, they were surprised to find that much of the region they had expected to explore had already been claimed by land companies and individuals.

This was discouraging, but they proceeded with their work. They examined the sterile badlands and waterless region of the upper Colorado, Brazos, and Wichita rivers but found no sites suitable for their purpose. Next they turned to the valley of the Clear Fork, where finally they decided upon a tract of four Spanish leagues (17,712 acres), in the Camp Cooper country, for the Comanches. Then, near the junction of the Clear Fork and the Brazos, below Fort Belknap, they established another tract for the small band of Caddoes, Anadarkos, Wacos, Tawakonies, and Tonkawas.

W.B. Parker, who accompanied Marcy and Neighbors on their journey, wrote a graphic narrative of their experiences in his *Unexplored Texas*, published about the time Lee came to Texas. He stated that on August 10, 1854, while the two dispirited men were returning to Fort Belknap, they were overtaken on the Clear Fork by Katumse, the Penateka chief, and two of his six wives. Katumse was every inch an Indian leader, about fifty years old, six feet in height, with a dark red-bronze complexion. His striking physique, however, was offset by his ludicrous attire. He wore corduroy leggings and buckskin moccasins, an old, torn, greasy, checkered-cotton coat, and a "six-penny straw hat," while his horse's bridle "was ornamented with perhaps fifty dollars worth of silver."

Parker described his wives as being hardly more than immature girls, one about eighteen and the other sixteen years old. The younger was chubby and dark; the older was lean, tall, and as fair as a quadroon. Their attire also bore the marks of long use. Both were dressed in dark calico shirts, with leggings and moccasins in one piece, like a boot. Their garments were dirty and common, and their heads were bare; their hair was short, thick, and uncombed. Parker thought that the younger was Katumse's favorite, for she had about her waist a wide belt studded with silver brooches, very heavy, showy, and costly.

Marcy entertained his red visitors at dinner. While they were eating, Sanaco's two subchiefs rode into camp, wearing umbrellas over their heads, much to the merriment of Marcy's party. The two Indians glared at the smirking Katumse and turned his self-satisfaction into furious anger when they denounced him to Marcy as a liar and scoundrel, with no authority to speak for the Penatekas. Only Sanaco had this right, they said. To prove this statement, they departed in search of him; and a few hours later they brought him in.

This rivalry for leadership of the tribe was of longstanding. On August 21, 1853, Sanaco had addressed a lugubrious appeal to T. Howard and "to whom it may concern, "asking for the censure of Katumse. He charged that his rival had urged the "commanding officer on the San Saba" to round up Sanaco and his band, and, if he would not mend his ways, to "fight me and kill me off."

While the subchiefs were away in search of Sanaco, at

sundown Katumse visited Marcy's tent holding in his hand a bundle of short stalks of grass. Seating himself before his host in dignified silence, he smoked his pipe for a few moments. Then he handed the stalks of grass, one by one, to Marcy, naming each as a chief or war captain of the Penatekas, and giving each one's attitude toward the whites. "After remarking upon four of high standing and three of mediocrity," Parker wrote, "he bundled the balance, eight in number, in a bundle, and handed them together, with a grunt and remark, "No count!" He affirmed solemnly that he alone could speak for the Penatekas and that he would accept in the name of his band whatever the Great Father in Washington had to offer.

The following morning Marcy's camp was pitched on the future site of Camp Cooper, near a spring and in a valley shaded by great elm and pecan trees, under which the Delaware scouts erected their lodges. Marcy arranged his wagons in a large semicircle, frontier fashion. Presently Sanaco led other bands to the valley, so that finally several hundred Indians had camped along the river.

Here, on August 20, Marcy opened his grand council with the Comanche chiefs and warriors. He told them that the Great Father at Washington had sent him to select a reservation for his red children, that they might have homes and learn to cultivate the soil and no longer pursue nomadic ways; for the buffalo and other game were fast disappearing, and shortly they and their people must resort to some means other than the chase for a living. Next, he warned the Indians bluntly that they must cease their depredations; if they did not, they would be hunted down and destroyed. The Great Father would not let them starve; he would send them agricultural implements and seeds and men to teach them how to farm; and he would give them food and clothing, until they had grown their first crops. Marcy assured them that he knew of other Indians who had taken his advice and who now had plenty. If they did so, too, they would soon be free from want.

At this point in his narrative Parker had interwoven comedy with pathos. Katumse sat attentively as Marcy spoke, expecting to be called upon for a response. But without invitation Sanaco arose, ignoring the glowering displeasure of his rival.

"What I am about to say," he began, "will be straightforward and the truth, and the sentiment of all my people. We remember what our former chief, Mo-ko-cho-pe, told us before he died, and we endeavor to carry out his wishes after he is gone. He visited our Great Father in Washington and brought us a talk from him. He told us to take the advice and example of the whites, and it would make us happy and benefit us.

"We are glad to hear the talk which has been sent us at this time; it makes our hearts warm, and we feel happy in knowing that our Great Father remembers his poor red children on the prairies.

"We accept this talk, and will endeavor to accede to all our Great Father requires of us." He then took his seat while his subchiefs nodded approval.

Katumse, frowning darkly, stalked away in silence when Marcy did not ask him to speak, too. But he was not too angry to rejoin his fellows a few moments later and accept some of the gifts which Marcy distributed. Eagerly men, women, and children crowded near. Printed cottons, handkerchiefs, blankets, knives, strouding for leggings, armlets of silver, and long wampum beads—all these were fabulous gifts beyond their wildest dreams. Then the council closed with another smoke, and Marcy invited the chiefs to dine with him.

At noon, under the great trees, the table was spread, and about it sat the expectant chiefs, who eyed hungrily the generous platters of bread, meat, and other good things until they were served. Yet they behaved "with great decorum," thought Parker, using knives and forks, but "wild Indian-like, never stopping until everything edible was consumed." Moreover, they returned for the next meal, and the next, until Marcy hinted broadly to them that his hospitality was exhausted.

Even then Katumse lingered, apparently still believing that Marcy would favor him over the other chiefs. But not so. Several hours later he came to the mess tent and asked the sergeant for corn and meat, only to be met by a rebuff. Then he and his wives mounted their horses and rode away, never once turning their heads to the right or the left or thanking their generous host for his hospitality.

While the chiefs were dining at Marcy's mess, beeves were slaughtered for the other Indians present. Marcy had also bought coffee, sugar, and corn for them at a near-by ranch. As soon as the beeves were killed, the Indian women began preparing them for immediate and future use. They consumed every extra edible part. Even the entrails, after they were slightly heated over the fire, were devoured while they were reeking with excrement.

They boned the flesh and then carved it into long slices, throwing them over poles to dry in the sun. "The caul, suet, and other inside fat, were dried whole, and the cannon bones and hoofs were first scorched before the fire and then hung up in the sun."

Those portions of meat intended for immediate consumption they placed upon a rude scaffold over a slow fire. This seared the meat, without depriving it of its juices, and prevented decomposition.

While the women were thus engaged, the warriors spent the day in gambling, in painting themselves and lounging about, or in wandering listlessly from lodge to lodge, expressing either surprise or pleasure by a grunt or a grin. They combed their hair in the middle, plaiting it in long queues and accentuating the divide across the head by a streak of yellow, white, or red clay. "A fat, chubby faced warriors" humorously wrote Parker, "painted a facsimile of a saw around his jaws in black, his cheeks red, his eyelids white, and his forehead and divide of his hair yellow, smearing his body and streaked his face with black, like a ribbed-nose baboon.

Katumse and Sanaco could not forget Marcy's food and gifts. He had promised other good things if they would accept Neighbors's reservation and raise corn, beans, and squash, like the Wichitas. Why should they not do this, they had asked themselves. Game had been driven away from its usual haunts and was increasingly hard to find. Every lodge was impoverished because of this scarcity—no skins for teepee covering and clothing, and no food. If they returned to the Clear Fork, at least they would have temporary relief for their women and children. Hardly had the first frost of fall whitened the grass about their High Plains lodges before they broke camp, band after band, and started eastward.

When Neighbors rode up from San Antonio to the Clear Fork in November, 1854, he was surprised to find about 1,000 Penatekas—Katumse's, and Sanaco's, and Buffalo Hump's—camped along the river above Fort Belknap. And hardly had he arrived before the chiefs came to him for a "talk." They urged him to hasten reservation arrangements, for their women and children needed food and a safe place to camp. Neighbors reassured them, stating that soon he would give them supplies and allow them to occupy the site Marcy and he had surveyed.

But presently the reservation plan met with near disaster. During the preceding spring, while Marcy was yet in the Indian Territory, he had employed a Choctaw teamster, who joined the survey party in order to have the privilege of trading with the Indians. He had loaded his wagon with tobacco, knives, beads, calico, and wampum; but he found the Indians too poor for profitable trading. He learned, however, that other traders who had met with failure had found a way out. When the Comanches could offer nothing in exchange for their goods, they would wait until the Indians could procure horses and other plunder by raiding the border settlements. While this practice had kept the settlements in a ferment of excitement, nevertheless the stolen horses had enabled the Comanches to deal with the traders. In fact, while Neighbors was at Fort Belknap, angry settlers came to ask Major E. Steen, post commandant, to aid them in recovering some stolen horses. When Katumse and Sanaco learned of their mission, they volunteered to accompany Steen to Comanche villages between Fort Belknap and Fort Chadbourne on the Concho to assist in recovering the lost animals.

By the time that Steen and the two chiefs had arrived near Fort Chadbourne, however, one of Sanaco's warriors overtook them, bringing a German trader's warning to Sanaco. He was urged not to eat, sleep, or rest until he had broken camp and had taken his people out of danger of white soldiers, who were moving northward to destroy them. Katumse discredited the report, but Sanaco hastened back to his village and sent runners with the alarming news to other near-by bands, and within a day's time nearly all of them had scattered over the plains, going as far west as New Mexico and as far north as the Arkansas. Only 180 of Katumse's followers had remained to begin the reservation experiment.

Neighbors and Acting Agent Hill censured Washington army officials for ordering out the expedition that had caused the Indians so much alarm. Captain P. Calhoun had been sent out from Fort Chadbourne with a body of cavalry to hunt down raiding bands of Tanima and Nakoni Comanches, and was told to attack any band found near the border.[1] Calhoun's blunder had sadly imperiled the government's reservation program. "Half a million dollars," Hill wrote on February 11, 1855, "will not produce the same quiet and calm condition of the Indian mind that existed on this frontier forty days ago."

But, unfortunately, censure could not repair the damage done. Neither Buffalo Hump nor Sanaco would ever again risk bringing their bands to Camp Cooper. In the end this was fatal. With only a part of the Penatekas on the reservation, the government's policy could not succeed. Neighbors and his agents could not keep the wild Indians from using the reservation as a base for their raids on the border; nor could they restrain Katumse's warriors from occasionally joining their wild kinsmen.

John R. Baylor of Lagrange, Texas, was the first regular agent of Katumse's Comanches. Lee learned that when Baylor had first come to the Clear Fork to establish the reservation, he found that the initial 180 Indians had been increased to 277, all "wild, restless, and discontented." Baylor had employed conciliation, for he had only a small detachment of infantry to protect the agency, and with this small force he could not compel the Indians to remain on the reservation. Well mounted, they entered and left the reservation at will. He convinced Katumse, however, that he had all to gain and nothing to lose by remaining. Later, in January, 1856, with the arrival of the Second Cavalry, he could speak with more authority, and order began to appear out of chaos.

A few days later, Baylor called the Indians into council. He told them that the season was right to start farming. Already he had employed a farmer and a day laborer, and they had plowed 100 acres of land, which were now ready for planting. Pleased, Katumse and his warriors set to work with a will, planting corn, melons, beans, peas, and pumpkins.

When Katumse's prairie kinsmen learned of this, they also came in from time to time, so that when Lee arrived at Camp Cooper in April, 577 Indians had camped along the Clear Fork. Lee also caught the spirit and planted a garden to corn, cabbage, and other vegetables.

This was the state of the Texas reservation experiment that Lee found. At last the wandering Indians had been assigned homes under the watch of troops at Fort Belknap and Camp Cooper. And here at the latter post Lee was to serve as commandant. Drouth was another discouraging factor with which Lee and Katumse's people had to deal. The Indians should have read the Great Spirit's message written across the sky; but if they did, they said nothing about it. Lee, the newcomer, knew little about Texas weather. Day after day dust filled the air and norther followed strong southwestern winds. The wind was hot and parched the skin, leaves on the trees drooped, and spring clouds melted as though they were of snow. Lightning flashed and thunder boomed along the Clear Fork, but little rain fell. Black night clouds of April and May slipped around to the west or east, and morning dawned on dry land.

It was easy to convince Indians who had accepted the reservation only halfheartedly that the Great Spirit was angry. Day after day the sky was red with sand. Then came more positive proof. One morning shortly after their corn had put forth its tender shoots, the northern sky was darkened, but it was not a norther—it was grasshoppers! And when these pests had finally moved on, they left a bare field. This was too much. The superstitious Indians abandoned all efforts to farm, and some joined the Yamparikas (Northern Comanches) on a buffalo hunt along the Arkansas. However, Katumse persuaded most of his people to remain. Even if their crops had failed, he reasoned, the Great Father in Washington would provide food and clothing for them.

Fortunately Lee did not witness the ravages of the drouth on his garden. While his vegetables were yet green, he had led his cavalry in a patrol beyond the frontier.

NOTE

[1] This is only one of many similar instances where Indian agents and border army officers worked at cross-purposes.

Notes Taken with Marcy Locating the Texas Indian Reservations

by W.B. Parker

This material is from notes taken during the expedition commanded by Capt. R. B. Marcy of the U.S. Army. The expedition traveled through unexplored Texas in the summer and fall of 1854. The author was attached to the expedition. This was first published in 1856. Rupert N. Richardson edited the work for this version.

The State of Texas, by an act of her Legislature approved February 6th, 1854, appropriated eighteen leagues of land to form a reservation for the settlement of Indians within her borders in case the government of the United States should accept the grant by locating, surveying, and inducing the wild Indians to settle on it.

Capt. R. B. Marcy was ordered by the Secretary of War and the Secretary of the Interior to repair forthwith to Fort Smith, Arkansas, and organize an expedition to carry out the provisions of the act. Marcy acted with his accustomed energy and left Fort Smith June 1, 1854, with a train of nine wagons. June 28, he was joined by a military force of forty noncommissioned officers and men. With some Delaware

Indians as guides the expedition moved into Texas, following the Fort Belknap road for some distance. However, he moved toward the Wichita rather than the Brazos, for he had instructions to explore the unknown territory about the head waters of these two streams before he should complete the main duty assigned to him—the location of the Indian reservation. An advance party reached the head of the Big Wichita. From this point the party moved south and occasionally southwest; and some four days of travel seems to have brought them to the Cap Rock of the plains where the South or Double Mountain Fork of the Brazos breaks away from the plains in Garza County. The party ascended the Cap Rock, but did not journey far into the plains country. They returned to their main camp on the divide between the Wichita and Brazos, feeling, "That the dangers we encountered and the privations we suffered had not been in vain, establishing as they did the facts that for all purposes of human habitation—except it might be for a penal colony—those wilds are totally unfit. Destitute of soil, timber, water, game, and everything else that can sustain or make life tolerable, they must remain as they are, uninhabited and uninhabitable."

The party then moved to the Clear Fork of the Brazos, and pitched their tents on that stream not far from where the road from Fort Belknap to Fort Chadbourne crosses it. Here they awaited the arrival of the Southern Comanches, who had been informed by Major Neighbors of Fort Belknap that the United States government desired them to assemble on the Clear Fork of the Brazos for a "talk" in regard to their location on the reserve.

W.B. Parker was attached to Marcy's expedition, and the notes he took of the experiences of the party were published at Philadelphia in 1856. We regret that we do not have space to give the reader a complete copy of Parker's book, which has long since been out of print. Few, indeed, of the books of American adventure make more interesting reading. However, his observations and imprecisions of the Comanche who assembled at the Clear Fork to "talk" with Marcy are especially interesting and valuable to students of history and ethnology, and we shall include that part of his book, beginning with the fourteenth chapter, which pertains to the dress, habits, and customs of the Indians he observed. (R.N. Richardson)

Chapter XIV.

August 14.- When Major Neighbors sent out runners to the Comanches, he intimated to them the plans of the government, and they in reply expressed their wish to be settled upon the Clear Fork, as it was their old hunting and wintering ground. Ke-tum-e-see having corroborated this statement, preparations were immediately made to explore in the vicinity of camp, but about 10 A.M., just as the party were about to start, two sub-chiefs of Se-na-ca's band rode in to hold a talk. Their names were Qua-ha-we-tah, or Tall Tree, and Oti, or Hunting a Wife. The latter was by birth a Tonkaway, but was taken prisoner by the Comanches when a child; he had adopted their habits and tribe and become a chief among them. Both were tall, powerful, athletic men, very savage in their appearance, scantily dressed, and fully painted. They rode into camp, bareheaded, with umbrellas hoisted, an incident which occasioned some merriment.

Previous to holding the talk, they improved their toilette, when I perceived what gave Oti his more than usually diabolical appearance, which I could not account for before on account of the load of paint with which his face was covered. Producing a small looking glass and a pair of rude tweezers, which he used with great dexterity, he proceeded to pull out every hair he could find on his face. His hair on his head was cropped close, except the crown tuft, from which depended his buffalo hair plait, and commencing at the roots of the hair on his forehead, he pulled out eyebrows, eyelashes, beard, etc., and then smearing the whole with yellow clay, streaked his eyelids with vermillion, spotted his cheeks with the same, and finished by daubing his chin with black, making a most hideous specimen out of himself in a very short time. The other was not so particular, but with his matted hair, hooked nose, and wide mouth was ugly enough without any effort to increase it.

They held their talk, and told us that we must not believe Ke-tum-e-see, that he was a liar and a scoundrel, and that they would go off and bring in Se-na-ca, who alone was authorized to speak for the tribe; they said the tribe was friendly, and would accede to the proposed settlement. Rations were then served them, and they passed the night under the trees in the valley, intending to leave early in the morning.

In the course of the afternoon Oti asked me for some sugar from the dish standing on our camp-table; and as our stock was small, I took out several large lumps and offered them. He shook his head and walked off, apparently angry. Pretty soon he returned, and pointed again to the dish. I nodded my head, and he deliberately poured the whole into his bag. The same thing happened with their rations; they refused them, and the commissary corporal immediately reported the case to the captain, who told him to double them; this was done, and they took them at once.

August 15th.—On coming out this morning, I was surprised to find the chiefs still lingering around camp, although having saddled up their horses. I found out that they had seen some whiskey and wanted to get it. Both were armed with bows and arrows in addition to their rifles. I tried to barter for a bow, quiver and arrows, offering goods and money to much more than their value, but no, they would trade for nothing but whiskey, and upon my offering it, (which I did to try them), were willing to give their bows and arrows for a bottle full.

Conner told me that this was their way—if they want anything, they must have it, let it cost what it will. He said he once got a mule, which he afterwards sold for fifty dollars, for a plug of tobacco, and, as I observed before, I could readily have got the two bows, quivers and arrows, for a short quart of whiskey. They care nothing about money, as they cannot use it. All they think of is the gratification of their appetite, even if this, as in this instance, should cost them the very means by which they sustain life. As I would not give them the whiskey, they mounted and rode off looking very glum and disappointed.

Conner told me that it was but a short time since the Comanches would drink whiskey, always refusing it and saying that it made fools of them and that they did not like it, but a colony of Germans settled upon the upper waters of the Canadian, and from frequently visiting them the appetite had been acquired by occasional indulgences, and now is quite prevalent among them.

He related a strange tale connected with this German settlement, which although savoring so much of the marvelous, I am obliged to believe from his earnest asservations of its truth, and my own observations upon the character of the wild Indians.

Shortly after the German emigration, a wild Comanche who had never seen them, met one in the prairie. The German wore his full beard, which with his hair was long and shaggy. Surprised at this unusual sight, the Indian shot him and skinned his whole head, the skin having been afterwards found in his possession, preserved and shown as a specimen of an unfound race of men.

Notwithstanding this bloody stretch of curiosity, Conner said that the Germans and Indians lived on terms of great amity, the former treating them with great hospitality whenever they visited the settlement, and a very straight road to a wild Indian's heart is through his stomach, as they are always ready to eat and drink.

August 16th and 17th were spent in explorations to find a suitable tract to be surveyed for the location of the Comanches, and finally one was selected about three miles farther up the stream from our camp, comprising every essential of upland and meadow with fine water and timber, the amount of land necessary being six square leagues.

August 18.-Se-na-ca and his party arrived today. He was very prepossessing in his appearance, about five feet eight inches in height, not stout, but his frame firmly knit, very dark complexion, with a countenance mild but decided. He dressed without ornament, and in this respect was a great contrast to his followers.

With him came Qua-ha-we-ti and Oti, the chiefs who had previously visited us, and Naroni, or little piece of meat thrown over a pole, and Straight-Fellow, two war captains, besides a large party of warriors, women, and children. A very interesting woman accompanied the party. She was the widow of San-ta-na, a celebrated chief who died about three years since, and still mourned her loss, going out every evening in the neighborhood of camp and howl and cry and cut herself with knives, according to the custom among them of persons in affliction. She had separated herself in a measure from the tribe, and formed a band of women, seven in number, like herself widows. She owned a large herd of mules and horses, and was a most successful hunter, having alone shot with her rifle fifteen deer in a morning's hunt. She was a fine looking woman, an Amazon in size and haughty hearing, rode astride, and dressed in deep black.

There was an invalid in the party, a chief, crippled with rheumatism and disease of the spine, drawn into a sitting posture by his ailments, emaciated to a skeleton, and a most pitiable sight, particularly distressing to us from our knowledge of the hardships and privations suffered by them in their wandering life.

The poor creature was perched upon a rude contrivance of sticks lashed on a horse, and bolstered with bags of grass, with a blanket and circlingle passed over and around the whole to keep him steady, and having the feeble use of his hands he guided the horse without assistance. A rude litter accompanied him upon which he could ride during heat and exhaustion. This was constructed by lashing long poles to either side of a mule, leaving the ends trailing upon the ground. Cross sticks were lashed upon the trailing ends, and skins slung to these made the bed, and by the addition of two poles bent in semicircles and fastened diagonally over the bed, a shelter from the sun was made by covering them with green branches.

He had a slave to lead or drive the mules and lift him back and forth. This was a boy about sixteen, a Mexican, taken prisoner in some foray, dressed and painted like an Indian, and apparently quite reconciled to his degraded life, the whole forming a wretched picture of misery and poverty, mixed with considerable ingenuity and contrivance.

Naroni rode in grand costume. He wore an old blue

military coat, with tarnished epaulettes, and covered with bullet buttons, a wampum necklace, almost equal to a breastplate, numerous earrings, finger-rings, and a large ring in his nose, completely encircling his mouth, and bright red leggings.

But his crowning glory was his head-dress. From the crown of his head started out four long eagle's feathers, two on each side. To the center was attached his buffalo hair plait, studded at intervals of an inch or two, with enormous silver medallions, of an oval shape, and at least four inches in largest diameter. This plate swept the ground, and he seemed to set great store by it, as nothing would induce him to part with one of the ornaments. A rifle and bow, quiver, and arrows completed his costume and equipments; but being slender in figure and short in stature, his appearance was not at all imposing.

Straight-Fellow was very miserably clad, dirty and ragged, with a very forbidding countenance, indicative of cunning and cruelty.

The women were ugly, crooked-legged, stoop-shouldered, squalid and dirty, with haggard and prematurely old countenances, their hair cropped close to their heads, and with scarce a rag to cover their nakedness.

They led, or drove off, the pack-horses and mules into the valley, and soon all was life and bustle—some cutting down green limbs to construct their temporary shelter, some building fires, cooking, etc., and others unsaddling, unpacking, watering, and tethering their animals.

Some of the visitors made their shealings on the prairie above us, so that, in a little while, we were surrounded by these wild creatures. Among these was a warrior armed with a lance and shield. The lance was a long, straight piece of steel, about two feet and a half long and an inch wide, tapering to a point. This was fixed into a slender handle of bois d'arc, about four feet and a half long, making the weapon seven feet in length; the handle was ornamented with tufts of colored cotton yarn and strips of cloth-worked beads.

The shield was round, and about two feet in diameter, made of wicker-work, covered first with deer skins and then a tough piece of raw buffalo-hide drawn over, making it proof against arrow-heads. It was ornamented with a human scalp, a grizzly bear's claw and a mule's tail, significant of the brave warrior and successful hunter and horsethief, and the fastenings for the arm were pieces of cotton cloth twisted into a rope.

During their stay, we endeavoured to get this man to show us his exercise with these weapons, but he peremptorily refused, and this I understood is universal with them, a proof of their cunning.

These Indians had plenty of horses and mules, but generally a very inferior stock. The rest of their camp material was meagre and scanty in the extreme.

August 19.-The first thing wild Indians ask for on coming into camp is something to eat. They are always ready and consume large quantities.

The Captain had an ox killed for them this morning, and the women were soon busy in preparing it for present and future use. Every edible part was consumed, even the entrails, which are considered a choice delicacy, were drawn through the coals and devoured, reeking with excrement.

The women boned the flesh and then split it, haggling and carving it into long chains of lumps and then throwing it over poles, dried it in the sun, when it looked like links of stale sausage. The caul, suet, and other inside fat were dried whole, and the cannon bones and hoofs first scorched before the fire and then hung up in the sun.

The portions of meat intended for present use were prepared by placing them upon a rude scaffold over a slow fire, in the same way as previously described among the Kickapoos, and which I have seen done by frontier squatters. It dries the meat, without depriving it of its juices, and prevents decomposition. A supply of corn from the ranch above us, together with some coffee and sugar, capped the climax of their happiness, and their bivouac wore a very cheerful appearance during the day.

The men of the party spent the day in painting themselves and lounging in their shealings, or wandering listlessly from tent to tent, expressing either surprise or pleasure by a grunt or a grin.

The intense heat—thermometer one hundred six degrees—caused them to denude themselves entirely, except the breech-cloth, so that with the yellow, black and red paint, they presented a motley appearance.

They parted their hair from the centre of the forehead back to the crown, and made a streak of yellow, white, or red along the divide, a custom in which they were greatly assisted by large beds of yellow and white clay, which they discovered in the valley some distance down the stream. I could not discover whether each had distinct style of daubing himself, but suppose this to be the case, as all were different.

A fat, chubby warrior painted a facsimile of a saw around his jaws in black, his cheeks red, his eye-lids white, and his forehead and divide of his hair yellow, smearing his body also with yellow.

The invalid painted his face red, his eyelids white and

streaked his face with black, like a ribbed nose baboon. Another painted one side black and the other yellow, continuing the process down to his waist. Another daubed yellow on one side and red on the other, his eyelids white and streaks of black upon his cheeks, in imitation of snakes. The boys also painted themselves; and several of the women had cheeks and hair stained with red. In short, all that savage fancy could do to increase savage ugliness was done, and a more diabolical, and at the same time ludicrous set, it would be hard to meet with.

About nine at night several of them collected upon the prairie to sing and dance. Seated on the ground in a circle, the leader commenced drumming upon a tin mess pan, accompanied with a low, guttural, monotonous chant, at intervals raising his voice louder, when a general grunt or a yell was added by the rest, and the whole strain ended with a prolonged "ugh."

They sang for more than an hour, occasionally two or three throwing their arms up and hopping around like what children call playing at frogs, ending by seating themselves again with a grunt.

I soon tired of the scene, which by the light of a low fire, looked more like a parcel of monkeys at dull play than anything else. Their audience of teamster and soldiers, however, seemed greatly pleased, and as a novelty it was somewhat interesting.

August 20th.-The usual morning toilette was gone through with by the men, but the intense heat—one hundred and five degrees in the shade—kept all quiet in and about camp, except the women; some of whom were unusually busy, conspicuous among whom were the two wives of the chief Ke-tum-a-see.

Our Delawares took the opportunity to have their deer skins, of which they had accumulated quite a large bale, dressed by these women, and the process was very simple but rapid. Having soaked the skins thoroughly, they drew them over a log leaned against a tree at an angle, and then taking a rib of a deer in both hands, removed the hair by scraping it against the grain; they then stretched and dried them, when they became beautifully soft and white. To color them, they tied several into a chimney shape, hung to a limb, and building smouldering fires under them they soon changed to yellowish brown on the hair side, and light yellow on the flesh side.

Great apprehensions were entertained that Ke-tum-e-see, (the chief who had gone out to bring in more of his people) had been waylaid and murdered, as he was absent so long, but about noon he rode in, and gave as a reason for his delay that he had spent the time in endeavoring to persuade his followers to come in, but without success. His two wives ran to meet him, and seemed quite overjoyed at his arrival, most probably because he had left them entirely among strangers, as I cannot imagine any affection in the case.

At dusk the chiefs were assembled in council, and seated on the ground around the light of candles and lanterns, pipes were smoked, and Captain Marcy addressed them, through Conner, the interpreter.

Captain Marcy told them that he had seen their Great Father in Washington, and he had sent him out to locate and survey lands for them, that they might have homes and learn to cultivate the soil and no longer lead the uncertain life they did; that buffalo had disappeared from these plains and deer and other game were fast disappearing; that in a few years they and their children would have to resort to some other means than chase for subsistence; that they would not be permitted to depredate upon the white settlements, and there was no alternative—they must learn to cultivate the soil.

He told them that their Great Father would send them agricultural implements and seeds, also men to teach them to farm, and that he would provide for them until a crop was raised. That he—Captain Marcy—had been among tribes in the North, who once lived as they were living, but who, on advice, had learned to cultivate the soil, and were now living like the whites, with plenty to eat and wear. That if they would do as their Great Father wished them, they would have reason to thank him in a few years. That an agent would be sent to reside among them, and with the assistance of the United States troops would see that they were not molested by white men, or other wild Indians if they remained friendly.

Se-na-ca rose and replied, speaking in a low, distinct and impressive tone, using but little gesticulation, but repeatedly placing his hand upon his heart. He said, "The chiefs and head men of the Southern Comanches have authorized me to reply to the talk which our Great Father has sent us by our friend, Captain Marcy.

"What I am about to say will be straight-forward and the truth and the sentiment of all my people.

"We remember what our former chief, Mo-ko-cho-pe, told us before he died, and we endeavor to carry out his wishes after he is gone. He visited our Great Father at Washington, and brought us a talk from him.

"He told us to take the advice and example of the whites, and it would make us happy and benefit us.

"We are glad to hear the talk which has been sent us at this time; it makes our hearts warm, and we feel happy in knowing that our Great Father remembers his poor red children on the prairies.

"We accept this talk, and will endeavor to accede to all our Great Father requires of us.

"I am pleased to see our friend, Captain Marcy, once more. I well remember seeing him five years since, near this place, when I stayed over night with him, and often inquired of the whites I have met, what had become of him, and I was much pleased, when I was told he was to meet us here."

He stopped, seated himself, and many questions were put to him, which he answered freely and favorably.

All this time Ke-tum-e-see sat like a statue, glum and silent, evidently displeased at not having been spokesman.

Although he and Se-na-ca expressed themselves anxious to meet the views of the government, they were evidently afraid often of their followers, and we anticipated that much perplexity might arise from this cause.

The presents—consisting of printed cotton handkerchiefs, blankets, knives, stroudding for leggings, armlets of silver, long wampum beads, paint, etc.,—were now handed in bulk to the chiefs, and, after another smoke, the council closed.

August 21. -This morning the chiefs distributed the presents, and great delight was manifested, particularly among the squaws, who kept up a continuous chattering.

It requires a good deal of knowledge of Indian fancies to select presents with judgment. Different tribes have different tastes. The Northern Indians like gay clothing and blankets, earrings, brooches, and beads of bright colors. The Comanches prefer dark clothes and heavy silver armlets, and long wampum beads, both the latter being very expensive, particularly the wampum beads, which are to be procured but in one place, a small town in New Jersey.[1]

Our stock of presents was very well selected, so that all were pleased and spent the rest of the day in painting and bedizening themselves, making many a funny show.

I surprised a party of women whilst they were bathing in the stream at mid-day, or rather they surprised me, as they bathed alongside of the road and in sight of camp. I observed, however, that they showed great dexterity in avoiding unnecessary exposure. Wrapping blankets around themselves, they entered the stream where a tree or a bush stood or hung convenient for them to place their blankets on as soon as they were immersed, and thus avoided exposure almost entirely.

The Comanche are very fond of bathing, both men and women, but cleanliness is only partially promoted by it, as they are either unable or neglect to change their clothing, but wear it in a filthy state.

The women observed the same modest caution in mounting their horses. They rode astride, and like all Indians mounted upon the right side of the horse. Drawing the left foot up, after placing the right in the stirrup, they extended it over the saddle at right angles to the right, instead of describing the arc of a circle, performing the feat and seating themselves with much ease and grace. This fact was common to all the females we met.

Towards sunset I observed one of the chief's wives leading a horse and mule slowly backwards and forwards through a slow fire, which scattered over quite a large bare spot of ground, made a dense smoke without flame, and at the same time I was sensible of an aromatic perfume pervading the valley. Upon inquiry, I found it was the process of hardening the hoofs by exposing them to the smoke and vapour of the wild rosemary—artemisia—large quantities of which grow in the valley of the Clear Fork.

August 22nd.-A little Mexican made his appearance among the Indians this morning, dressed in a gay dressing gown and pantaloons, and was immediately recognized by the Captain as a worthy he had seen during his Red River trip among the Witchitas. At that time, the Captain asked him why he did not leave the Indians and go home among his own people. He replied, "Me bin so long mong Witchita, me lie, me steal horse good as any, me big rascal, same as Witchita." If an honest confession is good for the soul, this certainly is a case in point, if there is any truth in physiognomy, for a more cunning rascally countenance no one ever saw.

He rode off in company with some of the party when they left, having succeeded in getting a handkerchief and some other articles, either by begging or stealing.

Se-na-ca and some of the chiefs, with their followers, left us during the day, shaking hands all round and apparently very friendly. They had dined and supped with us several times, behaving with great decorum, sitting at table and using knives and forks, but wild Indian-like, never stopped until everything edible was consumed. This peculiarity applies, in a great measure, to all Indians; so much so, that rations had to be issued to our Delawares for three days only at a time, for just as like as not, they would consume the whole in one day. They have no idea of economy or of tomorrow, but let that take care of itself.

All are proverbially hospitable, both to strangers and acquaintances, never turning a hungry man away empty as long as a scrap to eat remains in camp, but they are wasteful and improvident.

August 23rd.-But few articles could be obtained in barter from these Indians, as they were scantily supplied even with essentials, but what they had, and would part with, was readily taken up by different persons in the command, conspicuous among whom was a full-blooded Choctaw, a teamster, whom we had hired when we passed through the nation, a shrewd fellow, who had provided himself with quite a stock of goods, and obtained a good supply of white buckskins, bows and arrows, etc., in exchange for vermilion, looking glasses, and calico.

In connection with this subject, I may remark, that the present system of trading with the prairie tribes has a great effect in checking all efforts of the government to prevent depredations upon the frontier settlements, and in this way, viz., a number of Delawares, Shawnees and Kickapoos have for several years visited these tribes, with such articles as are most necessary for them, and which they will have at any cost, and have made large profits by the traffic. The articles they take are of small value, such as tobacco, paint, knives, beads, calico and wampum; and as the Indians have nothing of sufficient value to exchange for them, except horses and mules, they necessarily give them, and in large numbers. All these animals are obtained by marauding upon the frontier, and in proportion to the amount traded for, so is the corresponding amount of depredation.

A good plan to prevent this would be an annual donation by the government of such articles as are supplied by the traders, with the understanding that this should continue so long as no forays were made, and thereby depreciating the value of these articles, would render the trading business no longer profitable.

The tribes are accustomed to exchange presents in their friendly intercourse with each other, and have no idea of friendship under any other form; they also value the strength of attachment by the amount of presents received, as an incident related by Captain Marcy will illustrate.

He once held a talk with a chief of one of the tribes, and told him that the President of the United States was their friend, and wished to live on terms of peace with them. The chief replied that he was much astonished to hear this, for judging by the few trifling presents the Captain had given his people, he was of opinion that the "Big Captain" held them in but little estimation.

There is no doubt but that a small amount of money, annually expended in this way, would go far towards doing away entirely with the many and frequently bloody depredations of these people upon our poorly protected frontier.

August 24th.-The Indians continued to leave in parties of two or three, during the day, until all were gone except Ke-tem-e-see and the invalid, who seemed to be great friends.

Neither had anything to say, but lounged around under the trees, evidently with some object in view, which greatly excited our curiosity, but the weather was so intensely hot, that we could take but little interest in anything except the means of keeping cool.

Our larder had been most bountifully supplied for a few days past by a dragoon from Fort Belknap, who with a party, an escort to an invalid officer, had been spending a week with us, and discovered a colony of squirrels in a bottom on the opposite side of the Clear Fork. They were a large species, tawny on the belly and legs, and grey on the back, and so numerous that he shot fifty-five in four days, (going out for an hour at a time before the heat of day) which made into a stew were deliciously delicate and juicy.

August 25th.-Ke-tum-e-see disclosed his intention in

remaining this morning. He walked up to the Quarter Master's tent, and demanded more beef and corn, but was peremptorily refused, told that he must not expect any more, and must now look out for himself. He walked off very angry, and soon we saw his wives bustling round, preparing him to leave.

Some of us went down to his bivouac, and found him seated, looking as black as a thunder cloud, and taking no notice of anything.

The invalid was at the same time made ready, and when his slave had saddled and led up his horse, the women lifted him on and fastened him with great difficulty, every movement of the poor wretch being made with a groan.

Ke-tum-e-see's horse was then saddled and led up by his wives, when he mounted, and led the way across the prairie, not deigning to turn his head or grunt out a goodbye, and this was the last of the Comanches.

The knowing ones predicted trouble from this man, whom they said was revengeful and treacherous. We kept a good look out for him, however, and were constantly on the alert, as we had been during our stay in that wild spot.

August 26th.-The weather was still intensely hot—averaging one hundred and six degrees in the shade—and as the twenty-seventh was Sunday, the Captain determined to commence his survey on Monday, the twenty-eighth; the party was consequently busy all day in preparations, and those of us who had the opportunity kept as quiet as possible, as the most discreet plan under such a sun.

I thought we had done with the Comanches, but was mistaken. Towards evening one made his appearance in the distance, and proved to be Naroni; but oh, how changed from the Naroni of the council-fire. Dressed in an old torn vest, breech cloth and leggings, with a shabby straw hat upon his head, his buffalo tail, medallions and uniform laid aside, the little man looked smaller still, and miserably forlorn. He had shot two bucks, and came to barter the carcasses for corn. Lounging around for a time, and finding no trade, he rode off, and we saw no more of him.

August 27th.-Sunday, intensely hot, and a general quiet reigning in our camp.

Shifting their homes so constantly as these nomads of the plains do, they are very careless of offal about camp, and in time of plenty this evil accumulates.

Our visitors left their temporary abode in a very disgusting state—half gnawed bones, and masses of cooked raw flesh lying around, which soon, under the sun's intense rays, made us sensible of their locality.

As a sanitary measure, the Captain determined to break up our camp on the morrow, and move farther up the stream, and though we should miss the fine spring at this point, we should be nearer the land to be surveyed, which would be more convenient.

August 28th to September 4th.-Last night was one of great excitement in our camp. About midnight a general stampede of our horses took place, and as Ke-tum-e-see had left in such a bad humor, we concluded of course that the Indians had stolen them, but immediate pursuit being ordered, they were found in a ravine some miles off, much frightened, but supposed to have been by wolves, large packs of which had been prowling and howling around us every night during our stay.

We had scarcely got quiet again, when a mounted dragoon rode into camp, calling loudly for the Captain, and exclaiming that his comrade had been murdered at the ranch a mile above us.

An officer with the Doctor and a sufficient force were sent up, when it appeared that the express rider from Fort Belknap to Fort Chadbourne, with a single dragoon as escort, had arrived at the ranch about two o'clock A. M., and not wishing to disturb the inmates, were quietly tying up their mules to feed them, as was their custom at this place, when a young man, who was sleeping in the open air, being aroused, rushed to the house and shouted Indians. The man inside sprang out of bed, and seizing his gun, rushed to the door and fired two shots, both taking effect upon the poor soldier and mortally wounding him. He lingered insensible until eight A. M., and died. Our carpenter made a rude coffin, and we buried him upon a hillside, alongside of a dragoon who had been killed sometime before, by the Wichitas.

This incident shows how exciting is frontier life, and how constantly upon the alert the settlers must be against attack or surprise.

We moved camp six miles up the stream, on the same prairie and to a similar spot to the one we left, though the water was not so good.

Major Neighbors returned to his home near San Antonio, and took with him Conner, the two Jacobs and Jack Hunter, the Shawnee. We parted with the Major with regret, his fund of anecdotes of Indian life and customs, and his great experience on the frontier, imparted with so much affability and enthusiasm, had wiled away many an hour in camp and on the march, and we missed him very much.

We remained at this point until the fourth of September, the surveying parties actively employed in running the lines and marking them, which was done by raising mounds at intervals of half a mile along the line.

Our mess was well supplied with wild turkeys, catfish and turtles, and a stream in the vicinity, a tributary of the Clear Fork, afforded fine sport to anglers, with a fish called here a trout, but which proved to be a species of bass, very game and rising readily to the fly.

The soil was very fertile and the country around rich in mineral affording a fine field for geologizing.

The rock was limestone, appearing on the south-west edge of the prairie piled up in layers of rectangular blocks, looking in the distance like a regularly built fortification.

After the surveying party completed its work on the Clear Fork, the expedition returned to Fort Belknap, and a little later moved down the Brazos to locate a reserve for the "Caddos, Ionies, Ah-nan-da-kas, To-wac-ko-nie, Wichitas, and Ton-kah-was, who exist in this neighborhood."

NOTE

[1] Wampum is made of the thick and blue part of sea clam-shells. The thin covering of this part being split off, a hole is drilled in it, and the form is produced and pieces made smooth by a grindstone. The form is that of the cylindrical glass beads called bugles. When finished they are strung upon small hempen cords about a foot long. In the manufacture of wampum from six to ten strings are considered a day's work.

Life in the Town of Fort Griffin

by Ben O. Grant

T*he explanation given here describes life in the town of Fort Griffin.*

Fort Griffin was established as a United States frontier post in 1866. It was one of the forts of the second line of defense, and was, in the beginning, a post for military purposes only; but in the course of a few years buffalo hides became valuable, and because of the fort's location, it became the headquarters for the hide industry. Later it was the home of many frontier cowmen and was situated on the Western Trail of the great Northern cattle drives. Thus it was the center of much feverish activity and witnessed some of the lurid scenes associated with the last frontier. This discussion deals with the civilian community rather than with the military.

During the middle seventies the buffalo hide business attained huge proportions. Men who were lovers of sport and wild life came in large numbers to share in the profit which was to be realized by the wholesale slaughter of the buffalo. "Uncle Joe" McCombs, who now lives in Albany, ordered in one shipment two thousand pounds of powder and lead to be used by himself and his partner on the buffalo range in the fall of 1876, and on returning from one of his hunts he brought back sixty-four hundred buffalo hides.

Most of the hides obtained in this country found their first market in Fort Griffin.

The writer is indebted to Mr. McCombs for a description of the activity on the range. Sometimes the buffalo were stalked. If a watering place could be found where large numbers watered, the hunter would conceal himself and his horse and lay in wait. When the buffalo came as close as he thought they were apt to come, he would shoot down as many as possible, then mount and follow the herd. All the killer was interested in was in getting the buffalo down. Whether he was dead or not did not matter. There might be in a big "outfit" as many as a dozen "killers" and several times as many "skinners." The number of buffalo killed in a day depended upon the size of the herd, the topography of the country, and the skill of the killer in handling his gun. Shooting from horseback required unusual skill and not all bullets found their mark.

With the first "boom" of the killer's gun, the skinner began his march; following the herd, his work began with his first find. It took only a few minutes for an experienced skinner to strip off a hide. The wagon was stopped with the rear end to the head of the dead buffalo, the hide was cut around the hoofs, skinned up the hindleg to the hocks, and split up the belly to the mouth. Ropes were then tied to the loose skin on the hind legs and to the wagon. The buffaloes were fixed to the ground by means of stakes. The wagon was then started and the hide pulled off. The hide was thrown in the wagon and the meat left to decay.

About mid-afternoon the killers and the skinners returned to camp to stake out the hides. Each hide was stretched with the hair side to the ground, and pegs were driven through the hide into the ground, thus holding it in a stretched position. Sometimes in warm weather a little salt

York's Store in the town of Fort Griffin. It faced the river and was built originally as a bank building. It never housed a financial institution.

Fort Griffin Masonic Lodge upstairs, school downstairs.

Dutch Nance Store at Fort Griffin, 1868.

was rubbed on the hides, but generally they were cured by the dry wind and sun. At the end of a successful hunt, acres of ground would be covered with the hides. When the drying process was complete, the hides would be folded or stacked in the wagons to be carried to market.

Not all the hunters and skinners owned their own outfit but were paid according to the number of buffaloes they killed or skinned. The pay ranged from ten to twenty-five cents per buffalo.

When the buffalo wagons arrived in Fort Griffin and the company was paid off, a period of celebration began, and it was these celebrations which have added many tales of bloodshed and lawlessness to the history of the old frontier post. Even the old hunters say that it was no place for what they termed a "sissy." On one occasion, after a hunter had, as he termed it, "drunk a little too much" he "run all them — Yankees out of the mess hall." He was ordered shot by the captain of the post, but the sheriff of the county took him out and thus saved his life.[2] When the buffalo hunters came to town, trouble was expected, and it nearly always happened. However, they were welcomed because they spent money freely.

Not all the buffalo hunters were bad men. There were good men and bad men as there are in all walks of life, but generally speaking they were wild and reckless and some were viciously bad.

Fort Griffin jail in ruins.

Merchants, seeing the possibilities of this frontier post, began building temporary stores. Because of the demand of the soldiers and the buffalo hunters, each of these early stores was accompanied by a saloon. The town that sprang up around the fort was disorderly, wild, and lurid, yet colorful. It was more than typical of the communities along the last American Frontier. Within was to be found, in an exaggerated degree, every characteristic that made the Old West bizarre and thrilling.

Old Fort Griffin was built rapidly with little or no thought of beauty or permanency. It was considered more as a temporary camp than as a city, and no one felt any responsibility for its appearance. A few of the stores had sidewalks or porches in front of them, but many of these were in bad condition, more dangerous than rocky ground would have been. In many places on some of them, boards were missing or broken. The *Fort Griffin Echo* describes some of them as being traps for crippled people.[3] The paper refers almost every week to the bad condition of the town and asks people not to throw tin cans and boards with nails in them into the streets.[4] In keeping with the streets and stores most of the residences were crude and flimsy. However, there were some which were considered in those days good dwellings. In the terms of some of the men who were there, it was a free town; every man put his house where he wanted it.

After four years of camp life in Fort Griffin (1872-1876) merchants began to erect permanent business houses. Among the first men to erect good store buildings were Charlie Meyer and E. Frankel, about 1876. Each of these stores boasted the best saloon west of Fort Worth. Charlie Meyer's saloon kept ice almost all summer, which indeed, was not to be found in many saloons of the time. Why Frankel did not keep ice is not known, but he tried to offset Meyer's ice by keeping fresh sea food. This was almost a failure and, according to Frankel's statement, it was kept at a loss. Frankel's and Myer's saloon continued to be rivals during the life of Fort Griffin.[5]

The calico peddler and the tinware merchant found ready sale for their wares among the ladies of the town. The Fort Griffin Echo describes them as being as "thick as flies around his wagon," and according to the history of Fort Griffin, flies were plentiful.[6] Unless the trader wished to return and trade again, he usually charged the price he thought the customer looked as if he could pay.

Close on the heels of the soldier, the buffalo hunter, and the saloon keeper came the cattleman. Differing from the others he brought his family, so dwellings sprang up over the country as ranch headquarters. The rancher felt that because he was the first to use the land, it rightfully

Fort Griffin cowboys. Left to right: Berry Campbell, Lee Tuton, and Tull Newcomb.

belonged to him and, as a rule, was ready to drive out those who threatened to block his way on the range. His hired help, the cowboy, was often a reckless fellow. Although much of the cowboy's mischief was done in fun, the consequences often proved serious. The cowboys generally settled their quarrels with guns. Most of them were men of nerve, but some of them were not. Those who were not generally did not stay long in the cattle country, for they could not fit into the frontier life. Some were brave only when they had the advantage, but we cannot classify these as the true frontier cowboys. Most of them showed that they were not afraid of anything. Almost every week the *Fort Griffin Echo* told of the cowboys "shooting up the town."[7] We have no record of this ever being done with the intention of harm to anyone. Always when the cowboys "went on a spree," the concern was for the women and children. Apparently it did not occur to the editor that there was any danger of hurting a man.

The stealing of a horse in Fort Griffin created more excitement than the murder of a man. As proof of this statement there are to be found many instances where the soldiers, the Indian scouts, and the officers were called out to trail down horse thieves, but this was never done to catch one who had committed murder. Some were arrested for murder in Fort Griffin, but they were never punished. The files of the *Echo* carry numerous accounts of arrests and trials for murder, but the writer has not discovered a single instance where there was conviction. There were several reasons for this: first, as a general rule, the killings occurred among bad men and the people of the country considered that it was a good riddance. If the man who did the killing was bad, he would soon receive his punishment. Often the man who did the killing would leave before he could be caught. Many times these fights started in the saloons at night. The lights would be shot out and no one would know who killed the dead man, for no one was honest enough to admit it. If the murdered man had no relatives to bring charges against the murderer, the case was dropped or the murderer acquitted. A harmless Tonkawa Indian was shot down in the street because he accidentally got in a man's way.[8] The murderer's only punishment was that he was thrown in the calaboose until he sobered up. A peace officer attempted to arrest a man and ordered him to halt. Some say that the man was hard of hearing and did not hear the command; others believed that he attempted to draw a gun. The truth is not known, but the officer shot the man down and then turned to a bystander and offered to bet one hundred dollars that he could cover the three bullet holes with a silver dollar. The officer would have won his bet because only one bullet had found its mark and the single hole could have been covered with a silver dollar. A doctor was called, but when he arrived, the man was dead. This act caused the officer to receive severe criticism, but he was never tried. Of the twelve years of the existence of Fort Griffin, thirty-four men were publicly killed and eight found dead. Eleven of these were killed by the officers or the Vigilance Committee. "Cheap" John, one of the most widely known characters of the frontier, was killed after he had sold his store. People supposed the purpose was to rob him, but the man who killed him claimed that he was trying to collect a debt. He killed "Cheap" John out on the prairie and came back to town wearing "Cheap" John's eighteen dollar boots. Nothing was done about it.

Of course many of the tales of bloodshed and murder are magnified, but if we cut them to the minimum, we find that Fort Griffin was the murderer's and gambler's paradise, and the outlaw's rendezvous.

The role played by the soldiers in the town life must not be overlooked. Because of both white and colored soldiers, there was constant friction, nor were the military courts any more strict than the civil courts. A captain at the fort shot an enlisted man over a poker game. The captain was tried in the military court and acquitted, the decision being that under the circumstances it was the only dignified thing he could do.

Many of the colored soldiers were in accord with the Northern viewpoint concerning Southern slavery, and this difference of opinion was a beginning place for much trouble, which on one occasion, almost caused a battle in Fort Griffin. Both factions were armed and each just waiting for the other to start the fray. Only the good judgment of the post colonel kept down serious trouble.

It is no wonder that Fort Griffin was lawless in many respects. It was seventy-two miles to the nearest seat of centralized government, and much of the time not even a deputy sheriff was present. The people were left to shift for themselves. Not only did the extreme frontier location promote a wild life, but also the cosmopolitan population. Fort Griffin boasted at least one inhabitant from each state in the union, and from thirteen countries of the world. Not only disregard for law but ignorance of the Texas code of laws were responsible for many minor offenses.

Possibly one of the greatest hindrances to law enforcement were the "hangers on" who followed the trail drives through Fort Griffin every spring. These fellows who followed the herd were generally a tough group of men, judging from the number that were arrested at Dodge City, Kansas. Many of them were law "hide-outs" and secured positions from the cattle owners under assumed names. Dodge City, Kansas, became so severe with them that many a herd entered the city short-handed. The men who were wanted by the law turned back when they got close to the city. It is said, however, that what the herd lacked in men, the Texas cowboy made up for in swearing, because of the extra work put on him.

Unless we know how many of these characters passed through this frontier town, we might think their influence was slight, but the contrary is true. It is estimated that two thousand of these men visited Fort Griffin twice annually, going north with the herds in the spring, and drifting back through in the late summer or fall. In 1871 over five hundred thousand cattle passed Fort Griffin on the Western Cattle trail, and it is evident that a large number of men were required to handle this many cattle in a wild open country.

Because of these cattle drives Fort Griffin's night life was almost beyond description. Money and whiskey flowed like water, men quarreled, fought, and killed over imaginary insults, the dance halls were crowded, and disorder reigned supreme. The gambler filled his purse, the saloon keeper sold his stock, and the cowboy received as a general rule his next morning's headache, if he lived through the night. All too often the cowboy, like the katydid, sang and danced through the night and found in the morning that he had no evidence left of his labor on the cattle trail.

In the early days the professional criminal made of the frontier courts a farce because he and his gang could swear and prove what they wanted to. Because of this lack of justice the citizens of Fort Griffin organized themselves with a determination to stop, especially, cow and horse stealing. This organization became known as the Vigilance Committee. It is commonly said that this committee confined its work to Fort Griffin and surrounding territory, but it was active as far east as Rock Creek in Parker County. Whether in Parker County the same name was used is not known, but it is known that the two organizations worked together. In Parker County they were concerned only with horse thieves because there were not many cattle, but cattle thieves were held and turned over to the West Texas cattlemen. This accounts for the fact that so many men were taken out of the Shackelford County jails and hanged by the committee. We know little of this organization other than its workings. There are men still alive who doubtless belonged, but they choose not to talk. One of the sources of information concerning this organization is through men who were boys at that time and, of course, do not know the secrets of the order. It is known, however, that each member pledged himself to be fair in his judgment and report only what he knew to be facts. The organization was founded upon the principles of uprightness and justice, but as in all organizations of this kind, corruption and selfish justice came in. Possibly the first members were fair and unselfish, but as time went by men joined who used the organization to their own interest. It is generally believed that most of the cattlemen belonged, some because they thought it was the only way to stop cow stealing, and some because they felt safer in than out. The committee did some good; also it worked its share of mischief.

All was not bad in Fort Griffin. Besides the Vigilance Committee there was a minor element working faithfully, and trying to build up a people who would be obedient to law and order. They were in the minority, but they fought diligently and might have succeeded if the life of the fort had been long enough, but the moving of the fort came too soon for their work to be completed. It must be said, nevertheless, that in twelve years they had made very little progress.

For that time on the frontier, Fort Griffin had a well organized school system, and accounts found in the *Fort Griffin Echo* indicate that it was well attended. Instructions were given in reading, writing, Greek, Latin, mathematics, and grammar.[10] Mr. Lewis, who was the principal, had no help. He taught all subjects himself.

Fort Griffin also had an organization known as the Band of Hope. It was of a religious nature, but just what part it played in the life of Fort Griffin is not known. It seemed to be an auxiliary of the church. It is not known whether it was of the Baptist or the Methodist denomination. Both denominations held services, the Methodists on the first, and the Baptist on the third Sunday in each month. The preaching services were held in the school house. Before the building of the school house, very little preaching was done in Fort Griffin.

The church organizations of the community had many opposing influences to deal with, but because of the untir-

Lime kiln near Fort Griffin.

ing efforts of a few devout Christians they gradually gained a foot-hold. Members were added to the church very slowly, and because of the many temptations, many fell away who did belong. According to the old newspaper files the new church member's hardest fight was against whiskey and gambling.

Fort Griffin had a library society and a reading club. These societies did much to keep the people of the frontier town abreast of the times, more especially the reading club.

Ruins of C.K. Stribling house near Fort Griffin. Built in 1849 or 1850.

Barber Watkins Reynolds' house on the Clear Fork near Fort Griffin.

The literary society had regular debates which were often more of a quarrel than a debate. These debates resulted many times in hard feelings, which hindered the advancement of the society. Regardless of whether the subject for debate concerned the people of Fort Griffin, before the society adjourned two sides would be formed. These sides might hold to their contentions a long while, or they might be forgotten the next day. Because of this trouble the debating finally stopped.

W. H. Ledbetter picket house built in 1872 near Fort Griffin and moved to downtown Albany in 1953.

Fort Griffin citizens were not without amusement. They usually had a good baseball team, and the games they played were well attended. They were free to all who wanted to come. For this reason they were often attended by the whites, the blacks, and the red men. They had no bleachers on the baseball field, so the teams were unhooked from the wagons and the wagons put in a semi-circle about the diamond to be used for seats.

Fishing was a sport for nearly all, and a business for some. There were a few who kept Fort Griffin supplied with fish from the Clear Fork. Fish were plentiful and because they were, they were wasted. Hunting was another amuse-

N. L. Bartholomew house built in Reynolds Bend near Fort Griffin following the Civil War.

T. E. Jackson house built near Fort Griffin. It now serves as the headquarters for Fort Griffin State Park.

ment of the people of the fort and sometimes a necessity in order to have meat. Deer and turkey were the principal game to be found; occasionally a bear was killed, but they were few. Shooting, dancing, parties, and picnics were means of amusement, especially for the young.

Life in old Fort Griffin could not have been dreary. There the best mingled with the worst. There were good men and bad men, striving each in his way to extend the frontier; life was cheap and opportunities were few. No one cared for Fort Griffin nor regarded its future. It was a town where all lived in the wild flurry of the present. The gambler came because there was money, the outlaw for safety, the rancher for supplies, and many others to gratify their morbid cravings in wild excess. It was a place where money was squandered and recklessness disregarded. It was a place where man could let animal instinct rule, if he desired to die as he lived. There were characters that it has taken the ages to develop—the worst and the best. It was these characters who made Fort Griffin a part of the last American Frontier.

With the last of the buffalo about 1878 and the moving of the soldiers in 1880, Fort Griffin's wild life ceased. The merchant, the gambler, and the outlaw sought new fields, and the rancher was left in charge. Fort Griffin had served its time. Albany got its merchants, the ranchers tore down its buildings, and only a history remains.

NOTES

[1] Uncle Joe McCombs, Albany, Texas.

[2] "Uncle Joe" McCombs, Albany, Texas. John M. Larn

was the sheriff.

[3] *The Frontier Echo,* July 24, 1880.

[4] Ibid., June 30, 1875.

[5] *Fort Griffin Echo,* Sept. 17, 1881.

[6] *The Frontier Echo,* Aug. 17, 1877.

[7] Ibid., Nov. 19, 1875.

[8] Don Biggers, *Shackelford County Sketches,* p. 38.

[9] *The Frontier Echo* , Nov. 19, 1875 to 1881; also *Shackelford County Sketches.*

[10] *Fort Griffin Echo,* Aug. 28, 1880.

EXPLORERS AND EARLY SETTLERS OF SHACKELFORD COUNTY

by Ben O. Grant

        en O. Grant contributed this article to the West Texas Historical Association Year Book, *one of several that he wrote. In it he discusses several of the early settlers along the Clear Fork of the Brazos.*

    The coming of the white man to this continent did not affect the native life of Shackelford County for more than three hundred years. It is possible that the county was crossed by trappers and traders long before the nineteenth century, but their records, if any, were meager and very indefinite. The location of the county is such that it did not invite early exploration. The first white people to enter the region of Texas with which Shackelford County is associated were the Spanish, but there is no positive evidence that any Spanish explorer ever actually touched the soil of this county.

    In 1540 the Coronado expedition crossed the Great Plains from New Mexico and probably passed a few miles west of Shackelford County. However, the plains area was among the last sections to be explored thoroughly. Here nature has created barriers that make the country seem uninviting; consequently the plains were neglected for regions easier to explore. Also, after the Coronado expedition, the Spaniards had no desire for wealth such as the plains had to offer. Since the Spaniards had more inviting fields open to exploration, their attention was turned elsewhere.

The Spaniards succeeded in planting some settlements in Texas, but they were weak and located far from the Shackelford County country. There was Los Adaes, in what is now western Louisiana, a few missions around Nacogdoches, missions and a settlement at San Antonio, and two or three other communities of even less importance. The Spanish settlement nearest to the region dealt with in this study was the Mission and Presidio of San Saba, established near the present town of Menard, in 1757. It was harassed by the Comanches, however, and was of short duration.[1]

In an effort to pacify the Indians of north Texas, Athanase de Mezieres, a Frenchman in Spanish Service, in 1773, visited the country not far to the east of Shackelford County; but his efforts at exploring the region were of no great consequences. During the last quarter of the eighteenth century the Spaniards made peace with the Comanches both in Texas and in New Mexico. This pacification was followed by an effort to connect their settlements in these frontier provinces by a more direct route. That is, they sought a route from San Antonio to Santa Fe leading through the Rolling Plains and the High Plains of Texas. In order to lay out such a trail, the Spanish governor of Texas, Domingo Cabello, commissioned Pedro Vial, in 1786, to explore a direct route from San Antonio to Santa Fe. Vial went north, crossed the Llano, and reached the Colorado. He ascended the Colorado for some distance, but because of a fall from his horse, he returned eastward to the Brazos and camped at the Tawakoni village of Quisquate, where he remained for six weeks. Starting again in December, he ascended the Brazos sixty-two leagues and then turned northeastward to the Red River. At the Red River Vial turned west, followed the Red and Canadian rivers, and finally on May 26, 1787, arrived at Santa Fe. But this was far from the direct route that the governor had intended to explore; so in July, 1787, Jose Mares was sent out to improve on the route. Mares started out from Santa Fe to San Antonio but detoured so widely that his route was little better, if any, than the one followed by Vial. On the return trip Mares did some better, but the result was still not satisfactory; so Vial was sent out again. In 1789 Vial went north from San Antonio to the Clear Fork of the Brazos.[3] Here he turned northwest and went very close to, if he did not enter, Shackelford County.

The records do not reveal how white men first learned of the topography of this region. It may be that they learned about it from the Indians, but it is more probable that certain obscure, wandering pioneers visited it and passed their knowledge on to others who applied it but never gave the rightful parties credit for their explorations. At any rate Stephen F. Austin could draw a fairly accurate map of this region as early as 1829.[4]

The first explorer of this region of Texas who left records complete and precise enough to be of much value was Randolph B. Marcy, a captain in the United States Army. In 1849, by order of the United States government, Marcy started from Fort Smith, Arkansas, to Santa Fe, New Mexico, with a small expedition to serve as an escort for emigrants. On his return from Santa Fe, Marcy descended the valley of the Rio Grande to Dona Ana, in southern New Mexico. Thence be moved southeast to Delaware Creek and followed that stream to its confluence with the Pecos near the thirty-second parallel. He moved down the Pecos and crossed that stream into what is now Crane County. Thence he traveled northeast by the Big Spring, where the town of that name is located. Changing his course to a little north of east, he crossed the Colorado a few miles north of the present Colorado City, passed a few miles south of the Double Mountains, and continued in a comparatively straight course to Fort Preston on the Red River, north of the present Denison. From that point he made his way to Fort Towson and finally to Fort Smith, Arkansas. He did not touch Shackelford county, but did pass some twenty miles north of it.[5]

On this expedition Marcy observed the country carefully and suggested that the valley of the Brazos, at the places where he crossed it, would be a good location for a military post.[6] In 1850 Fort Belknap was located on that stream, near the present Newcastle in Young County, a few miles down the river from the site of Marcy's crossing. In 1851, Fort Phantom Hill was located on the Clear Fork of the Brazos, about eighteen miles northeast of the present Abilene, and a few months later Fort Chadbourne was located on Oak Creek, a tributary of the Colorado.[7] Marcy's report called attention to the resources of the country, and it probably helped to determine the policy pursued by the War Department in establishing the cordon of forts along the frontier. It was these posts that first brought white men to the Shackelford County country.

Captain Marcy was sent out again in 1854. This time he was within the present boundaries of Shackelford county and suggested that a fort be located on the Clear Fork of the Brazos. In speaking of the Clear Fork, Marcy said:

"This stream is here twenty-five yards wide, enclosed upon each side by high, precipitous banks, which contain the water at the highest stages, and are lined with pecan, hackberry, black walnut, and other trees, which in many places along the lowlands spread out over spaces of considerable extent, constituting a goodly amount of timber suitable for building purposes or fuel."[8]

The explorer foretold the possibilities of the quarrying industry, now carried on at Lueders, in the following statement:

"Limestone, which is here the predominating rock, is found in the greatest profusion, and is better adapted for building purposes than any I have ever seen before. It has been shaped out of natural causes into cubes and other symmetrical figures of convenient dimensions, with smooth surfaces and perfect angles in such a manner as to be already dressed for the hands of the mason."[9]

Marcy visited the farm on the Clear Fork which had been established by Jesse Stem, United States Indian Agent. After describing the success that Colonel Stem had at farming, Marcy wrote:

"These facts may seem foreign to the subject matter of a report of this character, but I have brought them to notice as an evidence of the fertility of the soil, and an argument in support of the adaption of this locality to the wants of the Indians."[10]

In this connection it is of interest that Marcy, aided by Major Robert S. Neighbors of the United States Indian Service, located the Comanche Indian reservation, which was established in 1855, just north of the Shackleford County line. A few months later Camp Cooper, a military post, was established there also.

Toward the last of the exploration period the more daring of the pioneers began to come into the Shackleford County region. Probably the first white man to come to Shackleford County to stay permanently was Jesse Stem, the Indian Agent already referred to. His headquarters and farm were on the Clear Fork of the Brazos, about six miles below the present site of Lueders, on the right bank of the river (looking down stream). He established himself here in October, 1852.[11] Mr. Stem was the official agent for the Comanches but had dealings with many other tribes who frequented the country. Besides looking after the welfare of the Indians, it was his duty to try to keep them from stealing, and when they stole to try to induce them to return the stolen property to its owners.

On one occasion Stem demanded the return of stolen horses. The Indians brought in only a few, and Major H. H. Sibley, on a scout in that vicinity, demanded the others. In order to be sure to hold the Indians to their promise, Stem demanded that some of them be held as hostages. Among these hostages was chief Koweaka, a Wichita, who persuaded Stem to allow him to send for his wife and child. Stem granted this request, not knowing the intentions of Koweaka. Not long after the wife arrived, Koweaka became very sullen and remained in his tent most of the time. Finally about mid-night, after a few days of this sullenness, his motive became apparent. He rushed the guards, killed one of them, and forced the others to kill him. When they examined his tent they found that Koweaka had killed his wife and his little boy, and then had brought death upon himself rather than to be humiliated by being held prisoner. Strange as it may seem, the other Indians said that Koweaka's wife had agreed to his plot. Koweaka had no hopes of ever leaving the camp alive; he had left his moccasins in his tent, which is a sign used by the Indians to indicate that they will not leave the place but will fight until death. The other prisoners were permitted to go at liberty.[12]

Horse stealing was a common occupation of these Indians, and no amount of persuasion on the part of Stem could have any effect on them. In one of Stem's letters he wrote that there was no hope of doing anything with them until force was used, that he had tried to reach them by kindness and had been repaid by one act of hostility after another. Stem said that he believed that Aqua Quash, chief of the Wacos, was honest because he had helped in recovering many stolen horses and also had given him notice of stealing parties. But, he said, Aqua Quash was powerless to manage his thieving followers.

According to Stem's account, he was visited in the winter of 1852 by the principal chiefs of the "Southern Comanches." They were Pah-a-yu-ka, Sanaco, Catumseh, and Buffalo Hump. Also he was visited by chiefs of Ta-na-was, No-co-nies and Yam-pa-rick-as. The chiefs represented the most numerous tribes of the Comanches.[13] In regard to these Indians Stem wrote:

"They sent a small delegation in advance, about the 24th of January, to communicate with me, and ascertain the disposition entertained by our government towards them. With these I held a talk, expressing my gratification in having the opportunity to see them, and talk to them at my agency, and assuring them of the great desire entertained by our government to be at peace with all the Comanches. They told me that their people were assembled in large numbers, about three days journey from the Agency, and on the head waters of the Big Wichita, a tributary of the Red River, where they were spending the winter to recruit their horses; that they would be willing to come to the Agency, and see me, but that the supply of beef and corn I had on hand was too small to justify them in coming down in such large numbers, out of striking distance of the buffalo.

"I distributed among them some blankets and tobacco, and a small supply of other presents; gave them some beef and corn,ʲ and sent them back to their people, apparently well satisfied."¹⁴

Though Stem was kept busy with Indian affairs, it is interesting to note that he found time for some farming.¹⁵ He planted corn and oats in 1853, and reaped an excellent harvest, which he sold at Fort Belknap at a good price. Thus he disproved the many reports that had been carried east concerning this section of Texas. Records show that this was the first attempt at agriculture in Shackelford County.

Stem's activity on the frontier was short. In the winter of 1853-1854, he was killed and his store was burned by two Kickapoo Indians."¹⁶ But Stem had proved to the government officials that some provision would have to be made for caring for and controlling the Indians of the frontier. His post on the Clear Fork was a forerunner of the Comanche reservation established in the same vicinity in 1855.

After the death of Stem and many other raids on the frontier settlements, the demand for a change in the control of the Texas Indians became so imperative that it could no longer be overlooked. For many years the Texas Indian agents had urged that the reservation system was the only solution presenting itself. So, in 1853, the state government offered to furnish land for the purpose and in 1854 the Department of War appointed Captain Marcy to organize an expedition to select suitable locations for the establishment of agencies.¹⁷ Major Robert S. Neighbors, special agent of Indian affairs in Texas, was instructed to join Marcy at Fort Belknap.¹⁸ These men were ordered to locate, if possible, land not occupied nor owned by individuals, but if this could not be done, to arrange for the purchase of land.¹⁹

Two reservations were located on the Brazos and its tributaries. The largest, which became known as the Brazos Reservation, was located at the junction of the Clear Fork and the Brazos, and the other, known as the Comanche reservation, was located in the present Throckmorton County, just north of the Shackelford-Throckmorton line. The Comanche reservation was to contain 18,576 acres and was to be ready in a short time for the Indians to occupy it. There was much delay, however. According to a letter written by Neighbors to Manypenny, January 8, 1855, the Indians were anxious to go on the reservation and the citizens along the frontier were anxious that they be located.[20] Nevertheless, the agents found some trouble in getting the Indians located on the reservation and were destined later to be even more sorely troubled in keeping them there.

Early in January, 1855, Sanaco and Buffalo Hump, influential Comanche chiefs, led their followers north off the reservation, claiming that they had heard that the soldiers were coming from Fort Chadbourne to attack them. All Comanches left except a few under Catumseh.[21] It was not until June, 1855, that Catumseh's band of about two hundred and fifty persons were located on the reservation land. Other Comanches came in from time to time, but the population of the reservation never exceeded five hundred.

The location of the Comanche reservation was never suited to its purpose. The buildings were on low ground which, when the river was high, would be under water. This fact gave the Indians an excuse to move every wet season. These Indians were not sedentary and had a way peculiar to all plains Indians of wandering off the reservation. Low ground was only one of their excuses.

It will be recalled that Camp Cooper was a military post established on the reservation. The place where it was built might be called a depression. It is surrounded by hills, except for the channel cut by the river at its entrance and exit. It is possible that this location was selected because it would be warm in the winter months; no other logical reason seems apparent. To the north is a chain of hills or mountains, to the west canyons, to the south, considerable hills and rock cliffs.

At first the quarters at Camp Cooper were only tents, which did not offer good protection from either the cold or heat. One of the tents was a hospital, which was too small and not suited for the purpose that it was supposed to fulfill. Much of the time water was scarce, and if wells were dug they produced salt water. The men who occupied the post were new recruits and unfit for hard work, since they had made a hard march to the camp.[22] Colonel Robert E. Lee, of the Second Calvary, was stationed at this post during 1856.[23] With the coming of the Second Calvary, Camp Cooper could boast of as good a staff of officers and fighting men as ever marched on the American Continent. The names of some of these men will always echo through the halls of fame; namely, Robert E. Lee, Albert Sidney Johnston, and J. B. Hood.

As soon as the arrangements could be made, the tents were replaced by stone buildings.[i] These buildings were strongly built and would have been of great historical value, but they were destroyed by the farmers who came later. Only cut stone was used, and each building was placed on a good foundation.

Besides the disadvantages incident to the topography of the region, there were other difficulties at the Comanche reservation. The Indians persisted in leaving the reservation, and it was charged that they continued to commit depredations on the settlements. Only a small minority of the Comanches were on the reservation. Those not confined continued to carry on their marauding operations, and the reservation Comanches were blamed for the acts of their wild kinsmen. Many of the settlers around Camp Cooper were extreme in their view concerning the Indians. When an Indian was accused of a crime by the settlers and proof could not be established, the officer in charge would refuse to punish him. This would make some of the settlers angry, especially those who believed "all good Indians are dead Indians." The officers, who believed that the Indians should be treated as though they were human beings, were criticized and held in contempt by the citizens. One of the leaders among the extreme radicals was John R. Baylor who, even his followers admitted, held extreme views. The difference of opinion among the settlers was so great that the agents were handicapped in their efforts to civilize the Indians, and the people of the community lived in the midst of great excitement.

In the spring of 1859, Captain Baylor mustered a group of men with the intention of driving the agents from the reservation and then dealing with the Indians as he saw fit.[24] This plan was not carried out because the soldiers supported the agents, and Baylor's men soon withdrew from the field with the threat to gather more men and return. However, this was never done.

The settlers' point of view toward the Indians was not without foundation. The savages committed many crimes and stole many horses. The settlements were so close that the Indians could leave the reservations at night, steal and kill, and be back by morning. However, much of the crime that the Indians were accused of was committed by mean, thieving white men who hung on the outskirts of civilization to avoid capture by the officers. Whatever the truth may have been, the frontier citizens continued to maintain a threatening attitude toward the Indians, and in order to avoid bloodshed, the reservation was abandoned and the Indians moved to the Washita Valley in the Indian Territory in August, 1859. During the winter of 1860-1861 the secession forces gained the ascendancy in Texas and became aggressive. In the military posts along the frontier were supplies and munitions which Texas and the Confederacy needed. Hence, bands of frontier citizens, sustained by bodies of state troops more formally organized, moved against Camp Cooper as they moved against other posts in Texas.

Observing that the "state troops and other armed bodies of citizens" were encamped in the vicinity and making hostile demonstrations, Captain S. D. Carpenter, of the United States Army, commanding Camp Cooper, demanded, on February 18, 1861, to know their purposes. W. C. Dalrymple, Aide-de camp to the Governor and Colonel commanding the Texan forces, replied by demanding that the post be surrendered.[25] On the following day Carpenter yielded to the command, protesting at the sad plight of the nation and explaining that he did so only to avoid civil war and unnecessary bloodshed. Dalrymple submitted terms which required that the federal troops surrender all arms, munitions and equipment subject to the proviso that they might march with their arms and deliver them to the state forces at San Antonio. The federal troops, numbering about 250 men according to the reports of the Texans, marched out on February 21, 1861.[26]

Dalrymple, who was commander of the "Texas mounted rangers," was assisted, it seems, by a party of citizens from the vicinity of Weatherford, under the command of H. A. Hamner. He left the post in command of Captain E. W. Rogers. Meanwhile Colonel Henry E. McCulloch, who had been commissioned by the Convention at Austin to take by force or to receive the surrender of all federal posts in northwest Texas, was on his way to Camp Cooper. He arrived there on March 6 and demanded that Rogers turn the fort over to him. Rogers readily complied. In his report to the Committee of Public Safety, McColloch complained that either the federal troops on leaving the post or the state troops and frontier citizens who entered it immediately thereafter had practiced waste and destruction. There the commissary houses had been opened and, it seems, various persons took whatever they pleased. Hence the quantity of goods and supplies taken by the state forces at Camp Cooper was much less than had been expected. McCulloch appointed J. B. (Buck) Barry to command the post.[27]

After the abandonment of Camp Cooper, the few remaining residents of this section of the western frontier were compelled to rely upon their own resource for protection. After several of the more isolated homes had been destroyed by the Indians, the few remaining citizens held a mass meeting and decided to "fort up."[28] The location selected for this fort was just across the line in Stephens County, then Buchanan County, on the Clear Fork of the Brazos. The ground upon which the fort stood is now enclosed in Mr. C. M. Cable's pasture. The place is about twenty miles northeast of Albany, Texas. At the time the fort was built, the land was owned by Mr. Rich Anderson and the place was named Fort Davis in honor of Jefferson Davis, president of the Confederacy.[29] In the true sense of the word Fort Davis was never a fort but simply a compact settlement where the citizens came together for mutual protection. There were never any soldiers stationed at Fort Davis. Among the citizens forting up at the place were T. E. Jackson, J. M. Frans, J. G. Irwin, H. Anderson, Phil George, Jim George, E. Christenson, N. McCarty, J. C. Musgrave, Jim Thorpe, Mr. Souther, Arch Ratliff, B. W. Raymonds, S. P. Newcomb, Mr. Lee, J. Wheeler, John Hittson, John Selman, R. A. Clarke, and J. G. Steele. These men were all married. Not all of them lived in

Shackelford County, but those who resided outside of the county were closely associated with its pioneer history.

Another "fort" at this time was known as Fort Hubbard. Like Fort Davis it was not a fort but a consolidated settlement. It was located on Hubbard's Creek, not far from where the old Lynch ranch house now stands, being about two miles up stream from the Big Hubbard bridge, which is on the road between Albany and Ibex, in the northeastern part of the county. The following men were at Fort Hubbard: C. C. Cooper, J. C. Lynch, W. W. Ray, John and Tom Boggs, George Hazlewood, Mr. Mercer, and Sam Lindley. All of these had families, who were with them at the post. Besides these there were the following unmarried men: William and M. V. Hoover, Jonathan May, and James Boggs. Most of these men were employed by either Cooper or Lynch. A brief sketch of the lives of some of these early settlers will be given later in this discussion.

Very little is known of the happenings in Fort Hubbard because no one kept an accurate account of them; but through the diary of Mr. S. S. (Gus) Newcomb, who taught school in Fort Davis, we have an account of life at that place. A few extracts from his diary will give us some conception of life at this isolated post.[30]

"Jan. lst, 1865. For the past year the Indians have been so troublesome coming into this section in large numbers, that a great many families have left the frontier and moved into the older counties and those who remain are forted up. Fort Davis is on the creek back from the Clear Fork and about fifteen miles below Camp Cooper. There are now about one hundred and twenty-five persons in the fort and others preparing to move in. There is another fort about twelve miles down the river, but it is not as large as Fort Davis. Fort Davis is three hundred by three hundred and seventy-five feet, divided into sixteen lots, each lot being seventy-five feet square, with a twenty-five foot alley running through the fort from east to west. This fort was commenced on the 20th of last October and there are now some twenty good houses here. That is good houses of the kind. They are built with pickets, covered with dirt, and the cracks are stopped with dirt, and while not very ornamental, they are very comfortable.

"A little child died here this morning, exposure doubtless being the cause."

In Mr. Newcomb's next entry he gives an idea of the anxiety that must have been suffered by the early pioneers:

"Jan. 2nd (1865) Messers. Jackson and Irwin, who left for Mexico with a herd of cattle, about three months ago and were expected back in about six weeks, but who were reported to have been pressed into the Confederate army, reached here tonight. They knew nothing of the last big Indian raid or about the people forting up, and when I conducted them to their families their mutual joy and surprise can be better imagined than described."

So many people trying to live together under such conditions created many problems. Many times the people of these forts had scarcely enough to eat. But they had to eat whatever they could get; there was no choice. Mr. Newcomb's entry of January 31, gives us an idea of the food problem in the fort:

"Jan. 31st. (1865) The crowd that left before Christmas for bread stuff returned this evening. They came in good time as there was not any rations of flour or meal in the fort when they arrived."

Even though the people were "forted up," Indian excitement ran high at times, and if the Indians could catch a person away from the fort, he was fortunate if he escaped with his life.

"March 12th. (1865) Indian excitement has been high here today. About nine o'clock this morning Mr. McCarty came upon a large body of Indians about three miles from the fort. They gave him a close chase but he reached the fort all right. The Indians were followed all day but made their escape. I think this will stir some folks in this fort into doing their share of the picketing."

That the long confinement made the people irritable is evident by this entry:

"July 8th (1865). A couple of the fort's leading ladies indulged in a fist fight this morning, the result of difference among children."

Since there were no stores, the people made their clothing and utensils or did without until a trader came along. The opportunity to purchase articles was rarely offered. Of course, if the need was great enough, a special trip was made for supplies. But only a scarcity of food or powder and lead would justify the risk of a long journey to Weatherford or Waco. Later two entries show the eagerness of the people to purchase a few simple articles.

"May 4th (1865). Mr. Wilson, a trader from Waco, displayed his goods this morning, and a large crowd of men, women, and children, and dogs gathered around. His stock consisted of a few pieces of home spun cloth, some shoes, a little tobacco, a few hats, some pins, needles, eyes, buttons, spoons, sewing thread, matches, knives, forks, teaspoons, guns, caps, combs, hairpins, pencils, paper and etc.

"May 7th (1865). T. B. Brownfield started this morning for Belknap to get a doctor for Miss Lucinda Selman, who is very sick. Several hours later he returned with some medicine but no doctor.

"May 12th (1865). The people are anxiously trying to learn whether Lee surrendered and the war ended."

"June 28th (1865). The first beef buyer since the war was here today. They are paying ten dollars per head."

The rest of the July 1865 diary is concerned with Indian raids. Mr. Newcomb's diary of 1866 deals with the closing of school and people leaving the fort.

"Jan. 29th (1866). My school is continually getting smaller. This is the second time a couple have quit school to get married."

"Jan. 30th (1866). John Hittson moved his family to Camp Cooper."

"March 2nd (1866). School closed, the teacher being heartily tired of his job and longing to wander around some."

With the exception of Newcomb's diary and the report of Jesse Stem, already referred to, there are very few records pertaining to the first settlers of Shackelford County. Information about these men and women must be gotten from oral accounts of persons who knew them. Indeed it is impossible to secure any information whatever about many of the people who are known to have lived at an early date in what is now Shackelford County. The concluding pages of this discussion will be devoted, nevertheless, to brief sketches of a few citizens concerning whom some information is available. After Jesse Stem, whose career in the Shackelford County region has already been recounted, the next man to use the lands of the county seems to have been Captain N. C. Givens, who was officially of the Second Dragoons.

Givens, whose military duties brought him to the Camp Cooper country, became involved in a quarrel with Robert

Marker at the Stone Ranch complex of buildings on Lambshead Ranch. Joan Farmer stands to the left.

S. Neighbors, Senior United States Indian Agent in Texas, and in the course of the controversy Neighbors charged that Givens owned a ranch and a herd of cattle, the ranch headquarters being located at what is now known as the Old Stone Ranch.[31] It was contrary to Army regulations for an officer to engage in any business or profession other than that of military service. Local tradition states that the captain denied the charge. He claimed that he did not own any land, which was doubtless true since it was not necessary to own land along the Texas Frontier in order to use it. Also, according to tradition, Givens' foreman assumed ownership of the cattle until the investigation was over. Hence, the Captain continued ranching until 1859, which made the life of his ranch about four years.

Among the first ranchers to come into Shackelford County to make their home was Judge John C. Lynch, a typical Irishman, of the Shamrock country. He was jolly and generous to the extent of bringing financial ruin upon himself on more than one occasion. He arrived in El Paso, Texas, in 1859, and, according to his statement, he did not know where he was going and did not care much. Mr. Lynch had been attracted to America by the tales of fortune to be had in California; but after staying there awhile and finding no gold, he decided to come east. Before leaving California he took out his naturalization papers; thus, feeling that he was a full fledged citizen, he started on his way to Texas. But this satisfaction was not to last long. Somewhere in New Mexico Mr. Lynch left the small party he was traveling with to get some game for food. After riding some distance he came in sight of a herd of deer. He dismounted and tied his horse with the intention of getting closer. He had gone only a short distance from his horse when he heard hoof beats. Turning he saw his favorite horse being led off by Indians; and his naturalization papers were in his saddle bags! However, Mr. Lynch considered himself fortunate to escape with his life.

When Mr. Lynch started east from El Paso, he had not gone far until he met a group of people going to California. After talking with the people for a time, he found that they were traveling under the direction of a man whom he had known in California and had come to regard as a scoundrel. The man denied the charge Lynch hurled against him and, being a Dutchman, carried the argument too far. Thus the Dutchman and the Irishman had to resort to their fists to settle the argument. However, one of the group persuaded Mr. Lynch against his own convictions to return with them to California. This man was Mr. Peter Gonsolus. Evidently Mr. Gonsolus' words were not as weighty as they first appeared, for at Santa Fe, New Mexico, Lynch married Gonsolus' daughter and returned to Texas with his wife in 1860, and settled on the north bank at the Big Bend of Hubbard's Creek. The place is about nine miles southeast of Albany. Here Mr. Lynch and his wife spent their lives. Mr. Gonsolus went on to California but did not find it to his liking; so he returned and settled in Stephens County, becoming one of the pioneer settlers of that county.[32]

Mr. Lynch had a nature very suitable for the hardships of pioneer life. Through war, Indian raids, and drouth he was generally cheerful. He acquired considerable acreage on Hubbard's Creek, and when the county of Shackelford was organized, in 1874, he was considered as one of the big cattlemen. In 1877 he was elected County Judge.

Judge Lynch's generosity caused him to lose all that he had. He had gone on notes for men who were not good for their debts, and he was forced to pay them. Thus all of his money and most of his land were lost. It was in this period that the Judge made the remark that he wished that he had never learned to write his name. To this his wife replied, "Well, it wouldn't have made any difference; even if you couldn't write, the whole country would be filled with your X's."

Losing his naturalization papers caused Mr. Lynch much trouble. In the early seventies the government agreed to repay the settler for the damage done them by marauding Indians. Since payment for such claims was made to citizens only, the request of Judge Lynch was not considered, and not until many years later did congress pass a special act under which the judge received his money. Also, he was granted citizenship at the request of the people of the county.

About 1867 Mr. Joe Matthews, later known as "Uncle Joe" settled on the Clear Fork of the Brazos, about two miles below where Fort Griffin was later located. "Uncle Joe" was said to have been one of the most influential men of the county; always his influence was for good. He became one of the big cattlemen of the county and accumulated much wealth in the form of cattle and land. Uncle Joe Matthews was a law abiding citizen and did much to influence the lawless characters of the frontier toward better ways of living.

Uncle Joe Matthew's son, Judge J. A. Matthews, is one of the outstanding characters of the county today, and the most prominent old settler. Judge Matthews is one of the big land owners of the county. Besides having served the county as judge, he is one of the most influential citizens and is possibly more widely known than any other citizen. Mrs. Matthews is of the Reynolds family, people who have also been very influential in the history of this region. While her husband is tending his vast herds of Herefords, Mrs. Matthews engages herself in writing the history of the Matthews and Reynolds families, which beyond a doubt will be a most interesting book.[ii]

Not long after the coming of Uncle Joe Matthews, B. W. (Uncle Watt) Reynolds settled in Shackelford County on the Old Stone Ranch, which was a part of the ranch owned by Captain Givens, not far from Mr. Matthews' holdings. Mr. Reynolds is spoken of as ever one of the kindest men of his time. Many say that he was never known to speak an unkind word, which is saying much for a man on this western frontier at that time. He was a substantial citizen, and his name will always live in the memory of the citizens of the county.

George T. and W. D. Reynolds, sons of Uncle Watt, are also among the outstanding pioneers. George T. Reynolds served in the Civil War, coming to the Fort Griffin section immediately after peace was signed.[iii] He and his brother, W. D. Reynolds, formed the Reynolds Land and Cattle Company, which was at that time one of the largest concerns of its kind in the West. Judge J. A. Matthews was at one time connected with the company. Few of the early cattlemen had more conflicts with the Indians than did the Reynolds brothers. Since their holdings were far flung the Indians thought they could steal cattle and get away without being punished. In 1866 the Comanches stole 500 head of cows and horses. In 1867 the Reynolds brothers and a number of cowboys trailed some Indians to Double Mountain Fork [of the Brazos River] in Haskell County, where a battle followed. Geo. T. Reynolds was shot through the abdomen with an arrow. He pulled the shaft out, but the head was lodged in the muscles of the back where it remained for sixteen years.[iv]

Also, ranking along with the first of the first pioneers are George and Cal Greer. Their father settled in Shackelford County in 1860, locating on Hubbard's Creek where the Greer Community is now located. Cal Greer, in company with

William King and Vol Simonds, receives the credit for discovering what became later known as the Ledbetter Salt Works. Cal Greer and his companions were driving cattle to the Concho country, and while on the return trip their horses got away and left them afoot. Late in the afternoon they came upon a small stream and decided to camp for the night, but when they went to get a drink they found the water was very salty, in fact so salty that it was impossible to drink it. When they got home they reported the discovery, and several people went to the place with kettles and laid in a supply of salt. The following account of operations at this place is taken from the Memoirs of Billy McGough, who at that time resided at McGough Springs in Eastland County:

"In 1862 we all got without salt. We had heard of a very salty place, to the northwest—kind of spring where, in hot weather, you could rake up pure salt, except that it was a little bitter. But bitter salt was better than no salt at all, so we concluded to go up there. There was no road through the country, but we got direction and knew that we had about sixty miles to go in a northwest direction into the Indian country. We fixed up and pulled out. We roamed and hunted over some of the roughest country in this section of Texas, but found our salt at last. It was a kind of salty flat lying between two mountains—open all around—very little timber in the neighborhood. In fact I do not think there was a stick of timber within ten miles. We had to haul our wood ten miles or more. We began digging shallow holes in the ground about three feet deep. We dug quite a lot of them, all close together. We had carried along with us several pots, barrels, and kettles, and by the time some of us got the wood with one wagon and three yoke of oxen, the rest of the boys had ten or fifteen holes dug, which holes would soon run full of water. The water was salty as brine, but bitter and muddy, and it would not settle or get clear. So we would dip it up in our kettles and boil it awhile, and then pour it up in our barrels. By the time it cooled in the barrels, it would be as clear as glass. Then we would pour it into our kettles and boil it hard until salt began forming on the top like ice, You could see it forming, and in a short time it would break and sink to the bottom of the kettle. You could then add more water from time to time as you dipped the salt out with a dipper with holes in it to let the water through. We made the prettiest and whitest salt I ever saw. After we got started, it did not take us but a few days to make lots of salt. We got three or four thousand pounds.

When we got home there was another crowd, Erath County men, that went up to the place. But they had hard luck. The Indians killed one of them and got their teams while they were out getting wood. I don't think they got much salt, and they lost one man and two horses. This was in 1862, as I have stated. In 1864 I went back again for another load of salt. At this time I found that a man by the name of Ledbetter had moved onto the saline flat and had preempted it."[33]

This place became so famous for salt that in 1863 W. H. Ledbetter began the manufacture of salt on a large scale. Citizens from Eastland, Stephens, Throckmorton, Jones, and Callahan counties had been accustomed to going to Fort Worth and later to Weatherford for their salt supply, but now it was at hand and of sufficient quantity to satisfy their needs. Most of this salt was used by the stockmen of the area, but it was also used on many of the tables. Ledbetter brought in several large kettles for the evaporation of the water, one of which is now placed on a stone foundation in the courtyard at Albany.[v] He found no trouble in finding sale for all the salt that he could make. It was not uncommon for people to come long distances with a number of wagons and load them all with salt.

The location of the old salt works was such that it invited Indian trouble. It was about eight miles southwest of Albany on the Salt Prong of Hubbard's Creek. It so happened that this place was a common crossing for the Indians, and Ledbetter's location made his place the object of many Indian raids.

Johnnie Ledbetter, the eleven year old son, is thought to have been stolen by the savages. The story of the lad's disappearance is one of the best known in all the saga of Shackelford County and will be related briefly.[vi]

In the early sixties there were no public schools on the frontier, so Judge Lynch, being a man of means, hired a teacher and invited all the neighbors' children to attend school free if they wished. He also invited those children who lived at a distance to make his house their home while school was in session. Johnnie Ledbetter was one of the children staying with Judge Lynch. He decided to go home one evening and slipped away without Mrs. Lynch's knowledge or approval of his going. It is supposed that he left just before night. At any rate, he was never seen again; at least, not until many years later. The searching parties searched all night and for several days but no trace of him was found. The mystery of his disappearance has never been cleared up and his fate is not positively known. It is stated that he was taken by the Indians, brought up as a warrior, and finally released to learn the ways of the white man. It is also stated that for many years he has lived in San Antonio, but will claim no relationship with the family. This citizen of San Antonio claimed that he was the lost boy but expressed a desire to have nothing in common with the family since his father and mother were dead. This person goes under the name of John Weatley [sic, S.W. Wesley] and does not use the Ledbetter name at all.[34]

Another of the outstanding characters of the frontier was John Hittson. Hittson appears in the records at Fort Davis. In 1866 he moved to Camp Cooper, and later engaged in extensive ranching in Texas and Colorado. From tales of his deeds as told by old timers, he seems to have been absolutely without fear. On one occasion, while they were residing at Fort Davis, John Hittson and Bill Hittson held a party of Indians at bay while a Negro, who was in their company, rode for help. In the fight Bill was wounded, and this threw most of the fighting on John. By the time help came, the Indians had left because of John's deadly shooting. They left three dead warriors on the field and carried some wounded men with them. This battle happened on Big Sandy Creek in Stephens County, just over the line of Shackelford. The place is a short distance below the Albany-Breckenridge highway bridge across Big Sandy. John Hittson was not only an Indian fighter; he matched wits with the most desperate cattle thieves of the time. On one occasion, he went to New Mexico and took stolen cattle away from the thieves and brought them back to their rightful owners in Texas. He was to receive for this only a percentage of the cattle he brought back.

The life of John Hittson was most colorful and almost constantly in danger. After the wild days of the frontier had passed, he moved to Colorado. Not long after he moved there, while going home from town one evening, he fell out of his buggy and broke his neck. It is strange that a life such as his should end in this manner.[35]

One of the best informed men concerning the early life of Shackelford County is John C. Irwin, who lives near Fort Griffin. Mr. Irwin has lived on the same land for seventy-five years. His father, John G. Irwin, was first sergeant of Company C of the famous Second Dragoons when John C. Irwin, was born at Fort Chadbourne, Texas, on February 7, 1855. Since the younger Irwin was the first child born at the post, they named him John Chadbourne. After leaving the army, the elder Irwin moved to the vicinity of Camp Cooper, in September, 1859, where he secured a contract to supply the troops at Camp Cooper with beef. It has already been stated that John G. Irwin moved with his family into the officers quarters at Camp Cooper when that post was surrendered to the Texans. The younger Irwin was then about 5 years old. He remembers the arrivals of the old Butterfield stage coaches, which at that time constituted the only means of communication between the Texas frontier and the outside world. There was a stable only a little way from Mr. Irwin's house, and he would watch them handle the teams.[36] Mr. Irwin said it was wonderful how some men could handle six horses.

The Southern Overland Mail, commonly called the Butterfield line, was established in September of 1858 and passed by Camp Cooper. This line linked St. Louis and Memphis on the east with San Francisco on the Pacific coast.[37] It provided semi-weekly stage and mail service, and its establishment was hailed all along the frontier as a great event.[38] There were stations approximately every twenty-five miles. Camp Cooper was made a "horse station," also passengers were served meals. Many of the early settlers still relate with pride the arrival of these coaches.

NOTES

[1] Gladys Collin, "Spanish West Texas 1735 to 1769, *West Texas Historical Association Yearbook,* 11 (1931), 99.

[2] H. E. Bolton, *Athanase de Mezieres and the Louisiana-Texas Frontier, 1768 to 1780,* II, 231.

[3] H. E. Bolton, *Texas in the Middle Eighteenth Century,* 128-132.

[4] Stephen F. Austin's Map of Texas, 1829, Archives University of Texas Library.

[5] Report of Captain R. B. Marcy's Route from Fort Smith to Santa Fe, Senate Executive Document No. 64, 31 Cong., 1 Sess. (1850).

[6] Ibid., 217, 218.

[7] C. C. Rister, *The Southwestern Frontier,* 49.

[8] R. B. Marcy, *Thirty Years of Army Life on the Border* (New York, 1866), 207.

[9] Ibid., 208.

[10] Ibid.

[11] Stem to Neighbors, October 8, 1852, University of Texas photostat copy of papers in the United States Indian office.

[12] Letter from Colonel E. H. Sibley in *The Northern Standard,* June 11, 1853. The letter was taken from the *Southwest American.*

[13] Stem to L. Lea, Commissioner of Indian Affairs, March 31, 1853. University of Texas photostat copy of papers in the United States Indian office.

[14] Ibid.

[15] R. B. Marcy, *Army Life On The Border,* 208.

[16] The Indians who killed Stem were tried by their own people and found guilty of murder. Their names were Polecat and Thunder. The Kickapoos were not supposed to be in this section; evidently these had wandered off their range. Hill to Neighbors, April 1, 1854, University of Texas photo-

stat copy.

[17] R. B. Marcy, *Army Life on The Border*, 170 ff.

[18] W. B. Parker, *Notes Taken on the Expedition with Marcy*, (Philadelphia, 1856), 10.

[19] W. A. Lewis, "Indian Reservations in Texas," (Manuscript, M. A. Thesis, Simmons University, 1928), 45.

[20] Ibid., 46.

[21] R.N. Richardson, *The Comanche Barrier To South Plains Settlement*, 217.

[22] Arrie Barrett, "Western Frontier Forts of Texas," *West Texas Historical Association Yearbook*, 1931, p. 134.

[23] Colonel M.L. Crimmins, "Robert E. Lee in Texas: Letters and Diary." *West Texas Historical Association Yearbook*, June, 1932, p. 5.

[24] R. N. Richardson, *The Comanche Barrier to South Plains Settlement*, 251 ff.

[25] *Journal of the Secession Convention of Texas. 1861* (E. W. Winkler, Ed., Austin, 1912), I) pp. 385, 386. It should be recalled that General D. E. Twiggs, Commander of the Department of Texas, had, on February 17, agreed to the surrender of all federal forts in Texas. It is evident, however, that the state commanders in the vicinity of Camp Cooper had not yet learned of this. Evidently they were determined to take Camp Cooper by force, if necessary, regardless of the decision Twiggs at San Antonio should make.

[26] Ibid., p. 388.

[27] McCulloch, at Camp Cooper, to Robertson, March 9, 1861, Ibid., 180 ff.

[28] J. C. Irwin, Fort Griffin, Texas, interview January 4, 1935.

²⁹ A.S. Swan, Carbon, Texas, interview, February 6, 1935.

³⁰ "The Diary of S. S. Newcomb," Manuscript, Albany, Texas.

³¹ Leeper to Neighbors, March 29. 1858. University of Texas photostat copy; Neighbors to Twiggs, March 29, 1858, Ibid.

³² Peter Gonsolus was the husband of seven wives and the father of 42 children. *The Dallas Morning News*, Sunday, July 8, 1934.

³³ From the memoirs of Billie McGough, manuscript, Hardin-Simmons University Library.

³⁴ This information is from family tradition and was given by Ethel Ledbetter, a niece of the boy who was supposed to have been stolen.

³⁵ A.S. Swan, interview, February 6, 1935.

³⁶ J.C. Irwin, interview, January 4, 1935.

³⁷ R.C. Crane, "Stagecoaching in the Concho Country," *West Texas Historical Association Yearbook*, 1934.

³⁸ R.N. Richardson, "Some Details of the Southern Overland Mail," *Southwest Historical Quarterly*, XXIX, 1-18.

EDITOR'S NOTES

[i] Opinions vary on the number of such buildings. The stones were used to construct the ranch house now owned by Mrs. J.C. Putnam and some other structures in the area.

[ii] The book entitled *Interwoven: A Pioneer Chronicle* was published in 1936, and is still in print. J. Frank Dobie in his book *Guide to Life and Literature of the Southwest* says it depicts "ranch life on the Texas Frontier as a refined and intelligent woman saw it" (p.62).

[iii] George T. Reynolds was discharged for complications of a case of measles after eighteen months of service.

[iv] More details are available in the section by George's brother Phin.

[v] Some of these pots are located north of the First National Bank in downtown Albany near the picket house constructed by Mr. Ledbetter on the Clear Fork after the Civil War.

[vi] See the more complete version of this story in a later chapter of this book.

THE FRONTIER ADVENTURES OF JOHN CHADBOURNE IRWIN

by J.R. Webb

This account of the life of a man who lived along the Clear Fork from his youth during the Civil War gives a broad survey of what living here was like in the time when settlement was just beginning. The Irwin family was one of the three earliest families to settle in the river valley. Mr. Irwin died in 1938.

I was born at old Fort Chadbourne in Tom Green Territory, Texas, near the present town of Bronte, Texas, February 7, 1855. My father, John G. Irwin, was then the First Sergeant in Co. C, 2nd U.S. Dragoons. Fort Chadbourne was established in 1852, and because I was said to be the first child born at the fort, they named me John Chadbourne, after my father and the fort.

We moved to Camp Cooper on the Clear Fork of the Brazos River, the site of which is about thirty miles north of Albany, in September, 1859. My father had secured a beef contract to supply the soldiers at Camp Cooper with beef and built a house at a big spring down the river from the fort. This contract was signed by Lieutenant Minter, and countersigned by Lt. Col. Robert E. Lee, afterwards commander-in-chief of the Confederate Army. Lee was then sta-

John Chadbourne Irwin

tioned at San Antonio, where the contract was sent to be countersigned. This contract is in my possession at the present time and is, of course, highly prized by me as a relic of the frontier days. I have heard that General Lee was once stationed at Camp Cooper, but I never heard my father mention it. At the time of the signing of the contract I have always understood that he was at San Antonio.

Camp Cooper consisted of officers' quarters and barracks and a sutler's store, which was run by a man named Harper. About a year after we arrived at the fort the Civil War broke out, and the soldiers were given orders by the Confederates to leave out. This they did, and the Confederates, under the command of the old Indian fighter Buck Barry, took charge. They stayed only a few days and abandoned the fort. They were the last soldiers ever to stay at the fort. It was never re-occupied after the Civil War.

Camp Cooper was located on what is known as the old Comanche Indian Reservation, a strip of country on the Clear Fork in Throckmorton County, ten miles long and six miles wide, set aside by the state of Texas for the Comanche Indian tribes. A couple of months before our arrival at Camp Cooper, the Indians had been moved by the government to the Indian Territory.

The Indian Agency was located about two miles down the Clear Fork from Camp Cooper. It consisted of a collection of about eleven drop-log houses.

There is nothing now to mark the site of the Agency, as the ruins have been hauled off and entirely obliterated, but it was in the Stribling field at the old stone fence only a couple of hundred yards from the river bank.

As the soldiers were leaving, Lt. Minter, in charge at Camp Cooper, gave my father permission to take charge of the Indian Agency quarters, and we moved into the house occupied by the agent and lived there until we forted at Fort Davis with the other settlers on account of depredations of the Indians.

At the time of our arrival at Camp Cooper there were ranches in our section owned by Judge J.C. Lynch and George

Greer about forty miles south of us on Hubbard Creek, and Bob Sloan was on Deep Creek. There were no ranchmen between Camp Cooper and those three early settlers, unless a man by the name of Snalum was on Snalum Creek.

When we arrived in 1859 the Butterfield Stage Line was running from San Francisco to St. Louis, and it continued to run until the outbreak of the Civil War, at which time it was discontinued for good. The stage line station was located where the Judge Stribling ranch house now stands, and they dug the old abandoned well to be seen there at the present time. The well is about all that is left to mark the site of the station, except a few half-buried rocks which were a part of the chimney. Stage Line Creek is named after the old stage line. The old crossing on the Clear Fork may be seen in the Stribling Field; also the road can be traced north of the station in the Stribling pasture.

I remember the old stage coaches quite well as they passed. They drove four to six horses or sometimes mules. A man by the name of McCluskey—Henry McCluskey—herded the stage horses kept at the station for stage changes.

When we arrived at Camp Cooper there were a few buffalo in the country, but after the soldiers left they came in by the thousands. I have seen them in their migration, both south and north, pass for a week at the time passing all day long by the thousands; the bulls would be in the lead, always coming ahead of the cows. Sometimes on the migration south, the old bulls when they reached here would be weak and would die in the Clear Fork bogs. I have seen them die in so great a number that we could not eat the fish from the river. There were lots of antelope, prairie chickens, and wild turkey in the country in those days. Speaking of buffalo, I remember that my father used to make me go out and keep the old buffalo bulls off the calf range around the house.

We were the first ranch people in the Clear Fork in that section and put in the first field on the Indian Reservation. During the Civil War, though, a number of ranchmen moved in. Among them were John and Bill Hittson, who moved into the officers' quarters at Camp Cooper, and Uncle Watt Reynolds, who established headquarters at the Old Stone Ranch on Walnut Creek. This ranch was formerly occupied, I have heard, prior to our arrival, by an army officer named Captain [Newton] Givins. He was not there when we arrived, and Mart and Bill Hoover moved there soon after the coming of Uncle Watt Reynolds.

In 1869 the Indians made a raid on Elm Creek north of the site of Throckmorton and killed several people who had come in during the War period. They captured Minnie and Lottie Durgan and the wife and children of a Negro named Britt and took them with them, supposedly to the Indian Territory. Britt went up to the Territory and succeeded in getting his wife and children and Lottie Durgan away from the Indians, but he found no trace of Minnie Durgan. It was only in recent years that Minnie Durgan was found, an old woman, the wife of an Indian and the mother of a number of half-breed children. I saw her at the old Settlers' Reunion at Newcastle. She has since died, so I have heard.

It was after that raid that the settlers decided to fort up for protection from the Indians. The frontier had no protection from the Indians, and they were becoming very bold in their raids. It was then that they built Fort Davis, which was not a fort in the sense of being a soldier establishment, for no soldiers were ever stationed there, either by the Confederates or after the war by the United States. It was simply a collection of houses built by the settlers in that section for protection against the Indians. As I remember, there were about twenty-five families forted up there during the War as follows: John and Bill Hittson, Uncle Billy Southerland, John Selman and his mother—Selman was called Sillman, at least it was pronounced that way, and he was afterward a noted outlaw. Uncle Henry Anderson, old man Musgraves and family, Rom and Arch Ratcliff, and the January family—I do not remember the initials. The Andersons and Edgar Christenson, descendants of whose family live at Breckenridge, also lived there. On the bank of the Clear Fork at the fort lived Uncle Watt Reynolds and family, and turning north, the Boswells from Parker County. There was a family named Steele, and next to them lived Jim Thorp, whose wife now resides at Throckmorton; then J.M. France, the keeper of the Butterfield Stage Station at the Indian Reservation before the war. Sam Newcomb, the school teacher, and T.E. Jackson and family about complete the list. So well do I remember Fort Davis and the people there that I could give the location of every family there at the time. The Confederate flag was the only one that ever waved at Fort Davis. It was destroyed by lightning and never replaced.

The T.E. Jackson referred to above was with George T. and William Reynolds, Jim Drake, Tom Lane, John Anderson, Andy and Bill Anderson, Si Hough and a man named Bozeman when they had the fight with the Comanches on the Double Mountain Fork of the Brazos. In this fight the settlers killed five Indians and a Mexican and Negro who were with the Indians. George Reynolds was shot seriously in this fight. He was shot in the stomach by one of the Indians and carried evidence of the fight for many years—an Indian arrowhead in the wound. Finally, years after the fight he went to Kansas City and had the arrowhead removed. John Anderson was also shot in this fight with the Indians, but his wound was not serious. I saw the party upon their return to Fort Davis. They had gruesome evidence of their victory, as they had the scalps of their victims and all of the Indians' equipment.

I remember another Indian fight that took place while the settlers were forted up at Davis. This fight took place on Tecumseh, in Throckmorton County in 1862. At the time, we were temporarily at our home at the Indian Agency. It happened in this way—John and Bill Hittson, Pres McCarty, and a Negro were cow hunting on Tecumseh Creek when they were attacked by a roving band of Comanches. All but McCarty took refuge under a bluff. It happened that he was a little way off from the others but in sight of the fight. Seeing he could not reach his companions, he made for the house, swimming the rising river three times to get there. The Indians were beaten off from the river, finally; but the Negro was killed, and John Hittson was hit just above the hips. Then Hittson, though wounded, made it to Fort Davis that night.

We lived at Fort Davis, as did the others, until 1867, the year of the coming of the soldiers and the establishment of Fort Griffin. Of course we were running our ranch at the Reservation and looking after the cattle, but all the settlers kept their families at Fort Davis during the latter part of the war.

After the War, in the spring of 1867, several companies of soldiers arrived and established a camp on the banks of the Clear Fork, about one-half mile from the site of Fort Griffin. Of course, there was no Fort Griffin then, nor had there ever been a soldiers camp there before the Civil War, as some now claim. At least there was none there in my day, nor did I ever hear of one ever having been there. I can recall nothing in those early days that indicated soldiers ever made a camp in the vicinity of Fort Griffin, prior to the arrival of the companies of soldiers in the spring of 1867.

For a few weeks this camp on the banks of the Brazos was called Camp Wilson, although it was my understanding that Griffin, for whom the fort later established on the hill was named, was in command. He left a short time thereafter, being superseded by General Sturgis. However, the fort, established a few months after the arrival of the soldiers, was named Fort Griffin. This fort was constructed from pickets but later reconstructed of rawhide lumber made mostly of cottonwood trees.

Here I will answer the question as to how Maxwell Creek got its name. It was named from an early settler by that name, who settled on this creek and who, it was supposed, was killed there by the Old Law Mob, a body of seven men similar to the latter day Vigilante Committee in that they took the law into their own hands. Maxwell was not killed, but in this connection I say that a lawyer by the name of King was hung, supposedly by the OLM, just below the new Albany-Throckmorton bridge. I saw his remains, which were never buried but tossed in a ravine. His only offense, for which he paid this penalty, was that he was employed by Mrs. Maxwell to obtain a divorce from her husband. Rumors had accused Mrs. Maxwell of trying to rid herself of her husband by foul means, and the lawyer was advised to leave immediately. This he failed to do, and the initials OLM were found pinned on his remains.

The name of Collins Creek was after a man named Collins who came to his end at the hands of the same organization that killed the lawyer King. At least, the same initials were pinned on his remains. His killing took place about where the old Ft. Griffin bridge now stands. It seems that someone wrote an anonymous letter accusing him of stealing some mules from Ft. Davis—government mules—and upon this evidence, he was shot.

In this day and time, people, or at least some people, seemed to have the idea that the stores, saloons, and dives just under the hill from Ft. Griffin at a later day and known as The Flat, existed from its establishment. This is a mistaken idea. There was no Flat, saloons, nor dives there until after the establishment of Shackelford County in 1874. Prior to that time, the land which afterward housed the tough dives and resulting lawlessness was under the jurisdiction of the government and, therefore, under martial law. Both saloons and dives were across the river, but they were not on government property.

However, after the organization of Shackelford County in 1874, all of the land except in the Fort proper was released to the county and thereupon sprung into existence that notorious part of Ft. Griffin known as The Flat, which took its name from being in the flat country just under the hill upon which the fort was built. It was then that the saloons, gambling halls, dance halls, low dives, and every form of vice and lawlessness invaded Ft. Griffin, and it looked to me like all of the bad characters from everywhere were swarming around there. It got so tough there that I was afraid to ride down the streets. During the buffalo and trail herd days it looked like the civil authorities were either helpless or controlled by the lawless element, and out of this condition sprung Vigilantes. During those days killings were frequent, and I helped bury a number of cowboys killed in shooting scrapes.

There were many names familiar to outlaw history around Ft. Griffin in those hectic days from 1873 to the 1880's. Two of the most notorious characters identified with the night life of The Flat were Hurricane Bill and his woman, Hurricane Minnie. The first and only Grand Jury to hold a session in Griffin found several bills of indictment against them for minor offenses. Two other characters well known to Griffin life were John Selman and Frank Smith. This was the same Selman that forted up at Fort Davis during the Civil War. Selman left Fort Griffin the night John Larn was killed by the Vigilante Committee at Albany and never returned there. He is credited with having killed the outlaw John Wesley Hardin.

Hurricane Bill was in the Albany jail at the time the Vigilantes got Larn. Both he and the guard at the jail left out that night. It was a couple of years after this that I saw Hurricane Bill in Sherman, and he told me about how badly scared he was at the time, as he thought they were going to get him too. He never returned to Griffin after that.

A few months before John Larn was arrested and taken to Albany, I was with a party deputized to arrest him at his ranch upon a charge of rustling cattle. Lieutenant Campbell, who was a State Ranger, and thirteen other men were in the party of deputies. When we reached Larn's house, Lt. Campbell ordered us to halt while he went in and conferred with Larn and served his papers. He was in there an hour or so and when he came out, Larn, John Selman, Selman's brother, and a man named Tom Curtis were with him. Larn started cursing our entire bunch of deputies and dared them to come through the yard. The Ranger remonstrated with him but to no avail. Well, no, we didn't go through the yard, but we did go around it and to the river just below his house where we fished out cow hides with grappling hooks. This was done in the presence of Larn and the Selmans. Those hides had various brands on them, but we found none with the brands of either Selman or Larn. Larn claimed that they had been planted there to frame him. Neither he nor Selman were taken to Griffin but promised to come over the next day. This they did, but I think all the charges were dropped.

About three months later, the deputy and Sheriff Kruger and a posse of eight men arrested Larn at his cowpen and took him to Albany, placed him under guard in the wooden shack jail, and there, the same night, the Vigilante Committee got him. I understand they gave Selman a horse and saddle to leave the country on before daylight.

I remember when the Hayes outfit was wiped out. I believe it was in 1872, at what is now known as Bushnob, in Throckmorton County. The outfit consisted of Bill and John Hayes, two James boys, one of whom was called "Hard Times," John Hazlett, and George Snow. All of them were killed. There was a boy member of the outfit who was let go. The killing was done by the soldiers from Griffin and settlers or ranchmen who were with them. John Larn and two men named Carter and possibly a cattle inspector named Beard went over there with the soldiers at the time of the killing. The Hayes outfit was accused by Larn of rustling cattle, but nothing was ever done about this. It was during the Reconstruction days after the war.

I have been asked who ran the first store at Ft. Griffin, known as the Outlaw's Store at the time. It was run by a man named Hicks, then by Adams, and later Frank E. Conrad, the well-known merchant pioneer, who later established a mercantile store—The Flat—and was known to be the biggest and best known on the Texas Northwest Frontier. Conrad advertised as having the biggest line of merchandise on the frontier, I believe.

During the time Fort Griffin was in full bloom, I freighted for the government, driving five yoke of oxen and traveling to Dallas, Fort Worth, and Weatherford. It took from three weeks to a month to make the trip to Dallas, depending on the weather.

I remember when General MacKenzie went west on his

expedition against the Indians, which resulted in the wiping out of the Indian village in the Yellow House Canyon and the slaughter of the big herd of their stolen horses, some of which were stolen at Griffin. MacKenzie crossed the Clear Fork at the Old Sod Ranch, so known now, and turned a wagon over in crossing. I was up there a day or so afterward and found where someone had dug the wagon out of the river and hid it in a thicket. Seeing a rifle in the river at the crossing, I waded out to investigate and found some sidelines lost when the wagon turned over. Those I took home.

I was present at what is now known as Newcomb's Grove at the Clear Fork when Shackelford County was organized in 1874. They were short of enough men to vote for the organization of the county as is required by law, so they wanted me to vote. But not being old enough, I refused. However, they voted a number of discharged Negro soldiers.

I was also present at the organization of Throckmorton county, which took place about 1879. This took place at Tecumseh Creek. The first justice court case in Throckmorton county was tried at the old Camp Cooper schoolhouse. The case was a civil suit—Marcus versus Wright. I was a witness in that case, and Judge A. A. Clark, late of Albany, represented the defendant. I don't recall the name of the lawyer representing the plaintiff.

Glenn Reynolds was the first sheriff of Throckmorton county. He deputized me to make the first arrest, as I knew the man I was after, and he did not. He was arrested, tried for a minor offense, and acquitted.

I attended the only Cattleman's Convention ever held at Ft. Griffin which, according to my recollection, was in 1873 or 1874. Although I saw buffalo hides brought to Ft. Griffin by countless thousands during the big kill from 1874 to 1878, I never killed a buffalo except for meat, and I never sold a hide. At the time Ft. Griffin was a great hide market, I saw high years that looked like, I would say, a great lumber year. The hides were stacked tier upon tier, in rows. At the time of the kill, the buffalo were west of Ft. Griffin.

The trail herds started coming through going north just about the time the county was organized, and they continued to come through from South Texas in increasing numbers, but the time of the big drives was after Albany was established in the late '80's, playing out altogether about 1890. The trail was not called the Chisholm or Chissum Trail then—it is only in recent years that I have heard it called that. It was just the Trail or the Southern Trail to us. I went up this trail in 1882 with six hundred cattle belonging to the JOM outfit, owned by McClintock and Woods. There were eight men with the outfit and we trailed to Caldwell, Kansas, and turned them loose on grass—the best grass I have ever seen. We shipped the cattle to Chicago and returned home two months later.

We lived at the Indian reservation until 1886 and then moved to the ranch house where we now live. The trail herd came right through this ranch. The main crossing on the river was about one half mile from the house. The herds would pass here almost daily and sometimes herd after herd a day, from spring until fall. The herds varied in size, but hardly ever over 2500 in one herd. At times a big herd of cows would pass in the spring and new-born calves would be left behind. I have had eight or ten young calves left on our ranch after the passing of such a herd. We raised several that came to our pens.

You asked what was Ft. Griffin's most prosperous time. I think it was 1876-1877. The buffalo kill that year was enormous. There were buffalo hunters, hide money, trail money, trail herd money, and soldier money, and too, it was the provisioning point for settlers going west and north, settling up the west. From the time that Albany was established, the handwriting was on the wall for Ft. Griffin. It is now, as you know, an abandoned fort where only a store and a small community school are left to mark a once prosperous, if wicked, frontier city.

I have in my possession tax receipts for taxes paid at Palo Pinto, Graham, Albany, and Throckmorton on our property where we now reside, located in Throckmorton county thus showing that though we have remained stationary, our county seat has kept moving nearer and nearer to us. My father, as a cattleman, brought me to this country, and now at eighty years of age, I am living only a few miles from where we settled seventy-five years ago, and am in the same business, not withstanding its many ups and downs all these years.

A Life Near The Heart of Texas History

J.C. Irwin of Fort Griffin lives richly in retrospect. His fourscore and more years have spanned three American Wars and the transforming of western waste into a growing empire.

As a lad he watched the stagecoach race along the Butterfield Trail, drawn by peppery mustangs. He saw Texas' Buck Barry haul down the Stars and Stripes and hoist the Confederate colors over Camp Cooper. The red men he knew in both their friendly and murderous moods. He was in Ft. Griffin when MacKenzie's scouts returned from a trip with stolid Comanche warriors tied to their ponies' backs.

He recalls how Cynthia Ann Parker was captured at the fight on the Pease River, and sent by Sul Ross to Camp Cooper within the shadows of the Irwin home. "Cynthia Ann had become Indian in all but blood," says Mr. Irwin. "Holding to her bosom little Prairie Flower, the child soon to die, and grieving for her Peta Nocona, she was the picture of inexpressible despair."

Born near Ft. Chadbourne, named John Chadbourne from that circumstance, Irwin's early life was linked with the Texas frontier. His father, previous to the war, had the contract to furnish meat for Camp Cooper and for a few years made it his pressing business to see that Uncle Sam's blue-clad boys were fed on grass-grown steers. Mr. Irwin exhibits a yellow and hallowed paper that is the meat contract between his father and the government, and which bears the signature of the great Robert E. Lee,

"All kinds of travelers came through on the Butterfield stages," says Mr. Irwin, "and I had ample opportunity to observe them as the stage stopped at the Clear Fork Station to deliver mail and change relays. The passengers who stepped out of the old stage coach were all types—prospectors, gamblers, cowmen, and assorted adventurers. The stage driver, too, was the cussing, whip cracking fellow the story books picture him."

When the Lee family, near Crystal Falls, Stephens County, was massacred by the Indians, Irwin was among the first to arrive on the scene, and helped bury the bodies.

"It was a horrible sight. The murder occurred on a Sunday afternoon in August of '71. Mr. Lee was on his front porch leaning out and singing a hymn. A young man was courting one of the Lee daughters, and others of the Lee family were enjoying a Sunday hour when the Indians stole up from behind a clay bank and shot Mr. Lee. They then attacked and killed or captured the others, except the courting swain who took to his heels and escaped. Both the parents were scalped, and the youngest daughter we found where she had been murdered in attempting flight." Two other daughters, aged fourteen and nineteen, were taken captives and remained with the marauders for almost a year. Their release was affected by a Texas Commission composed of Mr. Irwin, a Mr. Jackett, and Judge Walker, father of Breck Walker, founder of Breckenridge, Texas.

Mr. Irwin has somehow lived near the heart of history. He was living nearly where Kiowas and Comanches raided the Little Elm under Little Buffalo in '68, spreading terror with tomahawk and scalping knife. He knew the Durgan family whose child, Minnie, was captured in this raid and he lived to see her return as an old woman to her Young County home. John Larn, the Irish sheriff of Shackelford county, who, while in office was accused of cattle rustling and mobbed by Vigilantes, was a neighbor of Irwin's, and the splendid monument, erected by Larn's widow, over his body, can be seen from Irwin's spacious porch.

A son of Mr. Irwin's, Ennis, was among those who went to France in the recent conflict. This young patriot was among the first to fall on the battlefront. The Legion Post in Throckmorton bears his name.

Sound in mind and members, J.C. Irwin daily surveys his cleanly kept and well-balanced ranch of 2000 acres. He moves about in a world that he has seen grow from the ox cart to the airplane; in a society he has seen evolve from the six-shooter and hickory-limb era to an age of courts and technicalities. Through it all he has been straight-forward and sane.

ON THE CATTLE TRAIL AND BUFFALO RANGE

by Joe S. McCombs
Contributed by Ben O. Grant and J. R. Webb

One of the most famous buffalo hunters recalls what life was like on the cattle trail and buffalo range.

I was born in Randolph County, Alabama, on May 12, 1854. In the year 1868, when I was fourteen years old, we moved to Texas, coming by boat from New Orleans to Galveston, and then by the H. & T. C. Railroad to Calvert, Texas, then the terminus of the railroad and the destination of our family. The next year, we moved west to near Hillsboro, Texas, and later, 1869, again struck west and landed at Desdemona, in Eastland County. Of course, there was no town there then. Stephenville, in Erath County, was our nearest trading point. It was then only a village of two stores.

When I was 17 years old, in the year 1871, I struck out for myself, got a job cow hunting at $15.00 per month, and the same year made my first and only trip up the old Chisholm Trail as a cow hand with a herd of 900 to 1000 steers owned by Stewart, Strawn, & Bartholemew. The Strawn member of the firm was Belliol Strawn, for whom the town of Strawn was named. Judge N. L. Bartholemew was for years cashier of the First National Bank at Albany and closely identified with the early history of this section.

Our destination with this herd of wild and aged steers gathered out of the sand hills of Eastland County was the state of Colorado. There were only six or seven of us on the drive, and we had plenty of trouble, as there was stampede after stampede. However, we were not bothered with Indians on the way up, and the trip was uneventful except for those stampedes. When we reached Caldwell, Kansas, we wintered there, and as they sold the cattle there next spring, we never reached the state of Colorado.

I remember Caldwell then as a village of a store, a livery stable, and a saloon. The big drives up the Trail had not got well under way then. I don't recall having heard of a drive that preceded ours from that section. On the way home from Caldwell we passed through the Comanche strip and ran into a camp of Comanches. They surrounded our wagon, leisurely relieved us of what supplies they wanted, including all our tobacco, but otherwise did not offer to harm us. Back home after the drive, I failed to find a job either at home or at Weatherford where I went hunting one and meeting up with a young Frenchman who had plenty of names— Allison Edgar Cebron Dumas—I called him Dumas—we struck out horseback for Ft. Griffin, going by way of Metcalf Gap in Palo Pinto County. Reaching Ft. Griffin we found there a fort on top of the hill overlooking the Clear Fork of the Brazos River at which were stationed several hundred soldiers. At the foot of the hill was what was known as the Flat, being the village and trading point for the few settlers in that region as well as for the soldiers. According to my recollection there were three saloons and three stores there then. George Greer and J. C. Lynch were on Hubbard Creek, twenty-five or more miles south to southeast; Joe Browning was below Ft. Davis on the Clear Fork, and Uncle Joe

Matthews on the Clear Fork just below Griffin; John Larn was at the mouth of Tecumseh, and Mart Hoover at what is now known as the Old Stone Ranch. It is on Walnut Creek and was then the farthest ranch house west in all this section. Judge Ledbetter was just north of Ft. Griffin a few miles, and Judge Stribling in the Lamb's Head Valley above Ft. Griffin. The Reynolds family were then mostly ranching in the state of Colorado, according to my recollection.

There were no cattle going up the Ft. Griffin Trail to Kansas and other points north at the time. The herds were then still moving up the Chisholm Trail by way of Ft. Worth and Red River Crossing. The first cattle I recall going by way of Ft. Griffin was in 1874, and they were taken up by the Millet Outfit from South Texas; but from that time on cattle moved over this new trail in increasing numbers. The big rush was at the beginning of the Eighties during which in the spring and summer drives cattle came through in small and large herds daily and by the thousands. The big drives continued until about 1886, and from that time on they came through in diminishing numbers until they played out completely in the early Nineties.

It was in July, 1872, that Dumas and I reached Ft. Griffin, and we sure did start something, that is, I guess we could be accused of being the starting cause of General R. S. Mackenzie's raid on the Comanche Indian village in the Yellow House Canyon and the resulting slaughter of the Indians and about 1,500 head of horses.

It happened this way. We fooled around Ft. Griffin about a week after arriving there and, not being able to find a job, had decided to go to San Antonio. It was the night before the day we were to leave that we crossed over the river and camped in an old slough about a mile from the town. We hobbled our horses in a mesquite thicket and made down our bunk in the high weeds, doing both as a precaution against prowling and thieving Comanches.

About two in the morning the tramping hooves of horses and rustling weeds awakened us, and in the moonlight we saw Indians on horses making toward us. They passed by only a few feet from our beds, the horses even snorting as they passed, but if they saw us they did nothing about it, yet I feel they must have seen us. It is my opinion that a Comanche would not shoot a sleeping man.

After the Indians were well out of sight, we made a search for our horses and found, very luckily, our hobbles, which the Indians had cut and left in a path. We went immediately to the Fort and reported to General Buell, who was then in command, the presence of Indians and loss of our horses. He sent a scout troop to follow the trail, which led towards Crystal Falls. The scouts returned in a couple of days, reporting more Indians and more thefts in the vicinity of the Falls, and the entire band of Indians with stolen horses and cattle making their way up the Brazos by way of Ft. Belknap heading towards Yellow House Canyon. In a skirmish the Indians drove the scouts back. General Buell immediately dispatched more scouts to keep in touch with the general course of the Indians and sent General Mackenzie upon his historical expedition to intercept them. The troop—I don't remember just how many there were although I saw them leave—took along wagons, etc., and were well provisioned.

They headed up Paint Creek with Seminoles and Tonks as trailers, both of whom hated the Comanches. The trail made by Mackenzie on this trip was known and is still known to this day as the Old Mackenzie Trail, over which, at a later date, went many herds and settlers to the Plains. It can be traced to this day through the hills of Throckmorton County.

Strange to say, the horse of Dumas, the theft of which with that of mine at Griffin that night started out the scouts and afterwards General Mackenzie and his troops, was amongst the fifteen horses returned to Ft. Griffin. He was a sad looking sight though as the Comanches had cut off his tail and one of his ears, but Dumas took him back just the same.

Neither Dumas nor I went to San Antonio as we had intended before the Indians got our horses but stayed around Griffin. Dumas started back to Weatherford, Texas, after the return of his horse, and I heard he accidently drowned the poor old horse as he was crossing the Clear Fork near Ft. Davis. I haven't seen Dumas from that time to this but heard from him in Arkansas several years ago.

I stayed around the Fort working in and out for a year or so after this. I worked for Uncle Joe Matthews, and one year ran the government wood yard at the Fort. In the fall of 1872 I was out with a surveying party headed by Captain C. W. Holt. We were out locating the H. & T. C. Railroad surveys and went all the way to the foot of the Plains due west from Fort Belknap, and our same mission later carried us down south to the mouth of the main Concho River.

It was on the trip west from Belkanp that I saw the most buffalo I ever saw in my life. In fact we were in buffalo most all the way from the mouth of Miller's Creek, as far as we went. The largest individual herd though was near Kiowa Peak on the Salt Fork of the Brazos northwest of Haskell. (There was no Haskell then.) Our party estimated that there were 50,000 head of buffalo in that vast moving mass of buffalo heading south.

When we neared the Double Mountains on this trip we had what you might call a dangerous experience in a buffalo stampede, heading into a cloud of dust which we knew to be caused by a moving herd. The dust was not thick at first but animals scattering became frightened and started running, heading into the wind as always they did, and the ones behind kept following.

The dust thickened as did the herd. The wagons were ordered rounded together and all hands inside. It had begun to look squally. The herds were running blind, every animal with his tongue out and the dust so thick that they could hardly see the wagons, which was the only danger. It was soon over and my only experience of the kind. It would not have happened but for the blinding dust as a buffalo was always afraid of a man and there was no danger from one unless you crowded him.

On the surveying trip to the mouth of the Concho, we were out of bread and depended on buffalo meat. On our way home we ran into a burned strip fired by the Indians which extended from Mountain Pass, in Taylor County, to Fort Phantom Hill. There was not a living thing in this burned waste. However, we had some bear suet as we had killed a couple of bears in Mountain Pass. It was on this trip that a band of Indians which we estimated from signs at from 60 to 70 kept following us trying to steal our horses. Although they stampeded them one night, we only lost one horse to them on the trip. They never attempted to attack us.

First Buffalo Hunt Out of Griffin

About Christmas, 1874, John Jacobs, Joe Poe, and I rigged the first buffalo outfit ever to leave Ft. Griffin on a buffalo hunt for hide purposes. Ft. Griffin afterwards became the greatest hide market in Texas. We left out on Christmas Day, going out the Mackenzie Trail and up Paint Creek in Haskell County and established our camp six or seven miles northeast from Haskell near Mocking Bird Springs. There was no house or settlement west from the Stone Ranch at the time, but we did not strike buffalo until we got on Paint Creek—they always kept west of the white man. They occupied the prairies of Shackelford and Throckmorton Counties by the hundreds of thousands, so I am told, before Griffin's time.

Around our camp at Mocking Bird Springs, the hunting was good. I did all the killing, and Poe and Jacobs, the skinning. I would always shoot the leader of the herd, usually a bull, and if I could get him, the bunch or herd would start milling around until another assumed leadership and headed out, and then I would try to get him, the idea always being to keep shooting while they were milling but to get a leader in order to keep the milling going on. Most of the herds had moved south at this time of the year, but I killed 700 and we out two months. Nothing of consequence happened on the hunt—we saw neither white man nor Indians, nor did we hear any other hunters.

After returning to Griffin, Poe and I decided to leave Jacobs with the wagon to haul in the hides and to go further west on another hunt. So we rigged up a pony team and headed out up the Clear Fork of the Brazos by way of Fort Phantom Hill, finally locating our camp about where is now the town of Rotan, or near there. We stayed until May 1 and got 1,300 hides. After hauling in the hides of the first hunt, Jacobs followed our trail and located our camp, and we were sure glad to see him as we had been out of bread for ten days. It was on this hunt that one of our ponies slipped a shoulder, so we had to haul our hides into camp. We would just skin and peg the hide down on the ground, and when Jacobs arrived we hauled them in. In pegging down we simply stretched the hide and drove pegs at intervals in the ground using about fourteen pegs to the hide.

I remember a close call Poe had with a buffalo. I had downed several bulls right together. Poe, being only a short distance away, came over, and we approached the kill. When about fifteen feet from the downed bull, up he got and charged straight at Poe. I was behind Poe and shot by him and dropped the bull at his feet, Poe shooting with his pistol as he fell.

Our season's kill for the two hunts—there were 2,000 of them— sold at Griffin for $2.00 for the robe hides and $1.50 for the others. They were the first hides of any consequence marketed at Griffin. There had been some hides sold there from buffalo killed for beef, but this was the beginning of the great hide industry which ended abruptly in 1878 with the extermination of the herds—killed out completely for their hides. Conrad and Rath, to whom we sold these hides, were the big buyers there, and their hide yard in the big years of the kill, in 1876 and 1877, looked much like a cotton yard of today.

Buffalo hunters skinning a buffalo.

Third Hunt, 1875

In the fall of 1875 I organized an outfit of my own with three skinners, one of them was Bob Pitcock, now an oil man of Ranger, Texas. The other two were Wesley Tarter, who died in the '70's, and Sol Pace, who died in Ft. Worth several years ago. I had a span of mules and a wagon on this trip and took along 800 pounds of lead and five kegs of powder, a Sharps Sporting Rifle, and my reloading outfit. The rifle weighed 16 pounds. We struck out by Phantom Hill, going to where Sweetwater now stands, and camping there I killed several hundred before moving on to Champion Creek, just this side of Colorado, Texas. There we made permanent camp and stayed until April 1. My total kill was a little more than 2,000 hides. During this entire trip and hunt of over six months, we did not see any one outside of our outfit. In fact, there were no settlers in that country so far as I know, and

Buffalo hunters, 1876, drying buffalo hides.

the hunting had not got much under way. Upon my return to Griffin, I hired five or six ox wagons to go after the hides. Each buffalo wagon had a trailer, and six yoke of oxen were used to the wagon. They made two trips for these hides.

Fourth Hunt, 1876

By the time of my next hunt, the fall of 1876, buffalo hunters were becoming pretty thick. The northern hunters were following the herds on their migration south. I had about the same outfit and struck out on the same trail as the year before but did not stop until we reached Morgan Creek, which is over the divide west of Colorado City. There we made permanent camp, and our winter kill was 2,300 hides. All the time now the herds were being drifted west by the

A typical collection of buffalo hides piled high awaiting shipment.

hunters who were after them from morning till night. We could hear the guns of other buffalo hunters occasionally, but most of them were to the east of us. I always tried to keep on the outer edge.

On the way home we met several meat hunting outfits from the settlements to the east. It was this year, too, that hide buyers started following the hunters and buying the hides at the camps. I disposed of most of my hides in camp at $1.00 a hide straight through. The hides we hauled to Griffin brought $1.50.

1877 Hunt, My Biggest Kill

September, 1877, taking the same number of skinners and a Mexican to stake down the hides, and, as ammunition 1000 lbs. of lead and five kegs of powder, we struck the same old trail that we blazed two years before. But this time our permanent camp was at the Big Springs, where is now located Big Spring City. Later, however, we moved down to Mossy Rock Springs, which we named. They are near Signal Mountain, ten miles south of Big Spring. On this hunt from September to May, I made my biggest kill—same being 4,900, all of which I personally killed. Poe and Jacobs had an outfit north of us that killed 6,300. There were several camps around us as the hunters were getting thick. Two outfits stacked hides at our camp and we had 9,700 stacked there. I account for our big kill that year by being favorably located at these springs where these animals would come for water. I killed 1,000 bulls at Big Springs. The bulls always led the herds on the migrations, and they were usually thirty days in advance of the cows. At Mossy Rock Springs I killed 2,200 buffalo so close together that I could stand at one place and almost see this number of carcasses. We decided to poison our hides this year, due to a low market and carry them through the summer. After doing this I struck out in advance of the wagon for Ft. Griffin, but met a hide buyer, W. H. Webb, of Dallas, at Phantom Hill. He offered me $1.00 per hide, camp delivery, for the whole 9,700 hides and I sold, having authority to sell for the others, as well as my own.

He and I returned to camp, where he received the hides, and our outfits returned to Griffin. That was the last year of the big kill and the biggest year for the buffalo hunters in Texas. The hunters followed the herds north that summer and back again in the fall. All the time they were being hunted.

Last Hunt, 1878

Again in the fall of 1878 I went out and this time on my last hunt. This time I located camp at Mustang Pond, where is now Midland. This year, although I stayed out from September to the middle of March, my entire kill was 800 hides. Buffalo were scarce and wild and started north on their very last migration before their usual time. But they never got back to their summer ranges. Hunters finished their existence as herds on the one great ranges this spring of 1878, and all that remained of the vast herds of a few years back were a few straggling bunches, mostly calves. I do not recollect having seen a buffalo on the range after my return from my last hunt related above. There was no hunting after that.

Although I killed altogether about 12,000 buffalo while on these hunts, I never saw a white one. I saw some that looked white in the herd but killed several, and they always turned out to be a grizzly color.

A few months after returning from this last hunt I left Griffin and went back to Hill County for a girl I knew when I was a kid. Her name was Miss Betty Hale, but she became Mrs. Joe S. McCombs, June 29, 1879. We moved to Albany by rail in 1881, the year the road reached here, and have been here ever since.[i]

EDITOR'S NOTE

[i] Joe S. McCombs died at Albany, March 21, 1935.

FORTING UP ON THE TEXAS FRONTIER DURING THE CIVIL WAR

by Marilynne Howsley

During the Civil War, when troops were withdrawn from the area, settlers were left to their own devices for defense against raids by Indians. The Frontier Battalion was too widely spread to provide much protection. This account tells about families that moved to a common location and, by their very numbers, hoped to provide their own protection.

The settlers along Elm Creek, in Young County, were going about their business as usual that fateful day in 1864. The women were cooking the meals for the hungry men who soon would be coming in. The daughters were cleaning the houses or mending clothes. Everyone was working as everyone must do to survive in a frontier settlement, when suddenly down the valley swept a horde of Indians like a band of invading Assyrians. Their feathers and war paint gleamed in the sun, and their yells and blood-curdling screams struck terror into the hearts of those brave people who had thus far beaten the adversary of nature but now must contend with savages to keep what was their homes.

Common grave marker for victims of the Elm Creek Raid, July 17, 1867.

The Indians were there to kill and steal; what they couldn't take with them, they were set to destroy. Mrs. Bragg, the wife of Uncle Billy Bragg, was too far from the house to reach it by time the Indians arrived, so with her two children and their dog, she ran and hid under the protecting shelf of a rock down by the creek. She said that she had been afraid the dog would bark and reveal their hiding place, but he seemed to sense the danger also. The Indians came so close to them that she could hear the tread of their feet. She and the children had to stay under this rock all day, and when Mrs. Bragg returned to her house, she found it completely empty except for a bundle of raw wool tied in a blanket in a corner of the room, her spinning wheel, and loom. She said that the thing she regretted losing most was a suit she had just completed to send to her son at the battle front. The soldier by whom she was sending it had ten more days on his furlough; so she started work and spun the cloth. She made a suit in ten days when it would take most of us longer than that to make a suit out of bought cloth.[1]

After the Indians had left, the settlers gathered to check on who was missing, to care for the wounded, and to collect the dead; they found twelve people had been killed, and eight carried into captivity. Among the captives were the wife and children of a Negro named Britt, Mrs. Clifton, and her two granddaughters, Millie and Lottie Durgan. These poor people had supposedly been taken to the Indian Territory, so Britt went there and succeeded in getting all of them back except Millie Durgan. Some stories said that no trace of her could be found, while others said that she had been adopted by an Indian chief and his wife who had no children and refused to give her up. After sixty-six years, the wife of a Kiowa chief was identified as the long lost Millie Durgan. She herself was even unaware of her true identity.

It was after this terrible calamity of the Elm Creek Raid and other similar incidents that the settlers decided to move closer together to protect themselves from the Indians. Fort Belknap and Camp Cooper had been deserted at the outbreak of the Civil War, and the settlers were then left to their own resources for protection. Many gave up the struggle and returned from the frontiers of Northwest Texas to Central and East Texas. The weak were sifted out, and only the strong remained to fight for what they had thus far accomplished. The Indians, chiefly Comanches and Kiowas, became aware of the settlers' lack of protection, and thus started giving them more trouble than ever. The Elm Creek Raid was one of the results of the evacuation of the soldiers.

Fort Davis, in northwest Stephens County on the Clear Fork of the Brazos, about fifteen miles below Camp Cooper, was established by the settlers of that region. Even though it was not a fort in the strictest sense of the word, because no soldiers were ever quartered there, it being simply a collection of houses that formed a stockade, it was the best protection the settlers could possibly have since the soldiers had left them. There were about 25 families which moved into the fort. They called it "forting up." Fort Davis was a rectangle 600 feet long and 375 feet wide. It had a 25 foot alley running east and west through the fort. There was one stone house which was used as a refuge for the women and children when the alarm of an Indian raid was given. Some of the other civilian forts that were established during the Civil War were Picketville, Owl's Head, and Mugginsville in Stephens County; Bragg's Fort and Murray's Fort in Young County; and Lynch and Greer ranches in Shackelford County.

Life in these forts was much the same as in any other frontier settlement. Everyone joined in the work. The men were placed on sentry duty. The rules of the fort governing the period of service stated that a man was to do sentry duty one-fourth of the time and the remainder he was free to attend to his own affairs. The law said that under no circumstances was a man to be kept away from his family more than two months at a time, unless, of course, he was actively engaged in fighting or pursuing Indians. At one time the men must have grown rather lax in their sentry duty, as is seen from the excerpt from Sam Newcomb's diary for March 12, 1865.

"Indian excitement has been high here today. About nine o'clock Mr. McCarty came upon a large body of Indians about three miles from the fort. They gave him a close chase, but he reached the fort all right. The Indians were followed all day long, but made their escape. I think this will stir some people in this place to do their share of the picketing."[2]

The men had other duties, of course, besides doing sen-

The only building still left standing at Fort Davis on the Clear Fork.

try duty. There were farmers, hunters, cattlemen, and merchants. A school was soon established, and Sam Newcomb was chosen as its teacher. He kept a diary of the happenings of the fort during 1865 and 1866, and this little journal, written partly in home-made ink, is still in existence and is historically important. A portion of his dairy described his school thus:

March 13, 1865-Commenced school here today for a term of 14 weeks. I have only 19 scholars at present and most of them are rude, wild, and wholly unacquainted with school disciplines.[3]

On July 3, his diary gives another report from the school:

I have only 15 scholars now. The people are having a hard time getting books.[4]

On January 29 of the next year, he said:

My school is continually getting smaller. This is the second time a couple has quit school to get married.[5]

A Sunday School was organized at the home of J. M. Frans, a former keeper of the Butterfield Stage Line station at the Clear Fork below Camp Cooper. There was no Sunday School literature as we have today—only the Bible. They would read and discuss a few chapters from the Bible and then all of them, young and old, would have a spelling lesson from Webster's *Blue Back Speller*. Many of the people, even those full grown, married, and rearing a family had never heard a gospel sermon before W. B. Slaughter, a Baptist missionary preacher, started coming to the fort occasionally to preach a sermon or perform a marriage ceremony. Every time he did come, there would be a siege of baptisms and weddings. On January 23 there was supposed to have been a wedding, but the mother of the bride objected for some reason, and with a gun prevented the ceremony from being performed. She had won for awhile, but on February 10 the preacher arrived and the delayed wedding took place.

The men doing their hunting, farming, preaching, and school teaching were by no means the only ones who worked. The women whom they had chosen to share their lot in life and their children, as well, also shared the work. There was no cloth to be bought. It all had first to be spun into thread then woven, and at last made into clothes. Sewing machines were unheard of in this country at that time. The first sewing machine was brought to this region two or three years after the war. It was a small machine, clamped to a table like a meat grinder and turned by a crank. The name of the machine was "Common Sense." Mrs. Sallie R. Matthews in her book, *Interwoven*, recalls how all the women of the community flocked to her sister's house to take their turn at using this little machine. Some of the clothes were made from the tanned skins of deer and antelope. The women by using this buckskin, which was as soft as our present-day suede, saved themselves many hours of weaving. The suits were entirely useful until they happened to become wet, then the buckskin would stretch and become hard and stiff. Some of the women would learn to do one certain thing well and do this in exchange for other work. One would specialize in making buckskin gloves in return for weaving, while another might weave a hair net out of horse hair to get her candles made. All the candles and soap used had to be made by the women. The soap, and also the soda, were made from the lye bleached from wood ashes. The ashes were put into a hopper and thoroughly wet until they began to drip. The women had to do all the milking too, while the men sat on the fence and looked for Indians. With the family she had to rear and the meals she had to cook in addition to these other things, it was certainly true that a "woman's work was never done."

In spite of all the work to be done, the settlers still had fun. They had square dances, candy pullings, quilting parties, and feasts and dances at all the weddings. At the candy pullings the molasses candy was made in a wash pot out in the yard. The candy pullings were principally for the youngsters, but I imagine that the old folks enjoyed it fully as much as the young ones did. The women's quilting parties served a double duty. It afforded them entertainment, while at the same time, it accomplished one of the many tasks to be done.

The Indian raids in the vicinity of the fort were frequent, and the settlers were kept in a constant state of alarm. One of the more important raids took place on Tecumseh Creek in Throckmorton County in July, 1865. John and Bill Hittson, Pres McCarty, and a Negro were cow-hunting on Tecumseh Creek when they were attacked by a roving band of Comanches. All but McCarty took refuge under a bluff. He was too far away to reach his companions, so he started in the direction of the Irwin home; he had to swim the river, which was up, three times before he finally reached there. The Indians were finally driven off, but not before the Negro was killed, John Hittson shot through the thigh, and Bill Hittson wounded just above the hips. The Hittsons, though wounded, made it to Fort Davis that night.

The Indians also interfered with the fort's amusement. One night in 1866 the settlers at the fort were having a square dance, the music being furnished by Matt Frans. The Comanches had a dance by the same music on the bank of the river as mocassin tracks found the next morning indicated. Their dance was some twenty steps from the fort. Sentries at the fort must have been asleep or inside dancing, for after the dance the Indians got away with all the horses.

According to Mr. Newcomb, the Indian raids and hard

work were not the only disagreeable factors in being a settler in West Texas. The following is a portion of his diary of January 6, 1866:

"Sand storms are very common here in the spring, especially when it has been very dry during the winter. They are heavy winds that come from across the arid plains west of here, bringing with them great rolling, stifling clouds of sand, such as we read about in Africa. This country has some peculiarities that are very disagreeable. Among them are the sandstorms in spring, the awful northers in winter, the long, parching drouths in summer, and the swarms of grasshoppers in the fall."[6]

Some of the people in the fort decided that since they did call it a fort, they should have a flag. Invitations were sent out to some of the surrounding forts to come to the flag-raising ceremony and a feast afterwards on March 2, 1865. It was a Confederate Flag and the only one ever to wave at Fort Davis. It was later destroyed by lightning and never replaced.

By May, news had reached the fort that Lee and Johnston had surrendered, and soon the defeated Confederate soldiers were drifting home. The temporary civilian forts began to disintegrate, for they had served their purpose to protect the settlers from the Indians while the soldiers were away. The families remained at Fort Davis until 1867, when the United States soldiers came and Fort Griffin was established.

Bibliography

Biggers, Don H., *Shackelford County Sketches*, Albany: Albany News Office, 1908.

Matthews, Sallie Reynolds. *Interwoven*, Houston, Texas: The Anson Jones Press, 1936.

NOTES

*At the meeting of the West Texas Historical Association at Albany on May 10, 1941 Miss Howsley read this paper as the representative of the Albany High School Junior Historians. The Editor.

[1] Sallie Reynolds Matthews, *Interwoven*, 55.

[2] Don H. Biggers, *Shackelford County Sketches*, 17.

[3] Biggers. p.17.

[4] Ibid, p.18.

[5] Ibid, p.21.

SANDSTONE SENTINELS

by Joan Farmer

Graveyards reveal much about the people who lived in a place. This material provides details on individuals in the cemeteries in the Fort Griffin area.

On a spring day not so long ago I paid a visit to the site of the once bustling town of Fort Griffin on the Clear Fork of the Brazos. As I stood in the sunshine and looked down what was once Griffin Avenue,[i] I suddenly realized that there is virtually nothing left that would identify this place as a town with a glorious past. The little rock jail house has been moved to the city park at Albany; the Planters Hotel, Bee Hive Saloon, York & Co. store, the office of the *Fort Griffin Echo*, and many, many more have all passed into oblivion.

A breeze suddenly sent a tumbleweed scurrying across the porch of Art Newcomb's abandoned house. I felt a sense of sadness that all of the town of Griffin is gone. But this thought came to me: people lived, loved, and died here and must have been buried near the town. I soon found the cemetery, the one part of Griffin that would endure for years. Thus the thought became strong that many such places exist—old, forgotten cemeteries or single lonely graves which tell much of the history of this area. I began a search for these places, seeking old stories that would tell of how these people lived and how they died.[1]

The Griffin Cemetery is on the point of a hill overlooking the river valley, a peaceful place seldom disturbed by the sounds of a modern world. Here we find the story of Susan Thorp.

Soon after the close of the Civil War, Jim Thorp moved his family to Collins Creek near Fort Griffin. He obtained a patent on his land in 1867 and there built a rock house. Mr. Thorp operated a blacksmith shop in the "Flat" below the fort for a number of years. Susan J. Thorp was born June 3, 1869, in the rock house on Collins Creek. As a little girl she must have heard the beat of drums and weird shouts of the Tonkawa Indians encamped nearby as they held their ceremonial dances. Susan attended school in the old rock Masonic building. The school was under the direction of Professor Dalrymple. Susan had the leading part in the school play "Diamonds and Toads." In the year 1883 she was the proud possessor of an autograph album. The album contains the signatures of the Hourigan girls, the Bennett girls, Callie Stribling, Lottie Arendt, Lee Barber, and others. In January, 1883, a schoolmate of Susan's wrote this little message in her book: "Susie, remember thy Creator in the days of thy youth!" Susan had only youthful days, as she died of typhoid fever October 27, 1887, at the age of eighteen. In later years the Thorp family moved to Throckmorton. Susan's grave is found in the northwest corner of the Griffin cemetery.[2]

The majority of the stones in this cemetery are sandstone bearing no inscription. The oldest inscribed stone marks the grave of "Ellen Clayton, beloved wife of W. T. Clayton, departed this life Jan. 31, 1877, at the age of 26 years." Samuel J. Ward, who for many years occupied the rock house which is now enclosed in the Fort Griffin State Park, is also buried in this place. His death occurred December 16, 1881. The following article is found in the *Fort Griffin Echo*:

"Ward came to this country a poor cowboy in 1868 or

'69 and by his own industry and frugality he accumulated a competence, but like most of us he labored hard to add to his possessions and it is believed that overexertion, exposure, and mental labor were the prime causes which led to the disease which proved fatal to him. He has gone to join one of his children in another world, leaving a wife and five children, and a host of friends to mourn his death. He will be buried today by the Masonic fraternity, he being an honored member of that body."[3]

It is felt that many of the graves which are marked with sandstones date back further than 1877, but since they are not engraved and death records were not kept in those days, it is impossible to find any trace of their identity.

Southeast of the lower slope of "Government Hill," as the Fort was known, may be found a plot of ground enclosed by a tumbling rock fence. This was the military burial ground. Little is known about the men that were buried here. In the *Fort Griffin Echo* this item is found:

"The strains of the Death March came floating across from the Garrison on the evening air of Thursday, telling that another soldier was being laid in the Post Cemetery. We heard that he died suddenly but did not learn the particulars."[4]

After the fort was abandoned, the government moved all the bodies from this plot and reburied them in a government cemetery at San Antonio. In later years a new highway was put through from Albany to Throckmorton. During the building of this project one of the bulldozers uncovered a skeleton. The bones found, which consisted of the skull, two arms, and two legs, were carried to the general store and post office at Griffin. The skeleton was placed in a cartridge box and for many days proved to be the topic of conversation. Many stories were circulated as to the identification, and rumors were spread that a number of the soldiers had been uncovered. The mystery was solved when Mr. John C. Irwin made one of his regular visits to the store. He explained that the skeleton was that of a Negro who died near Fort Griffin years after the soldiers had been moved. Since digging a grave in the earth around Griffin proved to be quite a job, due to the rocky soil formation, it was decided that one of the soldiers graves could be easily dug out, as they had been filled in with loose dirt. Therefore, the Negro was buried in a second-hand grave. Upon completion of Mr. Irwin's explanation, the bones were sealed in the cartridge box and reburied in a pasture near the fort. Mr. Bill Manning, who was county coroner at that time, made a crude marker for the grave by chiseling a cross into a sandstone.[5]

Directly below the fort, also in an easterly direction, is another cemetery, which is enclosed with the State Park land. The passage of time has hidden the reason for Griffin having two civilian cemeteries. There are several theories. This second cemetery may have belonged to the Hervey family. The site may have been too small or high water may have necessitated moving to higher ground.

Up the river from Fort Griffin near old Camp Cooper are two graves enclosed by a well-preserved rock fence. One is a small grave marked, "Joseph B. Larn, son of S. W. and J. Larn, Born March 24, 1875, Died Sept. 17, 1875." The other grave is that of an adult, "John M. Larn, born March, 1849, Died June 24, 1878." Most historians tell us this man lived by the gun and died in violence; but facts become twisted and lost with the passage of time, and we know only that this man played his part in the history of this country, a part of which adds a sharp flavor to stories of the past.

Farther up the Clear Fork on the Treadwell Survey we

find a burial ground that was used by the Treadwells, Irwins, Gossetts, and Hursts. The oldest grave here is that of James M. Treadwell, who died in November of 1877 at the age of 24. Atlee E. Irwin, son of J. C. and Annie Harris Irwin, is buried here also. The Albany newspaper recorded his death with this item:

"On last Saturday, John Irwin while hauling with a spirited team near his house accidently let them run away. He got entangled in the wheel and was used very rough, but about the time he got free the horses made a circle towards his little boy who was setting playing in the yard. They ran over him, the wheel struck him and killed him instantly breaking his neck. The little fellow was a very bright child about 3 years old."[6]

Emily E. Irwin is also buried here. She was born February 14, 1833. In 1855 as a young woman of twenty-two years she was the wife of John G. Irwin, first sergeant in Company C, Second United States Dragoons at Fort Chadbourne, in present Coke County, Texas. Mrs. Irwin was the mother of John Chadbourne Irwin, so named because he was the first child born at the fort. In September of 1859 the Irwins moved to Camp Cooper on the Clear Fork of the Brazos, about thirty miles north of present-day Albany. Mr. Irwin secured a contract to supply the soldiers at Camp Cooper with beef. This contract was signed by Lieutenant Minter and countersigned by Lieutenant Colonel Robert E. Lee, afterward Commander-in-Chief of the Confederate Army. During the Civil War the Irwins forted up, along with other settlers, at Fort Davis for protection from the Indians. After the War was over, the Irwins moved back to their ranch on the old Indian Reservation. Mr. Irwin put in the first cultivated land in this section.[7] In 1867 or '68, Mr. Irwin made a trip into Kansas on business and never returned. His saddled horse was found near his home and an unsuccessful search was made for clues that would solve the mystery of his disappearance. Mrs. Irwin died February 14, 1903, at the age of seventy, the mysterious disappearance of her husband still unsolved.[8]

On the old Butterfield Stage Line near Lambshead Creek are a number of graves. These are believed to be the graves of people connected in some way with the stage line, either as passengers or employees of the line. Rock coverings two feet high have protected these graves from the elements, or they would have disappeared long ago.

Matthews and Reynolds are names that are woven like bright colored threads through the history of Shackelford and surrounding counties. These names are found in the discussion of almost any historical subject in this area. This subject is not an exception. Not many miles from Fort Griffin is Reynolds Bend. Here in 1876, shortly after he and his father, Barber Watkins Reynolds, established their ranch, B. F. Reynolds built a two-story stone residence. During the month of May, 1881, three-year-old Annie G. Matthews, eldest daughter of Mr. and Mrs. J. A. Matthews, came to Reynolds Bend to visit her grandparents. During this visit she became ill and her life was claimed by a disease which in these modern times seldom proves fatal. Annie was buried a short distance from her grandfather's house.[9] The following year, on June 1, Pearl Russell, daughter of Glenn and Augusta Reynolds, died at Albany, Texas. She was buried beside the grave of her cousin at Reynolds Bend. The death notice was printed by the *Fort Griffin Echo* and included this poem:

> Upon the hill in Durham Bend
> Another little grave was made
>   and close by little Annie's side

little baby Pearl was laid.

Darling little blue-eyed baby
 was tired and fell asleep,
Oh so tired but resting now,
Therefore, mother, do not weep.

Your precious little girl is safe
with ransomed throng above,
She sings her happy little songs
where all is peace and "God is Love."[10]

Also buried here is Barber Watkins Reynolds. He died on June 7, 1882, at the age of sixty-three years. Compared with the average life-span of today, this is not an exceptional number of years, but Mr. Reynolds and his wife, Annie Marie, came to this country at a time when it was firmly held by the coyote, buffalo, and the Indian's tomahawk. They came to Texas in 1847, and gradually moved west, until in 1860 they located at the Cantrell ranch, near what is now Breckenridge. In 1860 Stephens County was organized in their house. They moved from Stephens County to Fort Davis and from there to the Old Stone Ranch, which at that time was the extreme settlement to the northwest. It was from this house that the Reynoldses first caught sight of an army moving out of the south, coming to establish Fort Griffin. This event, in the year 1867, at last meant some protection from the Indians. In the years preceding Mr. Reynolds' death the country changed before his eyes. He saw no more the dust of huge buffalo herds as they trailed across the horizon, for they had been turned into gold by the hunter's gun. He saw the Indian's grasp upon the land broken, to be lost forever to the white man.

Through the years this little cemetery has been selected as the final resting place of the Reynolds, Matthews, and neighboring families. It is surrounded by rolling hills and beautiful old pecan trees which line the river bank near by. Curly mesquite and other native grasses softly cover the graves, which are marked by small old-fashioned stones. These stones have grown more beautiful with the passing of time until their texture and color seem almost a part of the surrounding scenery.

In the 1850's wagon trains, moving to California, turned their wheels through Texas. The gold-seekers chose this trail even though it was longer than northern routes, due to the fact that it could be traveled the year round. One and one-half miles from the mouth of Paint Creek in Throckmorton County may be found the graves of a few of these emigrants who started out so bravely with dreams of the gold to be found in California. One sandstone marker bears the inscription "Mary A. Died May 29, 1852."

South of Albany on Hubbard Creek is found the remains of the old Greer house. The George Greers settled in this county in 1860. Their son, Cal Greer, in company with William King and Vol Suvench, discovered what later became known as the Ledbetter Salt Works. The Greer cemetery is found on high ground near the creek. The oldest grave found here is that of Jackson W. Greer, son of G.W. and S. A. Greer, born August 27, 1858, died September 29,1862. George W. Crow, son of Wm. and E. C. Crow, is also buried here. He was six years old at the time of his death, the result of swallowing a cartridge shell.[12]

William Crow, who married one of the Greer girls, died April 26, 1884, and is buried here. *The Albany News* stated:

"Last Saturday night William Crow, an old citizen of Shackelford County, died at the residence of James Hart, on

Deep Creek in Callahan County of inflamation of the bowels. Mr. Crow was with a cow outfit at the time and on Saturday about noon he was sick and went to camp. Growing rapidly worse, he was removed to Mr. Hart's residence and a physician sent for. It seemed that he had a presentment that the end was drawing near and asked that his wife be sent for at once, which request was complied with. He grew rapidly worse, and Dr. Baird, the physician of the family, was sent for, but being absent Dr. Powell went in his place but was met about five miles this side of where Mr. Crow lay by J. H. Greer, informing him that Mr. Crow had died about eleven o'clock, his wife having reached him a short time before he died. He was buried on Sunday afternoon near Geo. Greer's residence with Masonic honors, the lodge from this place of which he was a member attending. Mr. Crow was one of the oldest citizens of this county and enjoyed the esteem of a wide circle of acquaintances."[13]

John R. Greer, who drowned near his home, is also buried here. On returning home from town one night he found the creeks and branches swollen by late spring rains. It is supposed that he swam several creeks including Hubbard and then drowned in a small branch. This seems a little odd, as he was said to have been an excellent swimmer.[14]

George W. Greer and his pioneer wife, who brought their children to this country almost a hundred years ago, rest here. The story is told of a man who was robbed of a large amount of gold by two Mexicans. The Mexicans were captured by Texas Rangers near George Greer's house. Years after the deaths of Mr. and Mrs. Greer deep ditches were dug in the old Greer fields as men searched for the gold that was supposedly buried there by the Mexicans.[15] While standing in this small hill top cemetery I could not help wondering if the spirits of these pioneer men and women buried here would not have smiled at this folly, for they knew the wealth of this country was not gold.

Among the first ranchers to come to Shackelford County was John C. Lynch. He married Florence Gonsolus at Santa Fe, New Mexico, and moved to Texas in 1860. They settled nine miles southeast of Albany on Hubbard creek.[16] Here, Mr. and Mrs. Lynch made their home throughout their lives. The rock house which they built still stands, and, though it is only a burned-out shell, it conveys the feeling that many stories wait within the walls needing to be told.

A short distance from the house is the Lynch Cemetery. This is said to be the place where many people, passing through the country in covered wagons, buried their dead in preference to burying them on the prairie.

Peter Gonsolus, father-in-law of Judge Lynch, is buried here. It is said that Mr. Gonsolus erected one of the first stores in the settlement that became modern Chicago. He left Chicago and migrated to California in 1859. He came to Texas in 1860 and became a physician, storekeeper, and leading citizen in old Picketville, which was the predecessor of Breckenridge. Gonsolus Creek, a stream on which Breckenridge is built, is named for him. He was the husband of seven wives and the father of forty-two children. He died at the age of eighty-five years.[17]

Icebenda C. Lynch, daughter of J. G. and F. J. Lynch, died in 1878, and is buried near her grandfather. In 1871 Mr. Lynch made a visit to the Reynolds family at the Stone Ranch. Susan Reynolds Newcomb made a note of this visit in her diary and tells of Mr. Lynch's great love for this little girl:

"Mr. Lynch left after quarreling (as he terms it) till he got tired. He took one of mine and Gus' pictures, also one of Bettie's for his little girl "Dutch" as he calls her, to put in her album. He says that he loves Dutch better than any one else living, better than his own wife. That does not seem natural to me that a man should love his child better than his wife. He must be a strange genius."[18]

Many stories have been written about the Civil War, but it is surprising to find a short story of this period chiseled into the smooth marble of a tombstone. Such a story is found in the cemetery at Moran, Texas:

In loving memory of our Mother Francis
Trammell, Daughter of Rev. D. R. Culberson,
Wife of William M. Trammell Died Aug. 2, 1900
Aged 73 years and 9 months.

On the reverse side of the stone:

Our father William Monroe Trammell a
Confederate soldier wounded at Atlanta Geo.
Died in a hospital at Griffin. Aged 45 yrs.
and 9 months and buried in Soldiers Cemetery
at Griffin, Geo.

At the foot of what is commonly called the "One Mile Hill" southwest of Albany is a cemetery which had its beginning in the 1870's and is believed to be the first cemetery plot laid out for the town of Albany. Weeds and brambles cover the twelve graves. It is possible that there were other graves here, but for many years this cemetery has been neglected and many headstones scattered and mounds dissolved by the elements.

In 1882, Mr. Weldon L. Rucker operated a rooming house

in the infant town of Albany. On a day in February of that year, a Mr. Evans got off the train in Albany, travel worn and ill. Mr. Rucker took the man home with him. The next morning it became evident that the stranger had smallpox. Upon his death he was buried in the cemetery north of Albany. The disease spread without control to members of the Rucker family. Joseph Jackson, son-in-law of the Ruckers, had a brother who had at one time had smallpox and survived. He was sent to care for the Ruckers. The best care available was not enough. The first to die was four year old Ettie Estellah, in February, 1882. Mrs. Rucker gave birth to her expected baby, and it too died. On March 3rd Mr. Rucker, his wife, and 21 year old Theodore Rucker died. Minnie M. Rucker, who died sometime in March, was the last to go. Weldon Leander Rucker, who at the time was a boy of twelve, contracted the disease but survived, carrying the deep pox scars through life. The Rucker family was buried beside the grave of little one-year old Georgia Rucker, who died in October, 1881, in the little cemetery at the foot of the One Mile Hill, west of Albany. The Rucker house with all its contents was burned to prevent further spreading of the disease. Alice Bennettie Rucker had married Henry Herron February 5, 1882, and they established their home in Albany. Mrs. Herron was not permitted the privilege of aiding her family during the terrible tragedy. Her grief was increased in later years when the little cemetery became a forgotten spot. Cattle left their hoof prints on the mounds and nudged over the headstones while grazing. Many years later the Rucker town lots were sold. With part of the funds received from this sale, Mrs. Herron had a metal fence built around the graves of her family.[19]

A diligent search has revealed the oldest marked grave in the Albany cemetery to be a child buried in 1877. Many pioneers of this area are buried here, and the stories to be found within this cemetery could not be limited to a few paragraphs or even confined between the pages of a single book. Following are sketches of the lives of a few of the pioneers sleeping here.

Found here is the grave of "Uncle" Joe McCombs. Uncle Joe was born in Randolph County, Alabama, on May 12, 1854. When he was fourteen years old he moved with his family to Calvert, Texas. The McCombs family made several moves west, and in 1870 they arrived in Eastland County.[20] At the age of seventeen Uncle Joe made his first trip up the old Chisholm Trail as a cowhand.[21] Uncle Joe rigged up the first buffalo outfit ever to leave Fort Griffin on a buffalo hunt for hide purposes. This was in 1874, and he made his final hunt in 1878. By then the buffalo had become scarce and the straggling remainder of a once great herd began their migration north. They never got back to their summer ranges, for this was the year the final big kill occurred. On returning from the last hunt, Joe went back to Hill County, married Miss Betty Hale, and moved to Albany by rail in 1881. They built a house near the present site of the residence of Mrs. C. B. Mauldin. Indians almost daily trailed in front of their house on their way to camps on the North Prong of Hubbard Creek. Mr. McCombs engaged in ranching and also served as Shackelford County Treasurer for several terms. During the latter part of his life he had a mercantile store in Albany.[22] On March 21, 1935, with many trails behind him and the sound of a moving buffalo herd a still familiar memory, Uncle Joe came to the end of one of the most colorful lives of the West Texas frontier.

Peace Officer, Buffalo Hunter, Cattleman—these titles were easily linked with the name of Henry C. Herron. He came to this country in 1875 and settled with his family two miles west of Albany. At this time Fort Griffin was beginning a career as marketing center for buffalo hunters and the Fort Griffin-Dodge Cattle trail. Mr. Herron became a deputy under Bill Cruger in 1878. He described Fort Griffin at that time and until 1882 as the "toughest place I have ever seen." From 1882 to 1886 he served as deputy sheriff under Green Simpson. He was elected sheriff of Shackelford County in 1886, serving two terms. He later served as a deputy under Sheriff Marshall Biggs. Mr. Herron went into the cattle business in 1890. He established one of the first herds of pure-bred Hereford cattle in Shackelford County. Mr. Herron's life-time spanned more than just years. He came to this county when it was a tough, wild place and the quickest mode of travel was a fast horse. When he died in 1944, the roar of airplanes had become a familiar sound in skies above pastures where once he had trailed the outlaw.[23]

Too little is written about the pioneer women who came to this western frontier with their husbands. They shared the hardships of frontier life as cheerfully as they later shared better days. Augusta Russel was married to Glenn Reynolds in Otero County in southern Colorado, March 2, 1876. As a bride of eighteen, Mrs. Reynolds came to Texas to live on her father-in-law's ranch above Fort Griffin in Throckmorton County. Her husband became the first Sheriff of Throckmorton County. In 1886 they moved to Holbrook, Arizona, and from there to a ranch near Globe, Arizona.[24] In this ranch house Mrs. Reynolds sat by her sick child and hopefully waited for the return of a rider who had been sent to Globe for medicine. He never returned, for this was during the Pleasant Valley war and the rider's arm was blown off by a gun blast. Soon afterwards the Reynold family moved into the town of Globe, where Mr. Reynolds was elected Sheriff in November of 1888.[25] After moving to

Globe, the four Reynolds children had scarlet fever, and little George, weakened from his previous illness, died. Mrs. Reynolds must have spent many uneasy hours waiting for her husband to return from his frequent man hunts into the Arizona wastelands. On Friday, November 1, 1889, Sheriff Reynolds began a trip to Yuma. He was to deliver eight Indian prisoners, including the Apache Kid, to the prison there. Mrs. Reynolds feared for the safety of her husband and pleaded with him not to go, as she knew the Apaches were desperate and dangerous men. As Mr. Reynolds kissed his wife goodbye he told her, "Gussie honey, let's not go over all that again; I'll make it all right: You just keep the pot boiling and the children happy, and don't you worry about me." The following day, Mrs. Reynolds was notified that the Indians had brutally murdered her husband while making their escape. Sheriff Reynolds was laid to rest alongside his infant son, George, in the Globe cemetery. The minister used as his text verses 9 through 12 of the Nineteenth Psalm, ending with the majestic lines: "So teach us to number our days, that we may apply our hearts unto wisdom." Mrs. Reynolds returned to Albany with her little family and lived out her life there, a useful and well-loved citizen, having a rich store of memories.

A stone brought over from Scotland marks the Matthews burial plot in the Albany cemetery. It is an impressive stone but it is overshadowed by the more impressive lives of those who sleep beneath the stone. Joseph Beck and Caroline Matthews, their son, J. A. Matthews, and his wife, Sallie Reynolds Matthews, are all buried in this plot.

Joseph and Caroline came west when their son, who was born in 1853, was only a baby. The settled in Stephens County. During the Civil War they lived at Fort Owl Head, seeking as did other early settlers, protection from Indians.

About 1867, they moved two miles below where Fort Griffin was located.[26] Mr. Matthews became one of the big cattlemen of the county. His son, J. A. Matthews, married Sallie Reynolds on Christmas day in 1876. They ranched in Haskell county and then moved to Colorado for a time, but returned to Texas and established the Lambshead Ranch in Throckmorton County. This ranch became the oldest operating ranch in the state in the hands of its original owners.[27]

Sallie Reynolds Matthews was a pioneer in the purest sense of the word. She entwined her personality into the hearts of all who were fortunate enough to know her. After reaching the age of seventy, she wrote *Interwoven*, an autobiography of her life on the frontier and a story of the interweaving of the Reynolds and Matthews families.

Ranchers, judges, storekeepers, law men, buffalo hunters, and a colored soldier from old Fort Griffin—it took them all to build this country. These pioneers who lie sleeping in these hallowed spots, whether in single, lonely graves or small family plots long forgotten, had enough trials to keep them strong, enough hope to make their hearts sing, enough sorrow to keep them human, and enough religion to give them value. The stories of their lives can never be erased from the pages of history for their dreams were the indelible fabric from which the history of this country was made. Sandstone Sentinels, Monuments to a Pioneer Past!

NOTES

[1] The Larn graves, Treadwell cemetery, Reynolds Bend Cemetery, Stage Line burial plot, and graves of the Forty-niners were all visited through courtesy of Mr. Watt R. Matthews, Albany, Texas.

[2] The Etta Soule Papers, property of Mr. Robert Nail, Albany, Texas

[3] *Fort Griffin Echo*, December 17, 1881.

[4] *Fort Griffin Echo*, September 25, 1875.

[5] Mr. Harvey C. Herron, Albany, Texas, interview, October 17, 1957.

[6] *The Albany News*, November 6, 1891.

[7] Memoirs of John Chadbourne Irwin as told to Hazel Overton, Albany, Texas.

[8] Mr. J. C. Irwin, Jr., Albany, Texas, Interview, October 3, 1957. For an account of forting up during the Civil War see Ben O. Grant, "Explorers and Early Settlers of Shackelford County," *West Texas Historical Association Year Book*, XI (1935), 17-31. For new information on this disappearance, see Lawrence Clayton, "A Gunslinger Confesses." *Old West Magazine*, Fall, 1982, pp. 17-19.

[9] *Fort Griffin Echo*, May 28, 1881

[10] *Fort Griffin Echo*, January, 1882. At the time this poem was written, the Reynolds Ranch was called Durham Bend because of some Short Horned or Durham cattle owned by the Reynolds family. Concerning B. W. Reynolds and the organization of Stephens County, see Lon William Hartsfield, "A Brief History of Breckenridge and the Stephens County Oil Field," *Year Book*, XII (1936), 100 ff.

[11] Ben O. Grant, "The Early History of Shackelford County." A Thesis. Hardin-Simmons University, 1936.

[12] Mr. Will Hatcher, Albany, Texas, interview, July 10, 1957.

[13] *The Albany News*, Friday, May 2, 1884.

[14] Mr. Will Hatcher, Albany, Texas, interview, July 10, 1957.

[15] Ibid.

[16] Ben O. Grant, as cited.

[17] *Dallas Morning News*, July 8. 1934, Section Two, page one.

[18] Diary of Susan Newcomb, MSS. February, 19, 1871.

[19] Mrs. A. W. Reynolds, Interview, July 9, 1957, Albany, Texas. During this epidemic a total of 13 persons died. The first log house built by the A. A. Clarks was used as a pest house and people afflicted with the disease were put in it, many of them to die. *Albany News*, May 13, 1937.

[20] Alvin B. Bernstein, Albany, Texas, Interview, July 4, 1957.

[21] Ben O. Grant and J. R. Webb, "On the Cattle Trail and Buffalo Range," by Joe S. McCombs, *Year Book*, XI (1935), 93-101. In *The Handbook of Texas* (II, 103), Ollie E. Clarke writes the name consistently McComb.(Ed).

[22] Mrs. B. E. Snyder, Albany, Texas. Interview, November 1, 1957.

[23] Facts about Mr. Herron's life obtained from *Albany News* of August 24, 1944, and Interview with Harvey C. Herron, Albany, Texas, October 10, 1957. The most comprehensive sketch of his life is that by J. R. Webb in the *Year Book*, XX (1944). 21-51.

[24] *Albany News*, July 1, 1943.

[25] Jesse G. Hayes, *Apache Vengeance* (Albuquerque: The

University of New Mexico Press, 1954).

²⁶ *The Albany News*, April 26, 1941; Sallie Reynolds Matthews, *Interwoven: A Pioneer Chronicle* (Houston: Anson Jones Press, 1936).

²⁷ Ibid.

EDITOR'S NOTE

ⁱ This street is now a gravel road designated as the Old Albany Road. It served as the road connecting Albany and Throckmorton.

John Calvin Ledbetter / S. W. Wesley: One Indian Captivity Narrative or Two?

by Lawrence Clayton and Morris Ledbetter

I ndian captivity narratives often reveal horror and death. This story, however, poses a mystery of whether the young Ledbetter captive returned later or not.

The numerous stories concerning abduction of whites, especially white children, by Indians on the American frontier have long intrigued whites, and Texans are no exceptions. We point with some sense of pride to the famous Cynthia Ann Parker, captured in 1836, and her remarkable son Quanah Parker, Chief of the Quahadi Comanche Indians in the 1870's.[1] People in West Texas, especially around Albany and old Ft. Griffin, still talk about John Calvin Ledbetter, the white boy stolen in late 1870 or early '71 by Comanche Indians. The mystery surrounding his disappearance and the person who appeared in Ft. Griffin some eleven years later, claimed to be the lost Ledbetter boy, but then denied that he was Ledbetter and claimed instead to be S. W. Wesley, makes this one of the most intriguing stories of

Johnny Ledbetter

its type. At least as interesting and not nearly so well known, however, are details of the later life of this man who claimed he lived with the Comanches before he returned to life as an Anglo, studied law, preached the word of God, became a successful business man, and later practiced chiropractory in San Antonio.

For the sake of focus, it is helpful to give a brief sum-

S. W. Wesley

mary of the family version of the story. The details of the capture are starkly brief when one considers the shock such an event would have dealt a family. By 1862 the Ledbetters had left the Clear Fork area and settled on the site of a saline spring south of present-day Albany, Texas, and had begun to produce salt for sale. William Henry Ledbetter, the father of the family and later to be the first elected judge of Shackelford County, had at that time two sons, Harve and John Calvin. As boys, playing around the salt works, the two had one game which was to become extremely significant later. In cold weather, the boys burned brands into corncobs near the fireplace. By bending a piece of strong wire, the boys could fashion a brand, which left its mark clearly on the fresh shelled corncobs. It was a common game for boys to put the cobs in "pens" and refer to them as cattle. Some collected all red cobs, some all white, and so on. At one time in this childhood game, whether by accident or by intention, Harve branded John in the small of the back, leaving a lasting scar.

Recognizing the need to educate the boys, Mr. Ledbetter sent them to a small boarding school on the Lynch Ranch, eight and a half miles southeast of present-day Albany and quite a distance from the salt works. Lynch, a man of some wealth and prominence, had built the school on his property but located it at the confluence of Deep and Hubbard creeks, approximately two miles from the house, probably in proximity to both the house and Ft. Hubbard, the site where families had "forted up" during the Civil War period, and the ranch house. This accounts for why in those troubled times the school was built that far from the relative security of the ranch house. On this particular day, as the eight or nine students who boarded with the Lynches were walking home from school, John lagged behind. When the other children reached the ranch house, John was missing. The search that followed turned up no trace of the boy but did reveal ample evidence of hostile Comanches in the area.[2]

The next family record indicates that a young man resembling Johnny Ledbetter rode a wagon into Ft. Griffin, the frontier town near which the Ledbetters had moved in the eleven years since the boy's disappearance. He was in the company of a man named Tiger Jim.[3] The older man had a load of buffalo hides he had traded from Comanches in the Palo Duro Canyon area. The trader indicated that he had obtained the boy from the Indians. The Ledbetters noticed the young man, who seemed unsure of his ancestry, and definitely thought he physically resembled the lost John. The trader apparently exercised no claim on the young man and left him to his own devices. Mrs. Ledbetter invited the stranger to stay with them and told the sons to take the young man swimming with them at the ford on the Clear Fork of the Brazos River north of the town. Harve immediately—and positively—recognized the scar that he had left on the back of his younger brother years before. The Ledbetters were convinced that this was indeed the lost son over whom they had grieved. The young man agreed that he was the lost son, at least for a time.

Oral history in the family indicates that Mrs. Nancy A. Thornton, now deceased, and a sister of the mother of John Calvin Ledbetter, was told the following story by the young man after his reunion with the family. She said the man told her that he was on his way home from school when he was kidnapped between five and six o'clock in the afternoon on that fateful day. He was then mounted on a horse in front of a squaw and in this fashion was carried by the raiders all night without stopping because they feared pursuit. At daylight the Indians stopped and ate some raw meat. The squaw, apparently realizing that the white lad's stomach would not tolerate that diet, broiled some for him. From there the group continued in the same northwesterly direction to the Palo Duro Canyon area, where the lad spent his years of captivity. This was the same area in which the buffalo trader found the young man. It seemed certain that this was John Calvin Ledbetter.

The adventures of the young man following his return can be gleaned from letters in the possession of the family. He did not remain in Ft. Griffin. First he went to school and, if the letters and later career are indicative, profited from the experience. In a letter dated April 15, 1885, and posted in Bryan, Ohio, the writer who signs himself, "Your son, J. C. Ledbetter," writes to Mrs. Ledbetter giving details of his life. He apparently began working for the railroad in Texas but quit that job to travel as an agent for an unnamed insurance company on a route from Cincinnati, Ohio, to Los Angeles, California. Concurrently, he studied law, for he mentions that he has mastered "Kemp's Second Volume" and has purchased for study four additional volumes of law. He closes by begging for news from home and by indicating that he has seen some old friends from his railroading days in Texas. There is one troubling note in the letter: he indicates that his Texas chums remembered him as "Wesley." Another letter, this time signed S. W. Wesley, is dated December 17, 1887, two years later. Penned to Mrs. Ledbetter from Navasota, Texas, it addresses her as "My Dear Adopted Mother." In this missive the writer expresses concern about how he would be received if he were to visit the Ledbetters at Christmas time and indicates that he is aware that the family is "contemplating prosecuting" him, an action that he does not understand. He states that he has discovered through a Sam Crowley from Missouri that his true relatives are from Missouri and Illinois, and he claims to have "gotten letters from all over the country telling me all about the Wesleys and Crowleys." He continues his denial that he is John Ledbetter: "I know that I am not." He even offers to file an affidavit denying his Ledbetter heritage and any claim to an inheritance from the family. He continues by saying that if he can be convinced that he is a Ledbetter, then he "will take the name and the place of a son with pleasure." One wonders what wrought the change.

Possible motivation for this change of allegiance is contained in this same letter. Mr. Wesley indicates that he discovered his father was Robert Wesley, a former steamboat captain on the Mississippi River during the Civil War. He also claims to have found a man who cared for him until he was eight years old. Then two key sentences appear. "These are all good citizens and many of them very wealthy. How can you blame me for doubting that I am a Ledbetter?" The Ledbetter estate at that time amounted to about six thousand acres of ranch land in West Texas. The discovery of oil on that land, by the way, came much later. He signs the letter "Your adopted son, S. W. Wesley." The letter is written in a fine hand on stationery which quotes John 3:16 and 17 at the top, for by this time S. W. Wesley had become Reverend Wesley.

A more comprehensive—but somewhat contradictory—account appears in an undated newspaper clipping in the Ledbetter family files bearing the title "A Strange Biography." Related is the story of the Reverend S. W. Wesley, who according to the writer of the article "has been doing splendid evangelical work in Texas." Here is the story:

"I was born in San Francisco County, Missouri, [and] at an early age came to Texas accompanied by my Uncle Sam Crowley, with whom I then lived, my father and mother being dead. A few months after coming to Texas, I drifted away from my uncle and wandered out West. There I fell in among cowboys, hunters, trappers, and Indian traders. Being a small boy—an orphan with no one to protect me—I was subject to all kinds of kicks and cuts from the frontier ruffians. I got tired of this and made the acquaintance of some Comanche Indians who came into the country to trade, and I determined to leave the white people and go among the Comanches.

Leaving the white men one morning, I struck out on foot for the Indian camp, which was in sight. Arriving there, I was received and treated kindly. This was something I was not used to. White men had never treated me thus, and I was determined to return to them no more. I remained among the Indians several years. I threw aside my own clothing and adopted those of the Comanches. My hair grew out, and my face, which was so sun tanned that it could hardly be called white, was painted. Although I looked rather "Injun," it was not long until I had mastered considerable of the vernacular. The Indians loved me and would deprive themselves of comfort for my sake. One thing was laid down to me very clearly. That was not to try to escape, or I might suffer for it. After residing among the Indians some years on and off the reservation upon hunts and the war path, I managed to get separated from them against my will, for by this time, I had become so attached to them that I did not want to leave.

I finally got lost from the tribe somewhere south of the Horsehead Crossing on the Pecos River and the next day ran upon a ranch outfit. The ranchman took me for an Indian until I explained that I was a white man, and they then suspected me of being a spy. After explaining that I was not, they with caution permitted me to remain at the camp that night. I stayed there several days hunting cattle and helping around the ranch until Mr. Rulin, the owner of the cattle, gave me a job at herding while the "boys" kept their eyes peeled. They knew if I was a spy that they had nothing to fear so long as I remained with them and had communication with no one. I was with them six months. Afterward in July, 1876, I went to Ft. Griffin, and now occurred one of the most remarkable episodes in my career. Judge W.H. Ledbetter, who in 1865, [sic] had a boy stolen by the Indians, claimed I was the stolen boy. I was convinced of it against my will, and for three years, I went by the name of Ledbetter. Having discovered the mistake, I made a trip to Missouri in 1881, and there met all my mother's people after first having come across Sam Crowley, the uncle with whom I had come to Texas. In Missouri, I found that I had forgotten my people, and I there secured a chain of evidence which has never been broken by the Ledbetters, who still claim me as their son. Having remained in Missouri a year, I returned to Texas and went on the range where I "punched cows" until 1883. I left the frontier in the fall of 1884 and undertook (that is, I tried to undertake) the study of law by spelling out Blackstone and Kent. In January of 1885, I quit law and went to Palestine, and there I attended the meetings of Major Penn and was converted and baptized. I then immediately went to preaching and have been knocking along with the Gospel, lariat in hand, ever since."

Another letter dated September 17, 1912, comes from Mr. Wesley, who was at that time Inspector General for the Federal Guaranty Company of Washington, D.C., but is addressed from Waxahachie, Texas. The letter is penned to Mr. Lee Tuton, John Ledbetter's brother-in-law, since Tuton married Susie, one of John's younger sisters. Mr. Wesley details some information of his family life, but more significantly he indicates that he has sold his banking business in Dallas but retains an office to which he travels as need demands. A sentence in the final paragraph of this letter is also revealing: "The 'Revolution' in Mexico caused me to lose over $50,000, but I have a few dollars left, and if that war ever stops I will be a very rich man in a few years." Mr. Wesley is obviously quite well to do financially and is in an influential position in the business world.

One of the greatest curiosities to grow out of the Ledbetter tale is, of course, the changed story reportedly told in Mrs. Thornton's presence and then later denied by the mysterious young man. It is clear that the decision made by S.W. Wesley caused him later to emerge a wealthy man, wealthier than he would have been had he been John Calvin Ledbetter perhaps. It is not difficult to imagine then that S.W. Wesley was indeed John Calvin Ledbetter and that he went on to a more financially rewarding situation by claiming the identity of the apparently lost child of the Wesley family. The man in question, whatever his true name, was certainly an energetic, skilled businessman who traveled widely and gained a good education. What became of his religious commitment in later life that allowed him to work for the Federal Guaranty Company of Washington, D.C., and hold an interest in a bank is, of course, an interesting question.

Discrepancies in versions of the story are many. In his interview article Wesley indicates that he came to Ft. Griffin in 1876 from the Pecos River area, not the Palo Duro region. The child was not lost in 1865, as Wesley says, for census records indicate the boy was in the home in 1870. Judge Lynch did not open his school until "1868 or thereabout," according to Biggers.[4] In letters to Mrs. Ledbetter, there is no indication that Wesley worked as a cowboy.

Instead he says that he was working for the railroad in the early 1880's. Wesley also leaves out any reference to his having gone to school, a fact omitted from the article altogether. In his interview Wesley says he was converted to Christianity in 1885 in Palestine, Texas, apparently shortly after January. To his mother he says that in April he is working for an insurance company traveling from Ohio to California. By 1887, as his letter indicates, he is preaching, so the 1885 date in the article could be just an error, perhaps of one year. The omissions of his education, railroad, and insurance experience are less likely careless oversights in the printed article. Since the article is undated, however, we can only assume it was published after 1885 (the last date mentioned in the piece) and certainly before 1912, the date of his letter to Lee Tuton in which Wesley indicates that he has sold a banking business and settled in Waxahachie. He has at some point been the Inspector General for the Federal Guaranty Company. He has also lost the $50,000 in the Mexican "Revolution," probably the result of an investment that would have taken some time to arrange.

These concerns are merely academic anyway and may be cited as proof by both sides. The lack of knowledge of the whole situation involving the Ledbetter boy may indicate that Wesley was indeed not the lost child. Yet in his own interview article and his letters, Wesley gives different details. One can only wonder why he was publicly showing a different side. What is known for sure is that Mrs. Ledbetter died assured that the man called S. W. Wesley was indeed her lost John, who had denied his true heritage. What became of S. W. Wesley after 1912 is not known for certain at present. One informant notes that Wesley lived in San Antonio, where he died and was buried. Rister, in *Ft. Griffin on the Texas Frontier*, confirms that Wesley lived in San Antonio.[6] Whatever the case, it is likely that further knowledge of him would shed no light on the story of the lost Ledbetter boy or convince those who know the story intimately that their opinion, whichever it is, is other than they believe it to be.

NOTES

[1] See James DeShields. *Cynthia Ann Parker* (San Antonio: Naylor Press, 1934) for details of that famous experience.

[2] Details of the story vary depending upon which of the numerous sources is consulted. This narrative is based on the family version known by Morris Ledbetter. See Carl Coke Rister, *Fort Griffin on the Texas Frontier* (Norman: University of Oklahoma Press, 1956), pp. 40-42, for a discussion of the event. See also Edgar Rye, *The Quirt and Spur*, Facsimile ed. with an Introduction by James M. Day (Austin: SteckVaughn, 1967). pp. 121-134.

[3] Letter, S. W. Wesley to Mrs. M. E. Ledbetter, July 25, 1887.

[4] Don H. Biggers, *Shackelford County Sketches* (Albany, Tex.: *Albany News* Office, 1908), unpaginated. See the chapter entitled "Ledbetter Salt Works."

[5] Interview by Morris Ledbetter of Rev. W. W. Jones of Raytown, Missouri, (who knew Wesley), September 1983.

[6] Rister. p. 41.

THE FRONTIER LIFE OF PHIN W. REYNOLDS

An Interview by J.R. Webb

The following material reveals a broad view of history in the Fort Griffin area and well beyond. The brothers of Phin, especially George and W.D., traveled extensively in the cattle business over the West. Phin's recollection offers a remarkable narrative of frontier life.

I. Bad Drouth from 1862-1864

Although a small child I can recall the severe drouth which began in 1862 and lasted into 1864. So severe it was that two-thirds of the post oak timber in that section died, and its effect on the timber could be seen for more than thirty years thereafter. I remember that my brother William and I walked up the dry bed of the Clear Fork for more than a half a mile hunting drinking water in 1863. We were then living on the Dawson ranch above Eliasville. I have never since then seen such a drouth.

Speaking of drouths, though, I remember that old Tonkawa White, an Indian I later knew while living near Fort Griffin and who looked to me to be almost a hundred years old, told me that a dry spell once drove the western Indians almost as far down the Brazos as Waco village for game and water. He was explaining to me the reason for what we early settlers called the Dead Mesquite Forest. This was a forest of dead mesquite trees which covered parts of Taylor, Jones, Haskell, Baylor, Scurry, Dickens, and other counties nearly to the foot of the Plains. At the time I first saw it there were standing trunks of large trees, the limbs having rotted away, but the hearts of the trunks being well preserved. There was no evidence of their destruction by fire, and there was no sprouting out from the roots. The strange part of it was that there was hardly a living mesquite in all that section and there were few even in Stephens County. This dead forest was there when the earliest settlers arrived, and it remained until fencing started in the early eighties. Much of it was then hauled away by the settlers for fence posts. The settlers in Shackelford and Throckmorton counties hauled their posts from the dead forests of Jones and Haskell counties. I tried to get more definite information from old "Tonkawa" as to the time this drouth occurred, but all he seemed to know was that it was "way back."

II. An Indian Scare

While we were living at the Dawson ranch shortly after we arrived in Stephens County, we had a little Indian scare. My two oldest brothers, George and William, and two cowboys who were working for us were out on the range working some horses, and they had taken with them all the pistols and guns that would shoot. We three younger boys, Ben, Glenn and I, were at home and out in the yard. One of the older boys had killed a panther and had brought it in, and we were busily engaged cutting into its tail to obtain some sinews to fix some arrows. A couple of our horses were hobbled out and grazing some fifty yards away. All at once we were startled by two Indians who swooped down on our horses, cut the hobbles, and drove them away. Three other

Indians could be seen on a nearby hill above the house. We gave the alarm, and our father rushed out of the house with an old gun that would not shoot; but it had its effect for they made no effort to harm any of us. Ben recognized one of the horses ridden by one of the Indians as belonging to Riley St. John, who had recently arrived from the Territory of Colorado. The horse had been stolen from him the previous night.

III. Trouble with Indians

For a few years after our arrival in Stephens County there were few Indian raids of any consequence until the big Indian raid down Elm Creek, in Young County, in 1864. Just prior to our arrival in the county, Jno. R. Baylor, who was a noted Indian fighter and hated the Indians, was desirous of avenging the death of the Browning boys; so he got up a party consisting of Tom Stockton (who was another noted fighter and who afterward established a ranch seven miles south of Raton, New Mexico, on the Santa Fe Trail), Min Wright, John Dawson, and two others, and they went on an Indian hunt up in the Phantom Hill country and brought back about a dozen scalps. The Stockton family were neighbors of ours, and there were three boys in the family—Tom, Rex and Thipe. A short time before their hunt the Indians had raided their place and killed around sixty sheep.

IV. The Settlers "Fort Up" for Protection

There was a great deal of excitement among the settlers after this raid, which occurred in the fall of 1864, as it was realized that the families, scattered as they were, were unable to protect themselves from the murderous bands of Indians prowling the country. Furthermore, we had no rangers or soldiers on the frontier as there was an acute shortage of manpower in the Confederacy in the last years of the War. It was up to the few settlers in the country to protect themselves. Many of the families abandoned the frontier and left for the interior settlements. Those who were determined to face the dangers and remain were called together for discussion as to the ways and means of providing protection for their families. It was decided to "fort up," that is, for the settlers in different sections to come together and build their houses in close proximity so that they would be gathered in groups, thus providing larger forces of men to repel Indian raids. This was done, and these communities of houses were termed forts, though they were forts in no literal sense as they had neither soldiers nor artillery. They did have men who were called upon for guard duty and scouting purposes. The settlers who occupied these forts or communities spoke of having "forted up" during the war, and it is so spoken of until this day. In our section were several such forts, one known as Fort Davis being the largest. It was situated on the banks of the Clear Fork in the southwestern edge of Stephens County, and its site is now owned by a man named Crousen, so I understand. Other forts in the section were Pickettville near the site of Breckenridge, Owl's Head, Clark, Mugginsville, and Hubbard, also known as Lynch's Ranch.

Our family moved to Fort Davis, which was built in the form of a square, and a picket stockade was started but never completed. It was to be constructed around all the houses, but as the scare died down somewhat, work upon it ceased. I can remember the houses and their owners and where each house was located. Our house was on the southwest corner of the hollow square; next door to the north was that of John Hittson, who was the wealthiest man in the country; next was the home of Jim Thorpe; and next to his was the house of Matt Franz. He had been the stage line agent at Clear

Fork Station of the Butterfield Stage Line until the stage line was abandoned at the outbreak of the Civil War. Next in order were the homes of Mich Anderson, A. Anderson, the Sutherlin family, and then the school house, which was the northeast corner of the square. Sam Newcomb, my brother-in-law, who taught the school and kept a diary of events at the fort, occupied a house within the square. John G. Irwin, who had a meat contract at Camp Cooper before the war, also lived within the square, and Arch Ratliff lived within the square also.

The Newcomb diary is still in existence, and my sister, Sallie Reynolds Matthews, quoted parts of it in her book *Interwoven* published in 1936. John Selman with his mother occupied the house on the east side of the square next to the school house. His mother gave me, while we were living at the fort, the first apple I ever saw. John Selman (pronounced Silman) was afterward to become a noted person and was run out of the country at the time John Larn was killed by the Vigilance Committee. Larn, the second sheriff of Shackelford County, was under arrest and was shot by members of the Vigilance Committee while in jail at Albany. This occurred in 1878. Selman afterwards killed the noted outlaw John Wesley Hardin. Selman was killed by George Scarborough, a former sheriff of Jones County, Texas. Next in order lived the families of T. E. Jackson, Alex Clark, January, Mich McCarty, Marion McCarty, Elgy Christenson, and last and next to our house was that of an old free Negro known as Aunt Maria [Williams]. When Joe Browning married Angelina McCarty at the fort, the bride borrowed her wedding dress from Aunt Maria. After this wedding they had a big candy pulling, and the candy was made from sorghum syrup boiled in a wash pot. Most all of the houses at the fort were constructed of pickets.

V. A Fort Dance and Uninvited Guests

I remember a dance at the fort in 1866 to which came uninvited guests. Not only were they uninvited, but they came unseen, danced to the fiddler's music only a few yards under the hill from the fort, and then took their departure, some on the horses of hosts and invited guests. Stealthily they came, danced, and left without the dancers being aware of their presence. When the dance was over and the men who had ridden in from a distance discovered that their horses were gone, the first evidence of the Comanche's raid was discovered. Not until the next morning when the circling moccasin tracks under the hill were detected was it known that they had dared to enjoy the fiddler's music while on their thieving expedition. I do not think they had any intention of making an attack on the fort.

As a matter of fact, I have never known of the Comanches making a night attack, with one exception. That attack was made in 1867 on the camp of Chas. Goodnight and Oliver Loving. It happened near the old Indian Agency at Camp Cooper. Goodnight was in that neighborhood several days putting up a herd to trail to Colorado, but some of which were sold at Fort Sumner. One night the Indians let loose on his camp and shot one of his men in the neck with an arrow. Goodnight was sleeping with this man, and the next morning several arrows were found under the bed roll, evidencing the fact that the Indians had crept up, discovered the bed, and were shooting low to get the sleeping men in their bunks. The supposition among the settlers was that these Indians were on the trail and had unexpectedly stumbled upon this camp.

It was this same herd, I think, which was supposed to have blazed what is known as the Goodnight-Loving Trail to Fort Sumner. This trail led out in a southwesterly direction from Camp Cooper, passed through Buffalo Gap in Taylor County, crossed the North and Middle Concho to the South Concho, thence up the South Concho to its head, then across the South Plains on a dry drive to Horse Head Crossing on the Pecos River, thence across and up that river to Fort Sumner, New Mexico. My brother William went with Goodnight and his partner Oliver Loving on this drive. After reaching the Pecos and driving a ways, Loving preceded the herd in company with another cowboy, and in a fight with the Indians was seriously wounded, although beating off the Indians in the fight. While his companion went for help, a freight outfit found Loving and took him to Fort Sumner, where he died from the effects of this wound. Before his death he expressed a wish that his remains be taken home for burial. In the meantime Goodnight had been to Colorado with a herd, so Loving was temporarily buried at Fort Sumner. After the delivery of the herd and their return to Fort Sumner, William Reynolds was in charge of an honor guard of three to take up Loving's remains and deliver them by wagon to Weatherford for burial. His partner, Chas. Goodnight, saw that Loving's request was complied with in every way. I might say that Goodnight and Loving were not the first ones to blaze this trail from this section to New Mexico, for in the fall of 1865, my brother George, Si Hough, and Riley St. John drove the same trail, though not then a trail. They had one hundred and twenty-five cattle, and their camp outfit consisted of one pack mule. They made it through to Santa Fe, New Mexico, undergoing some hardships but without having any Indian troubles. Their herd was sold at a nice profit.

VI. John and Bill Hittson's Tecumseh Creek Fight with Indians

At the outbreak of the Civil War, Camp Cooper, a well-known government fort which was located on the Clear Fork near the mouth of Tecumseh Creek in Throckmorton County, was abandoned by the Federals, occupied for a short time by Texas Rangers under Colonel Buck Barry, and then was permanently abandoned as a fort. John and Bill Hittson moved into the fort and were occupying it at the time of the Elm Creek Raid and continued to live there after most of the settlers had "forted up." A short while after this raid they were cow hunting on Tecumseh Creek and only a few miles from the fort. With them were two cowboys, Press McCarty and a Negro whose name I do not now recall. Suddenly and without warning a band of Comanches were seen charging down upon them. Outnumbered and taken by surprise, the Hittsons started a running fight and made for a well-known bluff on Tecumseh Creek, where there was an overhanging rock which would provide some shelter. Before reaching it both Hittsons were wounded by arrows, Bill being pinned to his saddle by an arrow through his thigh, but both were able to dismount and get under the rock. The Negro was further away but started racing for the same destination with the Indians in hot pursuit. In his haste he lost his hat. Instead of abandoning it to the Indians, he seemed to think more of it that he did the chances for his life; for he stopped, jumped from his horse to get it, and this move, or you might say the loss of that hat, cost his life. He was overtaken and killed before reaching the bluff. Press McCarty in the meantime, instead of joining the others and making for the bluff, left in the direction of Fort Davis and succeeded in reaching there without harm. The Hittsons, in spite of their wounds, backed up under the rock and fought off the Indians. One of them told me that the Indians were afraid to make a frontal attack but made repeated attempts to roll big rocks down from above, trying to make them hit a tree just in front of the shelter and bounce back against them. In this they failed and withdrew from the fight. The Hittsons reached the fort before a rescue party which was being formed had left there. After this they moved their family to the protection of the fort.

VII. The Old Stone Ranch

What has always been known in this section as the Old Stone Ranch was established or rather built of stone by Captain Newton Givens, and officer at old Camp Cooper. The date it was built was in 1856, or at least that date was carved in a keystone in the old ranch house. It is located on Walnut Creek three miles from the Clear Fork and in southwestern Throckmorton County. When Camp Cooper was abandoned at the outbreak of the Civil War, the ranch house was vacated. During the war it was occupied for a short time by Knox & Gardner, a cow outfit, but they too abandoned it. In 1866 the settlers started leaving Fort Davis and returning to their ranches or starting new ones on the range. My father in that year moved his family to this old stone ranch house. As we passed over the then-treeless prairies between the fort and our new home, it looked to me like we passed through herds of so many buffalo that there was upwards of a million head. While we lived at the Stone Ranch only two winters, we boys had to keep the buffalo off our calf range, and I guess we must have killed a thousand. Whenever we killed one, it was our custom to cut out and cure the tongue, and our smoke house always had a plentiful supply on hand. We had a little dog that learned to hamstring a buffalo cow and bring her down without assistance. She would do this by snapping at the cow's hamstring two or three times and down she would come on her haunches. She tried this several times on the buffalo bulls but had no luck with them.

When we moved to this ranch and while we were living there, it was on the extreme edge of the settlements. There was not a ranch house or a white man living west of us all the way to the New Mexico line. It was entirely unoccupied except by the Indians, and it was not then thought that the Plains would ever be settled on account of the lack of wood and water. In our immediate section the only settlers were the families of J. G. Irwin, Matt Franz, and Jim Thorpe, all of whom lived lower down on the Clear Fork. Twenty miles or more to the northeast there were a few families on Elm Creek, but I do not recall their names. The only settlers to the south of us in Shackelford County were J. C. Lynch and George Greer, who lived in eastern Shackelford County on Hubbard Creek, and Bob Sloan in the same vicinity on Deep Creek. Judge Wm. Ledbetter had a salt works at some salt springs some eight miles southwest of the site of Albany. Salt Prong Creek derived its name from these salt springs. Ledbetter's salt works furnished the settlers many miles to the east with salt, and some of it was freighted back to the Confederate forces in the field.

VIII. George Reynolds Shot in Fight with Indians

In the spring of 1867 the Indians raided down about Fort Davis, ran into a bunch of settlers out cow hunting, and they had a little fight, but none of the settlers were hurt. The next day eighteen of the settlers formed a "scout" and followed this band into Haskell County, where the Indians were overtaken. The Indians put up a stiff fight, and the settlers got the worst of it. One of the men got an arrow through his

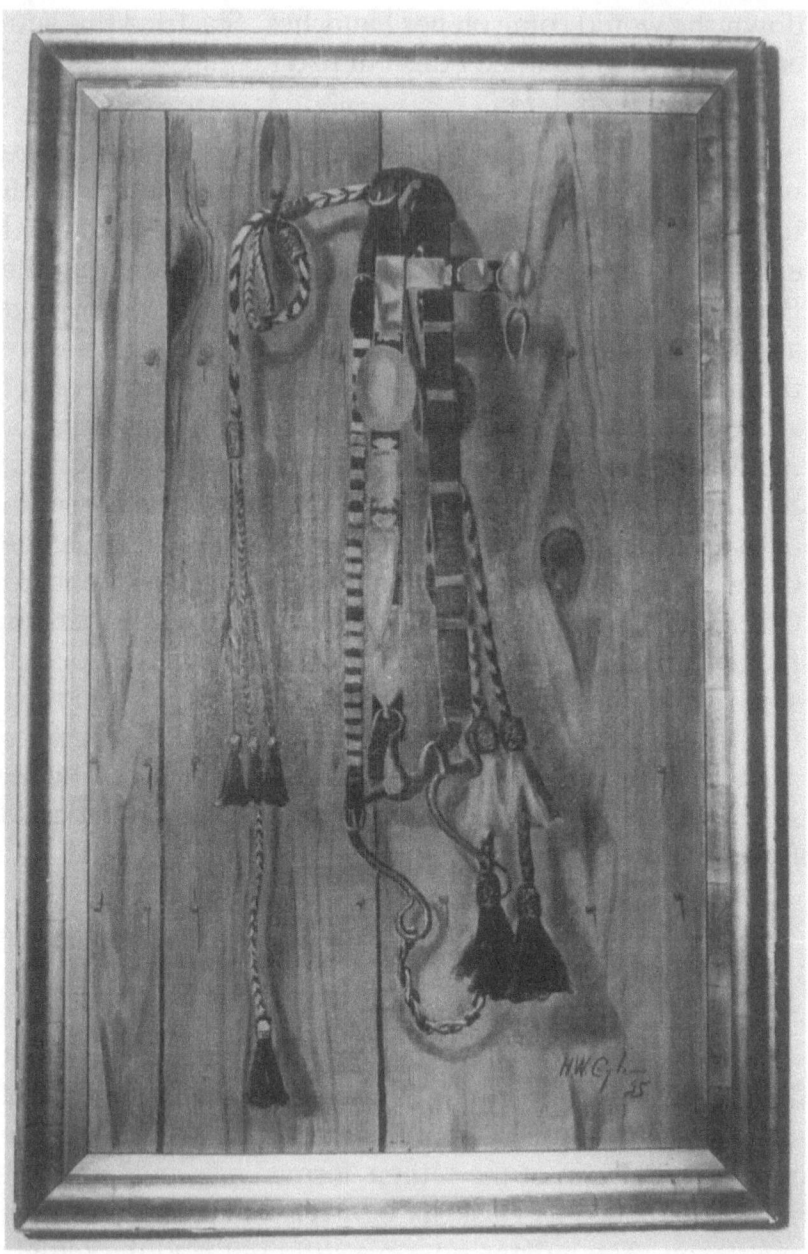

A painting of the bridle taken from the horse ridden by the Indian that wounded George Reynolds in the fight.

back, and the Indians were left in possession of the scene of the fight. The settlers came back by our house, stayed all night, and told us the details of the fight, admitting that they retreated, but only about six hundred yards one of them said, when the Indians quit following them. But anyway they admitted the whipping.

It was three weeks after this that Si Hough, T. E. Jackson, John and Mich Anderson, Steve Franz, Nelse Spears, Archie Baldwin, George and Will Reynolds, and a Dutchman nicknamed Little Joe formed a "scout," elected Jackson captain, and started west hunting Indians. On the Double Mountain Fork of the Brazos, forty miles west of the ranch, they ran on to a band of seven, killed six of them, and had only two casualties of their own. John Anderson got an arrow through his arm, and my brother, George, was seriously injured. An arrow pierced his stomach just above the navel and lodged in the small of his back. Although he pulled the shaft from the wound, the arrow head, which proved to be an iron spike, remained embedded in his back for fourteen years thereafter, until he had it removed by a surgeon in Kansas City. Too seriously wounded to ride his horse, a litter was made and placed between two of the horses, and he was placed thereon. This proved impractical, as the country was too rough, and the horses often had to go single file. So he was laid across his saddle, and in this way he was carried slowly, of course, until almost within sight of the ranch house. A runner had been sent ahead, and we had the information at the ranch a good while before they came within sight. I was on top of the house watching for them and counted them as they came in view and told the folks that all of them were accounted for and riding in. George had insisted that he be helped into his saddle, and he rode in as did the others so that the folks would not be too seriously alarmed about his condition. He suffered no infection from the wound, and it soon healed. However, it continued to hurt him until the arrowhead was removed fourteen years afterward.

I had my own experience with the Indians once, and a good many cattle driven off. My father had gone to Weatherford for supplies, taking Ben and my sister, Sallie, with him. All of the men, including George and William, were away except two, and Glenn and I were there with our mother. Fourteen Indians charged down toward the ranch house, and our two men guards made a good run for the house. I have often remarked that I that day saw two men in a horse race where neither one tried to "pull his horse." They got to the house safely and in a hurry. Although the Indians fired a few shots toward the house, they did not attack it otherwise; but they did drive away about five hundred head of cattle. We had in the pen a good many calves belonging to the cows put there for the purpose of locating the cows, and every cow that had a calf there got away from those Indians and returned home to her calf.

When Fort Griffin was established in 1867, my father moved his family over there for protection against the Indians and settled just above the town on the Clear Fork, at Reynolds Branch, which was named for him. The only store there then was the sutler's store, which was run by Frank E. Conrad. My brother-in-law, Sam Newcomb, built the first store in the civilian part of the town, called the "Flat," so known because of its location in the river bottom under the hill from the fort. Shortly thereafter Dutch Nance and T. E. Jackson built stores. Joe Bowers owned the first saloon. He was a bad man. He was at Griffin only a short time, but while there killed two white men and a Negro. One of the white men he killed was named Cockrell. He had two fights with Cockrell. In the first battle he wounded Cockrell, who got well. After recovering from his wound, Cockrell returned to the saloon with a Winchester to get Bowers, but Bowers fired first, getting him with a load from a shotgun. Bowers told me that he was from Prescott, Arizona, and was going under an assumed name. When we later moved to the state of Colorado, he moved up near us; but for some reason he had again changed his name and was going under the name of Kit Peppard, which he then declared was his true name.

IX. Move to Parker County

After two years spent on the ranch near Fort Griffin, my father decided to move to the settlements and try farming; so in 1869 we started for Parker County. We were only fifteen miles from our destination and had made what we thought was our last camp. The Indians visited our camp that night and relieved us of two of our work horses. They were still raiding deep into what we called the thickly settled country. While we were living near Weatherford, a band of seven Indians was discovered on the prairie gathering horses belonging to the settlers. The alarm was given, and it was not long before a party of about one hundred men were after them. The Indians took refuge in a big drift in the bed of a creek, and the settlers were unable to drive them out. But luck worked against the Indians, for it was raining, a rise came down, the water forced them out, and the settlers dispatched them in short order. I was not at the fight, but the scalps were brought to Weatherford, and I saw them there.

X. On the Move Again

Then we moved to Parker County George and William had gathered a herd and decided to drive them to the territory of Colorado and establish a ranch there. They did this and established a ranch on the north side of the Arkansas

River twelve miles below Rocky Ford. After making three crops in Parker County, my father decided to join William and George in Colorado; so in the fall of '72 we left by wagon for Colbert's ferry, near Denison, where we crossed the Red River and took the Missouri, Kansas, & Texas train. The M. K. & T. railroad had then reached a point in the woods three miles from the ferry and was heading for Denison. We went by rail to Kit Carson, Colorado, and freighted from there out to the ranch of George and William. We settled at the site of La Junta. My father tried farming, and during one of the two years he lived there, his crop of corn, just silking out, was totally destroyed by swarms of grasshoppers they called locusts. This was in 1874. In the fall of '75 the family decided to return to Texas and to the banks of the Clear Fork of the Brazos River in Throckmorton County. This they did in January, 1876, and settled at a new home near the mouth of Ranger Creek on the Clear Fork, not far from the old Stone Ranch. Here father continued to reside until his death in 1882.

XI. To the Neutral Strip in the Panhandle

I did not return to Texas with our family, but spent the winter of '75 in Colorado with William and George, so that I might assist them the next year in gathering and trailing their cattle to Texas, where they too decided to move. The following summer we gathered the cattle and drifted them down and turned them loose on Butte Creek about twenty miles south of Granada, Colorado. We left the herd there in charge of the cowboys. William and I, and Mart Gentry, who was afterward for many years foreman of the Reynolds Cattle Company ranches in Throckmorton and Haskell counties, returned to Fort Griffin. We went by rail from Las Animas to Fort Worth and by wagon to Griffin. The next spring we returned and established a camp in the Neutral Strip of the Panhandle, about three miles north of the site of the town of Guymon, Oklahoma. To this range we drifted our herd from Butte Creek. With us came the Turkey Track outfit, which was owned by R. E. McAnulty, with twenty-five hundred cattle, and the Bar CC outfit, owned by Hank Creswell, with six thousand head. All three of these outfits had wintered on Butte Creek, and we had thrown our camps together for protection against the Indians. We were not in any danger from them, but we feared we might be, as it was a wide open country and no other white people in "the Strip" but us. We rounded, worked, and branded together. I handled the irons and have branded many a "Turkey Track." I remember at one branding, two big mavericks were roped and drug from the herd. Neither McAnulty, Creswell, nor Reynolds Brothers would claim them. Creswell said, "Put Phin's brand on them," so the T- was placed on the mavericks. I owned a little bunch, which amounted to only thirty-seven head, when Reynolds Brothers sold out to Charles Goodnight the following year.

While we were in "the Strip" I went by an old stone house located on Carrizo Creek about two miles above where this creek empties into the Cimarron River. It bore the local name of "Robbers Roost." On several occasions I went by and looked it over and was curious about its name, a large hole in one of its walls, etc. There was a cowboy named Jimmie Folwell who worked for the O X outfit that ranched near Granada in Colorado who gave me his version of this robber hangout. He said that it was originally established by a well-known character, a Captain Coe, who headed a bunch of outlaws that depredated upon the freighters on the Cimarron cutoff of the Santa Fe Trail, and that this house was their hangout. Although I do not recall that he told me when it was established, it must have been in the late '60's, for Coe was hung by the Vigilance Committee at Pueblo, Colorado, in 1869. After Coe's death, the outlaws or a part of the gang continued their depredations and became so bold and such a nuisance that the Government took a hand and sent over a force of soldiers from Fort Lyons to destroy it. Folwell claimed to have piloted them over there. The house was surrounded by the soldiers and its occupants called upon to surrender, which order was refused. Whereupon the commander gave order to his men to open fire with a small cannon they had brought along. A hole was blown in the corner of the house, several of the gang were killed, and the rest surrendered; and that ended, according to Folwell, the "Roost" as a robber's hangout.

In December, 1877, a big fire started north of the Canadian and swept the range clean all the way to the Arkansas River. It burned a strip of country, I guess, that must have been one hundred miles long and fifty miles wide. At that time there was no one on this range to the south of us for three hundred miles. Our range was burned out, so we had to move. We gathered and trailed our herd down into the Panhandle of Texas and established headquarters near the old Adobe Walls, but on the south side of the Canadian River. When we moved to this new range, there was no one near us but Tom Bugbee, who, the year before, had come down from Colorado, passing our camp and staying there with us over night. Chas. Goodnight, who preceded Tom Bugbee from Colorado with his herd and who camped near us while we were on the Butte range, had established a ranch one hundred and fifty miles southwest of us in the Palo Duro Canyon. Hank Smith, formerly a merchant at Fort Griffin, was one hundred and fifty miles south of Goodnight in Canyon Blanco. He had come out in the spring of this same year. I remember that Hank told me that when he was going out to establish this ranch, he was just a day behind us as we returned from Fort Griffin to the Butte Creek range, in the spring of 1877. He said that he could see our fresh wagon tracks. While Hank has been credited by some people for building the old ranch house and establishing the first ranch house in Canyon Blanco, this is not true. A man by the name of Chas. Tasker started the house, although Hank may have finished it, or added to it. Tasker, who had come out to Fort Griffin, was quite a character at Fort Griffin. He was a bit "windy" and talked of going into the cattle business in a big way, always talking in big figures, even talked of buying out the Millett outfit, the largest in the country. They had headquarters on Miller Creek in Baylor County and were supposed to have around twenty-five thousand cattle on their range. It was not long until it was known that he had no means of any consequence, and he was given the local nickname of Lord Tasker, and he was somewhat of a joke. He did acquire a little bunch of cattle, and before he ran his course had succeeded in acquiring some unpaid debts. Anyway, he took his little bunch of cattle and trailed them out to Canyon Blanco and built his home there. Hank went out and took over the ranch and cattle on his debt.

As we returned in the spring of 1877, on the way back to the herd, I remember that we passed a dead Negro soldier lying near the Machenzie Trail. Someone had thrown a little dirt over his face. Later I heard that he had frozen to death after becoming lost while out on a scouting party. We struck a few buffalo hunters on Red Mud Creek on this trip. Bob Couch, who owned the Hashknives and had a big herd on Elm Creek near the site of Abilene, was with us on the trip. We crossed the Double Mountain Fork just above its mouth and then went a little north of west until we struck Big Stinking Creek and went up this a way. We went by McKamy, and we went to Tepe City on Hepe Creek. Tepe City consisted of a saloon, some women, and a store. We did not stop here, nor did we stop at McKamy, but upon the contrary went by McKamy in a trot for there was a small pox quarantine flag hanging out at McKamy's place. As luck would have it though, our road played out just beyond there, and William sent me back to ask the road. I wasn't afraid, though I observed that there were several there just recovering from the small pox with pits on their faces.

XII. Shooting Scrape at Bee Hive Saloon

In January, 1877, before returning to "the Strip," I was making preparations to go to Weatherford for some supplies. The afternoon before we were to leave, Bill Bland, a foreman of the Millett outfit, struck me on the street at Fort Griffin and invited me to go with him that night and do some night life in the town. I told him that I could not as I was on my way to Weatherford. He said, "Stay over, Red," as he called me, "and we will have one hell of a time." But I refused, telling him I had to be on my way. And it was a good thing that I refused and was out of town that night, for Bland and one of his men, Charley Reed, got in a bad shooting scrape at the Bee Hive saloon that night. It all started because they started shooting out the lights. Bill Cruger, the sheriff, and Jim Jeffries, county attorney, came in to arrest them and ordered them to throw up their hands. Bland was at the time taking sight on another light. Instead of obeying Cruger, he wheeled, faced Cruger, and started shooting. When the smoke had cleared away, men were lying on the floor dead. They were Lieutenant Meyers, who was not a participant, Dan Barron, and ———. Jeffries was lying on the floor shot through the lungs and critically injured. Reed left the country that night. The Bee Hive saloon will be remembered by old timers as having a sign painted on its front reading as follows:

> Within this hive we are all alive
> Good whiskey makes us funny.
> If you are dry step in try
> The essence of our honey.

After this killing, William Reynolds remarked that it should not have read that "We are All alive." [He] said the "all" part of it should have been omitted.

It was a couple of years after this killing that this same Bland, and Tom Peeler, another foreman of the Milletts, were "up the trail" with one of their herds, and it was reported that they with another one of their cowboys rode into Ogallala, Nebraska, and started plugging the lights. The citizens would not stand for this. Peeler was seriously wounded, and the cowboy who was with him and Bland were reported killed. Cap Millett, one of the owners of the Millett outfit, once attended a dance in Kansas City, and during the dance remarked that he wanted to show them how they danced in Texas: so he pulled his gun and plugged one of the lights. Peeler, by the way, was killed in South Texas, and was an officer, possibly sheriff, at the time, and I believe was acting in line of duty.

The Millett outfit sold to the Hashknife outfit, which was owned by Simpson and Hughes. The Hashknife was then one of the largest in Texas. They received around twenty thousand cattle from the Milletts and took over their range. This was in the early eighties.

Charles Goodnight and W. D. Reynolds visiting in their older years.

XIII. Chas. Goodnight Buys Adobe Walls Herd

In the summer of 1878 Reynolds Brothers sold their cattle at the Adobe Walls Ranch. They numbered four thousand head, which included six hundred head which Mart Gentry and I had gathered from those we missed on the Butte and in the Neutral Strip. In this herd, which was sold to Chas. Goodnight, were a half dozen mother-less buffalo calves which we had gathered in the roundup. Goodnight remarked to me a number of years after this that from these calves he started his herd of buffalo. I shall always remember the fine wild turkeys fattened on the sunflower seed along the Canadian River that we had at our Adobe Walls camp. They were the best turkeys I have ever eaten.

XIV. Up the Trail in 1882

The first herd I ever took up the trail was in 1882. Going "up the trail" in the early days meant driving a herd to the Kansas market, originally in my time to Hunnywell, Caldwell, or Abilene, or later to Dodge City, Kansas, or it meant taking them by trail to any of the northern or western markets which were then being stocked with Texas cattle. I was the trail boss over this herd of one thousand steers belonging to the Reynolds & Matthews M O outfit. The herd was put up in Throckmorton County. On this drive we were headed for Hunnywell, but we went up over the Dodge Trail. It was the popular trail in the eighties. Until the late seventies most of the cattle went up over the Chisholm Trail, which went by Fort Worth and crossed the Red at Red River Crossing. The Dodge Trail crossed the Brazos at Seymour and the Red River at Doan's Store. One hundred miles north from there we crossed the Washita. There we quit this trail, headed northeast until we hit the Chisholm Trail and followed it until we crossed the Cimarron at Red Fork about where the Rock Island railroad now crosses the river. Here we quit the Chisholm Trail, or at least we quit it when we struck the Kansas line, and turned east to Hunnywell.

About fifteen miles north of Doan's Store, we passed around a herd of 3,500 cattle belonging to Shanghai Pierce of South Texas. He was taking 7,000 head up in two different herds. After we had made camp that night we were visited by Quanah Parker, a chief of the Comanches, who came driving up in a carriage with one of his squaws. He was accompanied by four bucks on horse back. He asked to stay all night, explaining that he had passed Shanghai's camp and could have stayed with them, but they had Negro cowboys and he did not like that. I told him he could stay, which meant supper and breakfast for all of the Indians. We talked until bed time. He told me that he had been down to Doan's store for supplies and was on his way back to his camp further up the Trail on the North Fork of the Red River. He said, "I am staying on the Trail this year," which meant that he would demand one or more beeves from each passing trail herd. He said he would not ask anything from me, but as he departed the next morning, I gave him ten dollars anyway. During our talk I remember distinctly that he told me that he was thirty-five years old, I having first told him that I was twenty-five. When we reached Hunnywell, the cattle were sold to Dick Forsythe.

We returned home by the Chisholm Trail as far south as near Fort Sill, then took the government road from Fort Sill to Fort Griffin. When a short distance south of the Cheyenne Agency, we met a band of the Cheyennes and one of them wanted to match a horse race against a good-looking horse one of my men was riding. He proposed to put up one of his squaws against the horse on the outcome of the race. Just for curiosity I asked to see the squaws. He pointed to several and said I could have my pick. I took a look, shook my head, and told him I had a squaw back home. All of the squaws were dirty as well as hard looking. I had no intention in the first place to allow the race; in fact I would never run a race or allow one of my men to run a race with an Indian. But this incident accounts for the tale that the cowboys told on me that I refused to match the race after I had taken a look at his dirty squaws.

XV. The 1883 Drive

The year following our drive to Hunnywell I took 1,200 big steers belonging to Reynolds & Matthews up the Dodge Trail from Throckmorton County for delivery at Caldwell,

Kansas. On this trip we came very near having serious trouble with Old Roman Nose, who is to be remembered by trail drivers as a chief of the Cheyennes. His country lay between the two Canadians in the Indian Territory, and as we passed through it the previous year I had to avoid trouble by giving him two beeves. But during the winter at Fort Griffin I had heard a good deal of talk from the cowboys out of the Panhandle country whom we called Pearlhandlers, so nicknamed because they wore pearl-handle six shooters. These Pearlhandlers boasted that they would not give the Cheyennes anything, but upon the contrary they would pistol-whip any of them that held up their herd.

When we reached the Cheyenne country, Roman Nose and five of his bucks rode into our camp one day for dinner, and I made no offer of beeves. He sat on his haunches, scowled, and looked surly enough after eating dinner and demanding a beef, which I refused. Then he threatened me, put an arrow in his bow, and pointed it my way. At that I whipped out my pistol and leveled down on him. Seeing I had the drop, he threw down the bow and arrow and made for his rifle. It was an old army gun of .50 caliber known as a Needle Gun. With an oath he threw a cartridge in the chamber and made out as if he intended to use it. He had judgment enough not to attempt or make a move to level down on me, seeing I had the drop. It was a touchy moment, for I was going to let him have it if he made another move; but he never did. I gave orders to the boys to drift the cattle to the river, the South Canadian, for water. The Indians followed along. As the cattle started drifting out on the other side, the old chief sent a buck to the point of the herd who attempted to turn them back. I paid no attention to this for a time as I wanted the cattle held up until all had watered and we had started forward on the drive. However, when we did attempt to get them going, the buck started yelling, kept trying to turn the point, and did everything he knew to excite and confuse the cattle. I rode forward, caught hold of his bridle reins, and started leading his horse away from the herd, to which the buck meekly submitted. Old Roman Nose, whom I had passed between the river and the point, then sent two more of his bucks to that one's assistance. They in turn caught my horse by the reins, one on each side of me, but I wrenched their hands loose—an Indian doesn't have much physical strength. At that they left me but started charging into the herd, whooping and yelling, with Roman Nose yelling at me that he would drive them back to Texas. We had the best horses, and I motioned to our men to drive them forward; but the herd was becoming excited and confused. I soon saw that the Indians were getting the best of it. They might cause a stampede, which would mean the loss of a lot of flesh on those big steers. I decided the best thing that I could do under the circumstances for the best interest of the owners of the cattle was to give in, and that is just what I did.

I called to old Roman Nose, addressing him as "John," for all Indians were called by that name in those days, and they addressed the whites by the same name. I said, "All right, John, I'll give you a beef." Seeing he was getting the best of it, he replied with an oath, and asked for two. After a parley I succeeded in talking him down to one, which I cut from the herd and had his bucks drive away for the kill. Although the Indians shot him in the stomach and other parts of the body with arrows, they could not bring him down. By signs, the chief motioned me to come out and kill him and indicated that he wanted him shot between the eyes. Luckily I got the steer between the eyes with my first shot, and this seemed to impress the old Indian.

Before leaving the Cheyenne country, we had to furnish

two more steers to another band. I found this to be the best and cheapest way through, and I have always held it against those Panhandlers for their bad advice and what might have resulted in some pretty serious trouble for me and our outfit on that drive. Shortly after we went through, there were eight herds from the Panhandle going through, driving close together. This same band of Indians demanded beef and were refused. Some of the herds were stampeded and lost around one hundred beeves. In revenge some of the cowboys shot into an Indian tent and wounded a buck and a squaw. The following year Roman Nose was killed by men from a horse outfit that was passing through his country.

We passed out of the Cheyenne country a little beyond the North Canadian and struck the Cherokee Strip. The Cherokees did not molest us, and we delivered the herd to Caldwell, Kansas, where they were sold to George Miller of the 101 outfit.

XVI. The Drive to Dakota

Our next drive was to be a long one and started in the spring of 1886. We had 2,850 stock cattle belonging to Reynolds & Matthews and were headed for a free range in the northwest corner of North Dakota, located on the Little Missouri and eighty miles north of Dickenson. We started from the Throckmorton County ranch, going up the Dodge Trail to the North Canadian for 100 miles to pass around Kansas, which had a quarantine against Texas cattle on account of the tick fever. From the Cimarron we drove pretty much up the Kansas line. I admit that I took some short cuts across into Kansas in the southwest corner, as I knew the country pretty well and could save miles of driving. Excepting these short cuts, the Kansas line was followed from

A marker in North Dakota indicating the path of the cattle trail blazed by the Reynolds Brothers.

the Cimarron to the Arkansas River. From the Arkansas we trailed to Hugo, Colorado, where we struck what was known as the New Mexico-Colorado Trail, which we followed to its crossing on the South Platte at a place called Brush. Thence we followed the trail to the North Platte, and up this river for fifty miles to cross the river on a bridge at Fort Laramie. From here the trail led north to the Cheyenne River, which was up. Here we had to stop and build rafts and float our wagons across the river. We swam the herd across, of course. This crossing was on the Shipwell Ranch. North of Laramie there were no towns along the trail, which went west of the Black Hills and to the head of the Little Missouri. From the crossing on the Cheyenne we followed what was known as the Hashknife Trail almost to our destination.

A little incident which took place while we were on this

The bridge named for the Long X Ranch in North Dakota.

drive shows how well known this trail was to Texas people living in Dakota. It will be remembered that the year 1886 was one of our worst drouth years, and a good many families left our country in Texas for other sections. One of our cowboys, Brights Carter, had just married a girl in Stephens County, whose family was pulling up stakes and leaving for Wyoming. It was understood that Brights was to come on up with the herd and later join her in Wyoming, so she went by wagon with her people and reached their destination long before the slow-moving trail herd. They had homesteaded ten miles east of the trail and west of the Black Hills. As we were trailing along up there, I noticed a stick with a note

Reynolds Brothers Cattle Company cowboys: (l-r) Jim House, Charlie Sebastian, Watt Reynolds, Elmer Reynolds, Mart Gentry, Tom Witby, Charlie Blount, Glenn Coffee, John Bennett, John Taylor, Beverly Mitchell, Fos Crowson, Bob Stevens, Glenn Penniston, Unknown, Will Larn.

tied to it standing beside the wagon trail. That meant that it was for someone coming up the trail. I examined the address and saw it was for Brights Carter. We were trailing in two herds, and Brights was with the back herd, which was in charge of Tobe Butler. I left the note in place, and Brights got it as their herd came by. His bride knew that in all probability he would get that note. Carter went on with the herd to its destination and then returned to her from there.

We had a sad and fatal accident to one of our cowboys while on this drive. Tom McFaddin was critically injured when his horse fell on him. It occurred on Elk Creek in Indian Territory. He was carried along in the wagon for two days, but he died this side of the Washita River, where we buried him along the trail. Will Moore lost his foreman near the same place and at about the same time. Steve Best took charge of his herd. Tim Murphy, who was taking up a herd for the W O O of Shackelford County, also lost a cowboy this same year and near the same place.

XVII. The Pleasant Valley War in Arizona

On the year 1887 Reynolds Cattle Company, owners of the "Long X" brand, put 1,500 head of cattle on a range near Holbrook, Arizona, and the following year I went out there to gather and dispose of these cattle. That was the year that the cattlemen and sheepmen were having a local war over their rights to the range. It has been sometimes called the Pleasant Valley War, and is also known as the Sheep and Cattlemen's War. It is the same one which is written up by Zane Gray in his book *To the Last Man.*

I had a wagon and a few men, and we worked with the Hashknife outfit. This outfit had a big lot of cattle on the range. The Hashknives were mixed up in the war and had several men killed. I kept my mouth shut and took no part in it. I remember that Tom Tucker came into our camp one night with a bullet wound in his breast, which we doctored. He had gotten it several days before in the fight at the Tewsbury house. Tom Payne, one of the Hashknife boys, was killed in the fight and two more of their men wounded. In this war, Andy Cooper, a brother-in-law of Henry Jacobs, a former sheriff of Shackelford County, was killed. I think he was killed by the local sheriff or comadore. I was there when he was killed. He was also known as one of the Blevins boys.

My brother, Glenn Reynolds, was a recent arrival there, and he took part in the war on the side of the sheepmen. A year after the trouble had terminated, Glenn was elected sheriff of Gila County, the only Democrat in the county to be elected that year. It was only a short time after taking office that he was killed in line of duty. He was taking the well-known outlaw, the Apache Kid, and seven other Indians and a Mexican to the Yuma penitentiary. When near Riverside and while Glenn and six of the prisoners were out of the stage coach walking up a long hill in order to lighten the load on the horses, the Indians in some way overpowered them, and Glenn and Holmes were killed. The stage driver was seriously shot, but he recovered. The Indians escaped. Mexican custom guards afterwards recovered Glenn's watch in an encounter with some Indians, either from a prisoner or a casualty, and through diplomatic channels it reached Glenn's wife, who had moved to Albany. The Apache Kid was the one who is supposed to have done the killing, but, no doubt, all of them had a part in it except the Mexican.

XVIII. The Snow Storm

The winter of 1891, the Reynolds Cattle Company, Webb & Hill of Albany, and I, had each wintered a herd on the range of Colonel Charles Goodnight, near Goodnight Texas. It was a severe winter and our respective losses amounted to about 40 percent of the cattle we had put up there. In the spring our outfit bought the remnant of the Webb & Hill herd amounting to a 1,000 head, and that of mine, amounting to

200, which together with 3,200 head of their own, made up a herd of 4,400 head for the spring drive to Dakota ranch of Reynolds Cattle Company.

Cutting the cattle in two herds, I put Tot Richards of Throckmorton in charge of one herd and Tom Matthews, now living at Albany, as foreman of the other herd. Will Poer, now (1938) of Marfa, Will Matthews living (1938) at Olney, and a Negro named Bill Avery, who later called himself Tige, and Louis Shoffitt of Albany, were some of the cowboys I remember as being along. The drive started at Goodnight, and the trail we followed took us to a crossing on the Canadian River fifteen miles above the Adobe Walls. From here we headed for the Arkansas River and a crossing at Lamar, Colorado. Here we struck a new trail then known as the Northern Trail, which passed by a town on the Missouri Pacific called Chevington. Beyond Chevington fifteen miles, we struck the same trail driven by us on the '86 drive. We were following this trail and were on the Divide twenty-five miles north of Hugo, Colorado, at the head of the Republican River. It was the night of the 31st of May, 1892, a date I have never forgotten, that a blizzard and driving snow storm struck us, which continued until noon the next day, and left eighteen inches of snow on the level to cover the country. I was with the lead herd, having passed 10,000 cattle in four herds belonging to the X I T outfit. Our back herd was ten miles to the rear of the X I T herd. It started snowing early in the night, driving from the north. I was not on night guard nor did I go out, for I well knew what it would mean. The cattle would start drifting south with the wind and there would be no stopping them by all the men we had so long as this blizzard lasted. All of the men in the outfit, however, except me was out with the herd and did their best to turn them, but it was no use. The same thing happened with our other herd and with the four X I T herds. All the hard work and hard riding in the bitter weather failed to turn the cattle and these fourteen thousand four hundred cattle, belonging to the two outfits, and which prior to the storm were being held in six herds, drifted in a big mix-up thirty miles to the south until they struck the right-of-way fence of the Union Pacific. They drifted up and down this fence, trying to find an opening. The ground was tramped into a loblolly after the thaw started. A small bunch of two hundred fifty head did find an opening under a railway bridge, and, strange to say, every hoof of them were cattle belonging to our herds. We were sure in a mess. On the 2nd of June I telegraphed George Reynolds at Albany a summary of what happened, which I quote: "A snow storm struck us on the high divide 50 miles east of Denver, Colorado. Six herds in one and drifted 30 miles south. Twenty-eight horses frozen to death. Fresh horses here. Men all accounted for." There were in fact twenty-seven horses and one mule, and they were chilled to death instead of frozen. They were old horses and rather in a bad condition anyway and had been ridden hard.

The old Negro, Bill Avery, has told about this snow storm many times, and has always insisted that when he saw a mule leaning up against our wagon frozen stiff, he got so cold that he went and got in bed with the boss, meaning me, and would for emphasis add that "he would have gotten in bed with Jay Gould himself." Old Bill, dead now, told this story so many times that he got to believing it. Of course the mule was not leaning against the wagon, and this was not the night that Bill got so cold, nor did he get in the bed with me. It was on the 4th of June while he was on night duty with me, that he got so cold that he said he was just about to freeze to death and begged to go to camp, and I sent him in.

The fresh horses spoken of in the telegram were some

that had been sent down from the Dakota ranch to meet us, and luckily had arrived before the storm. The old horses were to be sent back when these arrived, but the storm got most of them. We were exactly eight days in gathering, separating, and getting the herds divided and back to the wagons. Dan Cole, trail boss of one of the XIT herds, was given a box of cigars by a cowboy whom he had discharged the night before this storm. They were presented in gratitude by the cowboy for the discharge given in time to keep him out of all that hard riding, hard weather, and hardships. Cole handed me the box and when I took one, he said for me to get a handful, for after they were gone he could get more by just discharging another cowboy! It is the first time I have ever known a man to receive a present for discharging a man. Two of our men and several of the X I T cowboys quit before we got the cattle separated and on their way. After getting the cattle in shape, I turned the cattle over to the two trail bosses, Tot Richards and Tom Matthews, for the balance of the 1,500 mile drive, and I returned home by train to Albany.

XIX. The Last Drive

In 1902 there was a bad drouth in the Davis Mountains and in the Pecos country, where Reynolds Cattle Company and George Reynolds owned ranches and upon which two ranches there were around 20,000 head of cattle. They decided to ship part of these cattle to a free range in Montana. It was near the town of Malta and along the Canadian border. In order to save expense and a long haul, it was thought best to ship to Billings, Montana, and drive from there the 300 miles to the Malta ranch.

I was put in charge of the cattle, 2,000 from the Davis Mountains ranch, loaded at Kent, and 1,650 from the George

Reynolds ranch, loaded at Pecos City. Nearly all of both shipments were yearlings and poor and weak. Two weeks ahead of the cattle went two loads of horses, twenty-five to the load, one from the Davis Mountains ranch and the other from the Pecos City ranch.

Colonel Rush, foreman of the Pecos ranch, sent a load of good horses, as he had an axe to grind. He expected to be put in charge of the Montana ranch, so he would have at least one load of good mounts. But Sam Selman, foreman of the Reynolds Cattle Company ranch at Kent, cut out and shipped a load of the sorriest horses on the ranch. This was always the way, absolutely, with a ranch foreman. Since he wanted to keep his best horses, the trail boss would get the worst of it. And this was the reason why I had the heavy loss in horses during the snow storm on the 1892 drive.

I left with the shipments from Kent, but left them at Dalhart and took a passenger train to Billings, in order to get fixed up to receive the cattle upon arrival. When I did arrive and saw the sorry horses that Selman had sent me, I immediately bought an additional twenty-eight head for the drive.

The cattle were eight days in getting through to Billings, and, of course, the cowboys came through with the stock trains. In the crew were eight boys, all Reynolds relatives or friends of the family. In the crew were Eaton and Will Reynolds of Albany—Will is now foreman of the Long X Ranch at Kent; Joe and George Reynolds, sons of Ben Reynolds of Throckmorton; John Conrad and my son, Ben G.; Tom Tucker, whose daddy went up the trail with me on the '86 drive; John Honeycutt, now of Sierra Blanco, was another one of the boys. In addition to the boys who were out for trail driving experience (which they sure got), I had two men who understood the business—good hands—a man named Blackjack and Walter Christenson.

Having lost eighty head in shipment, we left on the drive out of Billings with around 3,600 head, the largest herd I ever put over the trail and much too large for a good drive, especially for one over a hard-watered country we had to pass through. In fact, it was about as large a herd as I have known to be put over a trail, except the two herds of Shanghi Pierce of about the same number which we passed around on our drive up the Dodge Trail on the '82 drive. But it was one thing to put a herd over an open country like the Dodge Trail and something different to put one over a trail scarce of water and mountainous like that from Billings to Malta.

We drove north from Billings to the Musselshell River and then down the Musselshell for a couple of days when we swung off east to the head of the Big Dry Creek. I would send one of the boys ahead to scout for water always, knowing in this way a couple of days in advance where I could water the herd and make camp. I sent Eaton Reynolds on a two day's scout, but on his return he missed the herd in the hilly country we were passing through. We saw him to the right of the herd a mile to the rear, leading his horse, which had given out. I sent another of the boys, John Conrad, back for him; but he in some way missed him and he was away from the herd for a week. The boys were getting some experience and little sleep, as the days were long and the nights very short—it was toward the last of June in Montana. All the boys had to go on night herd. The herd would not bed down until 9 o'clock, and the cattle were stirring by daylight, before 3 A.M. John was short of sleep and bedded down at a horse or sheep camp until he caught up on his sleep.

As we headed down the Big Dry, I scouted the range which was our destination, which lay to the other side of the Big Missouri, this side of Malta, and decided that the range on the Big Dry was just as good if not better than across the river. So I decided to turn loose on that free range. We took a day and a half scattering the cattle on this range. Then word reached me that George Reynolds wanted the cattle across the Missouri. He had shipped another 1,000 cattle from Texas, intending to trail our herd, but upon reaching Billings, decided to send them by rail to Malta. So we gathered the herd and struck the Big Missouri at the mouth of Musselshell, at a town called Kismet, consisting of a post office, a store, and a saloon, all housed in one building.

Here we spent three days trying to swim the cattle across the river, which was 400 yards wide and swimming depth all the way across. We would cut the herd in bunches of three to four hundred and try to swim them across. There were skiffs there, and I hired three men with skiffs at $10.00 per day each, and would keep them on the lower side of the swimming herd in an effort to keep them headed across. But the water was so swift that it would drift many back or around until they headed back to shore on this side, and the ones coming back were of course hard to put across again. At last we made it across with all but 600 head. We had to give it up on these and leave them on this side, and were two years in getting that bunch together, so badly did they scatter. The big bunch was turned loose on the other side between there and Malta. We swam the horses—I led one in behind a skiff and the others followed. The wagon was crossed on a small ferry boat.

On this short 300 mile drive we had all kinds of experiences, and it was by all odds the most troublesome and the hardest drive I ever made, due mostly to poor cattle, rough country, scarce water, and the unwieldy size of the herd. This was my last experience with a trail herd and, I repeat, the hardest.

Letter To Harry E. Crain From W.D. Reynolds

Foreword to
*Letters From Old Friends
And Members of The Wyoming
Stock Growers Association.*

At the annual meeting of the Wyoming Stock Growers Association, held in Cheyenne, on Tuesday, April 7, 1914, the following resolution was adopted:

Resolved, That it is the sense of the Association that the President appoint an Historical Committee to gather data for a history of the Association and development of the cattle business in the state of Wyoming, said committee to consist of three members, with power to appoint a sub-committee consisting of one member from each county in the State; and that every old member of the Association is earnestly requested to furnish said committee all memories and available data, that they may be able to properly commemorate the pioneer history of Wyoming.

Honorable John B. Kendrick, who was then President of the Association, appointed the following committee: Mr. N.K. Boswell, Mr. B.J. Erwin and Mr. Harry E. Crain.

Mr. Boswell notified the Secretary that it would be impossible for him to serve on the committee, and requested that Mr. Crain be delegated to assume the duties of the chairman.

Mr. Crain communicated with a number of the old-time stockmen, requesting them to record their experiences of early days on the range. But few are left to tell the story, and we are publishing in this little pamphlet the letters written in response to Mr. Crain's request, printing them in the order in which they were received. They contain much of historic interest—memories of the picturesque days of the cattle business—typifying the character of the men who rode the range and laid the foundation of Wyoming's greatest industry.

THE COWMAN—GOD BLESS HIM!

Cheyenne, Wyoming,

June 5, 1923.

Fort Worth, Texas, February 8, 1917

Mr. Harry E. Crain,

Cheyenne, Wyoming.

Dear Mr. Crain:

While I was in Cheyenne I promised to write you some of my recollections of the early trail.

In 1867 Mr. Goodnight and Loving drove two herds of cattle from this country to Colorado by way of New Mexico. That was about the beginning of the trail drives from Texas. I went up as a cow hand with the second herd some two or three weeks behind the first herd. We went up the Pecos

River to New Mexico and Colorado. Mr. Goodnight and Mr. Loving both went with the first herd until they got some distance up the Pecos River. Then Mr. Loving, with one of his men, one-armed Billy Wilson, left the herd, expecting to go to Fort Sumner, New Mexico, and have the cattle sold when the herd got there. A day or two after they had left the herd, they got up on what is known as the Black River, coming into the Pecos River from the Guadalupe Mountains. Here a band of Indians attacked Wilson and Loving and ran them down to the Pecos River, just a short distance to the east, and wounded Mr. Loving in the arm very seriously. Wilson and Loving took refuge in the tall cane breaks, and the Indians did not venture in after them, but the Indians got away with their horses and saddles. Along in the night Loving persuaded Wilson to go down to the Pecos River, swim down a distance, and make his way back to the herd, saying that he was wounded himself and could not get away. Wilson did this and walked back on the trail about two days, without food, before he met the herd.

He was lying out under a bluff near the trail when the herd came along. A man by the name of Mose Cooch saw him lying here and went over and woke him up. Wilson reported what had happened, that Mr. Loving had told him to go back to the herd as he didn't expect that he could get away, and they drove the herd on to Fort Sumner, which was about 200 miles up the river. At first they doubted Mr. Wilson's statement, but after seeing Mr. Loving, he, of course, corroborated what Wilson had said. The Indians, it seems, left the place after running the two men into the cane breaks, and Mr. Loving came out in the morning, got to the trail, and tried to make it to Fort Sumner. About fourteen miles west of there he came upon some Mexicans with ox carts, and they hauled him into Fort Sumner. When he arrived at Fort Sumner, the wound in his arm was so serious that although the arm was amputated, blood poisoning set in. He died and was buried at Fort Sumner.

The herd I was with came along later. We had no trouble with our herd on the trail. We drove them up to southern Colorado, arriving there the middle of December. About the first of February, Mr. Goodnight sold the cattle to John Wesley Iliff, who drove these cattle to Cheyenne right in mid winter. Our outfit then started on its return trip to Texas. We got an extra wagon and a pair of mules, exhumed Mr. Loving's body, and hauled it to Weatherford, Texas, where he was buried. Mr. Loving was the great-grandfather of the Secretary of our Texas Association, Mr. E.B. Spiller. Mr. Charles Goodnight is still living at Goodnight, Texas, forty miles east of Amarillo, on the Ft. Worth & Denver Railroad line, and has a famous herd of buffalo. In 1879, I went over the same trail all the way to Colorado and started a ranch on the Arkansas River just north of where La Junta is.

The next spring I drove 1000 head of cattle to Salt Lake, going out east of Denver and by way of Greeley, just at the time when Greeley was being first settled, then southwest of Cheyenne up Dale Creek and out by Laramie City, where Bill Nye used to run a newspaper. He had his office up over a livery stable and had a sign up to show his friends where to find him, which read something like this: "Go through to the back, and take the ladder, but if you are in a hurry, wring the mule's tail and take the elevator." We drove all the way to Salt Lake that year. As there were no other cattle on the trail to bother, it was like a summer outing to me. From Laramie we went west. There was all sorts of game along the trail, including elk and lots of fish; also fine grass for the stock. When we got to Bitter Creek, the water was bad and grass was scarce, and we had a pretty hard time until we got west of Green River, when we struck good country again.

We crossed Ham's Fork, Black Ford, and Bear River and then reached the Mormon settlements. They were very nice to us, and we could buy everything at reasonable prices, and if our stock got into their crops, the damage bills were very reasonable. We made our way around to Corinne, where Bear River runs into Salt Lake. There we bought a small bunch of California horses and returned to Colorado over the same trail, reaching there in November. Iliff, Hutton, and Cratton at that time handled most of the cattle that came into that country.

In 1871, I made another drive and went over what was known as the Chisholm Trail, which went through by Fort Worth, where I now live, to Wichita, Kansas. Then, instead of going by Abilene, Kansas, to Ogalalla, Nebraska, I turned up the Arkansas and went to Colorado, where I ranched for eight years. It is my memory that year there were 450,000 cattle driven over the Chisholm Trail to Abilene and Ogalalla. Since then I have driven a number of herds through the Panhandle and up through Colorado and crossed the Union Pacific tracks east of Cheyenne and into North Dakota.

I was very pleased to meet, while in Cheyenne recently, an old Texas cowboy by the name of J.B. Kendrick, who is now Governor of Wyoming, and was recently elected to the U. S. Senate.

Very truly yours,

W. D. Reynolds

An Account of The Death of Glenn Reynolds

by Jess G. Hayes

An Account of the Death of Sheriff Glenn Reynolds at the Hands of the Apache Kid and Others Near Globe, Arizona

EDITOR'S NOTE

The following account is taken from that presented by Jess G. Hays in his Apache Vengeance (University of New Mexico Press, 1954). Hays wrote an excellent and very readable account of the entire incident involving the Apache Kid, one of the most notorious outlaws in the history of the West. The following focuses on the unfortunate death of Glenn Reynolds, brother of George, W. D., and Phin. Glenn was at the time the sheriff of Globe, Arizona. It was Reynolds's duty to transport the Apache Kid and several other Apache outlaws and one Mexican to prison in Yuma, Arizona, where the outlaws were to serve sentences for a variety of crimes of which they had been duly convicted. The narrative below begins at the start of the fateful journey of Reynolds and the other members of the group headed for Yuma, one of the most detestable prisons in the early West.

All arrangements for the trip having been made,

Reynolds spent most of the next day with his wife and children and made his personal preparations for departure the following morning.

It was Friday, November 1, 1889. An hour before sunup Sheriff Reynolds arose, calm and refreshed after a restful night. While his wife prepared breakfast, he went to the stable and saddled his best horse, Tex, which he would ride as far as Riverside Station. He saddled another horse for the Mexican convict, Avott, in order to lighten the load of the stagecoach on the steep, rough mountainous grades.

Mrs. Reynolds's fear for the safety of her husband was very real. When he got out in the desert wilds, he wouldn't have the army and Al Sieber to help him. Could only he and Holmes handle all those convicts? When her husband came back into the kitchen for breakfast, she appealed to him once more to change his plans.

"Gussie, honey, let's not go over all that again." The sheriff spoke gently and with no impatience at her insistence. "I'll make it all right. You just keep the pot boiling and the children happy, and don't you worry about me."

Reynolds kissed his wife good-bye and led the saddled horses the short distance to the courthouse. In the pre-dawn darkness he could see Middleton's stagecoach and horses outlined by a yellow shaft of light that shone from the jail office window. He tied Tex and the extra horse to the hitching rail and entered his office to pick up the commitment papers and the $400 expense money.

The prisoners already had been served breakfast, and the deputies and Stage Driver Middleton all were on hand when Reynolds entered the jail. The sheriff was pleased and his voice was brisk but genial. "Good work, fellows. We'll get the prisoners and load them in the stage now."

"Hold on there, Sheriff! I'm not going after any Apache prisoners!" declared Middleton. "I'll just climb up in my seat on the stagecoach and wait there while you load 'em. If you need any help with them out on the road, I'll be ready, but until that time comes, I'm takin' care of the teams and stage and you herd the prisoners."

Reynolds grinned as Middleton strode out and, picking up the jail keys, ordered Deputies Blevins, Ryan, and Holmes to follow him to the cell block. One by one, handcuffs snapped around wrists and the Apache convicts were marched into the hall. Watching this procedure in the dim lantern light was Nah-diez-az, left behind to await his execution. In the Apache language, and paying no heed to the Mexican prisoner who still occupied a cell, he bade farewell to his Apache brothers. The cool November air was piercing when the Apache convicts went out of doors, and they drew their worn and dirty coats closer around their scrawny bodies. They remained stolid and unresisting while they were being loaded into the stagecoach. When all were seated, shackles were locked around their legs.

"How about this hombre, Reynolds, will he ride inside with the Indians?" Holmes asked, as he brought the Mexican embezzler from the jail.

"That boy isn't dangerous, he's just a spendthrift," said the sheriff, but in a more serious tone he added, "The Mexican will ride on this extra horse alongside of me. Holmes, you ride inside the coach behind the Indians." As Ryan helped the hapless Mexican to mount, Reynolds quietly surveyed the whole scene, mentally checking his arrangements. Middleton carried a pistol. Holmes possessed a lever action Winchester rifle and a six-shooter, and he himself was armed with a .45 Colt and a double-barreled shotgun, loaded with buckshot. Each man being an expert marksman and fast on

Glenn Reynolds

the trigger, there appeared no chance for the convicts to commit foul play or even try to escape. Satisfied, he mounted Tex, motioned the Mexican to precede him, and called to Middleton. "All set, Gene. Let's move."

Middleton tightened the reins and the prison-bound stage, drawn by four bays, rumbled out of Globe as the sun broke through the November mists over the mountains.

The four-mile run south from Globe to the 66 Ranch was made in record time. Here the stage was stopped at the tollgate that gave access to the Globe-Pinal Summit Toll Road. The gatekeeper reckoned the charge at $7.00—twelve people at 25¢ each, six horses at 50¢ each, and $1.00 for the stage. Eight pairs of greedy Apache eyes watched Reynolds take out his leather pouch and thumb through a roll of bills to pay the toll.

The management of the Globe-Pinal Summit Toll Road kept a colony of monkeys at the gate to entertain the wayfarers. The presence of these hungry-looking and curious little animals stimulated the sale of peanuts, popcorn, and candy, which were offered by the management. While the gatekeeper was reckoning the toll charge, Reynolds bought a bag of peanuts to feed the chattering monkeys. He felt a tug at his gold watch chain. "No, you can't have that, you little thief," exclaimed the sheriff. "That is my most valuable possession, next to Gussie and my children." Once again the monkey reached for the chain as it glittered in the early morning sun. "Hey, no monkey business, little fellow." He handed the monkey a paper bag half filled with peanuts. Laughing at the would-be thief, Reynolds walked over to the candy stand and purchased several bags of sweets for the prisoners and his assistants. After passing out the candy, the sheriff paid the toll and gave the command to move on. The toll road clearance signal was given, and the gate opened. Middleton released the brake shoes. The bullwhip cracked, the horses lunged forward, and the chain traces jingled until the slack was picked up. The cacti and mesquite soon disappeared and scrub oak, mountain laurel, manzanita, and cedar and pine trees appeared, as the prison-bound party climbed slowly toward Pioneer

Pass. Before reaching the summit, they stopped to rest their horses where a number of lumberjacks were felling trees. Sheriff Reynolds waved and spoke to the lumberman who approached him.

"Sheriff, I'm mighty glad to see you!" exclaimed the foreman of the lumberers. "Thar's been an Apache molestin' our camp for a right smart spell and packed off nearly half our grub."

"Might have been a skunk. These mountains are full of them," suggested the sheriff.

"It was a skunk all right, one of them stinkin' Apache kind," the lumberman continued. "I laid eyes on him last night fer the first time, trying to steal my saddle horse, Thunder. He nearly got away with it, but Thunder is plenty smart. Recognized my whistle and came running towards me. I shot three or four times, but guess I missed him."

"Ma-si!" Reynolds gasped. "When he sneaked out of the dragnet at San Carlos, army officers told me that he probably came back to this area."

"Sounds like that Apache killer," Holmes confirmed, speaking from his seat in the stagecoach.

"Send one of your men to town and report this to Chief Deputy Jerry Ryan," instructed Reynolds. "Maybe this time my boys'll bag that slippery devil."

"I hope that damn redskin stays away from us, Sheriff. We got plenty of 'em as 'tis," Middleton shouted and without waiting for Reynolds to give the order, he cracked the whip and started the stage up the rutted road.

The officers and stage driver rode without speaking. Their eyes glanced nervously from time to time to huge boulders, large clumps of bushes, big tree trunks, and overhanging vines. Once, when a deer darted across the road, Middleton felt his heart skip a beat.

Pine-scented, cool, and invigorating air helped the straining bays pull the heavy stage over the summit of Pioneer Pass. Brakes were set, and the stage made a gradual descent to the mining camp of Pioneer.

The arrival of the stage caused the little camp to bustle with activity. A crowd gathered around and watched the officers as they released the Apache prisoners from their leg irons. Handcuffed in pairs, they were taken to the dining room. As the prisoners and their guards ate dinner, hostlers changed horses and greased the stage.

An old prospector who had seen every stage come and go for a number of years watched the procedure of handling the convicts. Sauntering up to Sheriff Reynolds, he asked in a cracked, high-pitched voice, "How the devil did ja catch them Apaches in one bunch, Sheriff? I remember some of 'em, by cracky! Some officers brought 'em right through here a while back, taking 'em to Casa Grande ."

"We just rounded them up, Granpa," explained Reynolds, as he smiled and looked at the old man. "Then the judge did the rest."

"Them thar redskins are still wild and plenty mean," the prospector said. "Better be extry keerful with 'em. I heared thar was a bad Apache causin' a lot of hell with them lumbermen up in the Pinal Mountains."

"So they told me. I think he is Ma-si. We'll pick him up before long, I hope," said Reynolds, mounting his horse just as Middleton started to pull out with the prisoners.

Traveling up one hill, then down another, the passengers bounced and rocked as the weaving stage reeled off the miles, finally reaching the deep, irksome sands of Disappointment Valley, now called Dripping Springs Valley. At this point, the Indians seemed to relax. They became less sullen and began to talk to each other in their own language. The apparent easing of the tension in the stage was a relief to Deputy Holmes. The spruce old fellow was a poet of sorts and a born entertainer, and the sullen mood of his fellow-travelers in the stage had begun to tell on his nerves. Now that the Indians had, seemingly, decided to be a little friendly, Holmes relaxed and let loose with some of his rollicking "poems." Glancing into the stage periodically, Reynolds saw that the Apaches apparently were enjoying Hunkydory's performance.

Holmes was going through his repertory happily as the stage started up an incline known as Chalk Hill, about two miles long. This was one of the steepest pulls and the horses were rested frequently. During these rest periods, Sheriff Reynolds demonstrated his markmanship by drilling holes in prickly pear cactus with his .45. By midafternoon the party had reached the top of the hill. Storm clouds were gathering in the west. The sheriff put his six-shooter back in his belt holster and buttoned his overcoat. Riding alongside the stage driver, Reynolds shouted to Middleton, "It's getting colder and looks like a storm's coming. We'd better crowd the teams, Gene, and try to make Riverside before the storm opens up."

Middleton trotted the horses down the last seven-mile grade, endeavoring to reach the Gila River before the drizzling rain broke into a downpour. Finally, they arrived at the river's north bank, and Middleton and Reynolds made a survey to determine if it would be safe to cross the stream. During the high water, stages did not attempt to ford the dangerous stream but waited for stages coming from the opposite direction. Passengers, mail, and cargo were conveyed across the stream in a box running on a cable that was stretched across the channel high above the water. After the exchange was made, stages turned around and went back to their terminals. This procedure, although necessary at times, caused delay, inconvenience, and more work on the part of stage operators and passengers alike. Just a short time before, a passenger by the name of William Murphy lost his life here. When the box was about halfway across, Murphy got dizzy by looking at the swirling water and fell into the river. His body was recovered the next day about a mile downstream. The incident was fresh in everyone's mind, and again there was an ominous silence in the stage.

Middleton concluded it would be just as safe to take a chance on crossing the stream in one group as it would be to transfer the prisoners across one at a time. Furthermore, Middleton's distrust of the Indians was profound; and Reynolds's confidence did not displace his fear that the three were no match for the Apache renegades, despite handcuffs and shackles. He chose to risk the river hazard.

At the crack of the whip the horses plunged into the Gila, dragging the heavy-laden stage behind. The water was belly deep on the saddle horses, so the sheriff and the Mexican convict held their feet high. "Better hold your feet up too, Hunkydory!" Reynolds shouted to Holmes, "The water is running through the stage!"

By the time the travelers crossed the river, without incident, the heavens had opened up, raining harder and harder. The Apaches sat huddled in the stage, cold, miserable, and too moody to talk. The horses needed no urging as they neared the end of their run, sloshing along over the muddy road.

Lights were springing up in the station when they rounded the last slight bend in the road.

Riverside, a station stop situated on the Gila River some forty miles south of Globe, was established to serve traffic. A hostelry with a good well of cool, fresh water offered accommodations to travelers who ventured into this rough and isolated section of the Arizona desert. It was the post office that served ranchers living along the Gila and San Pedro rivers, the two streams making their confluence some fifteen miles above the station. Just as Middleton's stage stopped at the station, the Globe-bound stage from Tucson also pulled in for the night layover.

"Howdy, Gene," greeted S.C. (Shorty) Sayler, driver of the Tucson stage. "This sure is a night for Satan and his imps!"

"Hi, Shorty," responded Middleton, wrapping his reins around the brake lever. "Can't speak for Satan, but we got his imps with us in this load of Apache convicts!"

"You have!" Sayler shouted in surprise. "Those redskins enjoy a night like this, and I'm not unloading my passengers until I know it's safe."

At this point, Sheriff Reynolds rode up to Sayler's stage, assuring him that the prisoners wouldn't molest his passengers.

While hostlers took care of the saddle and work horses, the prisoners were unloaded and taken into a large room for the night. Built of adobe, the room contained a long table, wooden benches, chairs, and a pot-bellied stove. This was the dining and waiting room. On this particular night, after passengers had been served their meals, it would be used as a sort of jail. The woodbox was piled high with mesquite, and a couple of lanterns hanging from the ceiling threw out their dim light. Served by the management in this room, the tired convicts, officers, and stage driver feasted on Irish stew, rice pudding, bread, and coffee.

After supper, Sheriff Reynolds made plans for the night watch. A couple of cots were set up so the officers could alternate in getting a little sleep. Middleton was to sleep in one and be close by in case he was needed. The Apache convicts sat at the table placed cornerwise with their backs to the walls facing their guards. They were securely fastened in irons, so any sleep they got would have to be in a sitting position. Avott was allowed the privilege of sitting in a chair without being handcuffed. Sheriff Reynolds had explained that on tomorrow's trip the saddle horses would be left at Riverside and all twelve of the party would continue in the stage.

"If you catch the four o'clock afternoon train at Casa Grande for Yuma, we should leave here not later than five o'clock in the morning," Middleton told Reynolds. "Up the road a spell, there's a steep grade, heavy with sand. My four horses can hardly pull an empty stage over it, so your passengers will have to walk up it to lighten the load."

"I remember the hill," the sheriff said. "Last spring when I brought some prisoners over this way, we all had to get out and push. I believe the sand was a foot deep. None of the wagons can make it without some help."

"You won't have to push—just walk. That's the reason I've got my four best horses on this run. Once we hit the flat, desert country, my blacks will make good time," Middleton concluded.

The Indians jabbered in Apache, but neither Middleton nor the officers understood them. They had one advantage over their escorts, inasmuch as they could piecemeal their guards' conversations and knew what the next move would be.

Middleton didn't rest much. He was up and down all night long watching closely the eight Apaches in the same room with him. He would breathe easier when he knew these redskins were behind the bars at Yuma.

The rain had stopped, the temperature gradually dropped to near freezing, and the valley at Riverside remained pitch dark. The hours passed slowly for Sheriff Reynolds during his first-trick watch. The apprehension, trial, and conveyance of these Apache convicts had been a physical and mental strain. All day he had maintained his composure without effort, but during these dismal hours on guard over the dark, hunched figures he could not but have felt some apprehension. Apache Kid and Hos-cal-te seemed never to take their eyes off him even when it meant shifting their uncomfortable positions to follow his pacing about the big room. It is not unlikely that he remembered, now, his wife's whispered "May God be with you" as he left his home in the early dawn of that day.

Holmes was to relieve him at two o'clock, and Reynolds paused beside the turned-down lamp to look at his watch. Apache Kid's voice came out of a shadowed corner, "Givem watch—me keep time."

"Never give up, do you, Kid?" replied Reynolds as he replaced the coveted watch in his pocket.

The voices aroused Holmes and Middleton, who were up in a flash. They suggested guarding the rest of the night together and persuaded the sheriff to lie down. Reynolds was in deep slumber when Middleton shook him by the shoulders, "Wake up, Glenn," he called. "It's four o'clock and time for breakfast."

After the meal, Middleton went to see about the stagecoach, and Reynolds conferred with Holmes about seating arrangements in the stage. Apache Kid and Hos-cal-te would be shackled, handcuffed, and placed in the front seat and not permitted to get out and walk when the party reached the grade. Reynolds took no chances on these young, notorious cunning convicts. The other six Apaches, being older men, would be handcuffed in pairs, leaving each person one free hand. He didn't consider them particularly dangerous in the present circumstances.

Middleton yelled into the waiting room that the stage was ready. The horses were fractious, and the hostlers were having trouble holding them. Middleton was in the driver's seat and repeatedly called each horse by name in an effort to quiet them. Whether the cool, crisp morning, the smell of Apaches, or the sense of danger caused the horses to act this way is not known. Nevertheless, at a later date, when Middleton wrote to Mrs. Reynolds describing the trip, he said, "I never saw horses act in such an unaccountable way."

"It's too dark to sit next to those fellows," Sheriff Reynolds whispered to Holmes; but in a louder tone he said, "You ride in the rear boot, and I'll climb up in the seat beside Gene. When we get on top of the hill, we'll rearrange the load."

Holding his watch near the lantern by the innkeeper, Reynolds checked the time. It was five o'clock on the morning of November 2, 1889, when he took his position alongside Middleton.

Middleton gave slack to the reins, and the horses were off like a flash. Following the winding road, they raced across the country along the river's bank. Using all the tricks of his teamster career, Middleton guided the runaway team while the stagecoach swayed and bounced. Reynolds held the butt of his shotgun between his legs, and clenched the barrels with his right hand. He held tightly to the rail with his left hand. Holmes, riding in the rear boot, held firmly to his hat and guns. They dodged scratching catclaw and mesquite branches as best they could.

During this excitement the Apache prisoners inside the coach braced themselves and whooped it up. The ex-scouts believed that they had been punished enough for having served a term in the Ohio state prison for wounding Al Sieber. To think they were being sent to another prison for the same offense was something they did not and never would understand. The fact that they were originally tried in a court which lacked jurisdiction meant nothing to them. They were not responsible for the bobble made in the original court which illegally convicted them. It would not have occurred to them, however, that Sheriff Reynolds was equally innocent of responsibility in that fiasco. That he was merely an officer of the law who carried out the edicts of the court after they had been tried, convicted, and sentenced would have carried no weight in his favor, even had they been aware of it.

Undoubtedly, they had been formulating plans of escaping if and when the opportunity presented itself. They had learned that Reynolds carried the keys to their bonds, and they knew just how many guns their guards carried. They also discovered that Holmes was not too active in his movements. They knew that Middleton would have his hands full with the stage when they arrived at the sandy grade where some would have to get out and walk. The ex-scouts had walked over this spot before, when federal officers had them in their custody, but on that trip they were too heavily guarded to attempt an escape. This time it might be different. Once they were out of the stagecoach into open space, their chances of escape had possibilities. They had declared previously that they would rather die as Nah-deizaz would than be doomed to die of consumption in the Yuma prison. They were desperate, but Sheriff Reynolds didn't realize it. The terrifying ride did nothing to lessen their desperation. At last Middleton gained control of the horses, and they slowed down to a trot and then a walk. The travelers relaxed and sat back in their seats.

The yellow wheels rolled off the final yards, and the bottom of the sandy grade came into view. The horses voluntarily made their customary stop. "Pretty smart horses, Gene," exclaimed Reynolds.

"Sure they're smart, Glenn. They know it's time to lighten the load,"' the stage driver spoke. "But I don't understand why they were so disturbed when we started this morning."

"Guess they smelled the Apaches and were afraid of 'em,"spoke Deputy Holmes from the rear of the stage.

"Maybe you're right, Hunkydory," replied Reynolds, as the two officers climbed down, preparatory to unloading the stage.

"Come on, Avott, you and the six convicts handcuffed in pairs, get out," Sheriff Reynolds ordered in a level cold voice. "The Apache Kid and Hos-cal-te are staying in the stage."

"Are you sure these two Indians in the stage can't get out?" Middle asked Reynolds. "It's nearly a half-mile to the top of the hill."

"Those fellows are handcuffed and are in shackles. They couldn't break loose from those irons in years unless they got the keys, and I have them," Reynolds assured him. "Pull ahead, Gene—All is well."

As the cold light of dawn broke over the Arizona desert

wilds Middleton looked back and shouted, "Watch those damn Apaches, boys. They strike hard at dawn. An Apache is an Apache, so be careful! I'll wait for you on top of the hill." He gave slack to the reins but not before his hand dropped to his gun belt to assure himself that his own gun was in working order, obviously intending to use it if the convicts made a false move.

Those on foot began the ascent behind the stage, which was soon out of sight when it rounded a bend. Jesus Avott led the group, looking neither to the right nor left, but carefully picking his way along the rut made by the stage wheels. Sheriff Reynolds walked with sure slow steps behind the Mexican. He allowed what he considered a safe distance to intervene between him and the six Apache convicts who walked behind him. Cautiously, he carried his shotgun, his fingers on the gun's triggers. The piercing cold caused him to button his heavy overcoat tightly around him, and his Colt .45 was in its holster strapped around his waist under his coat.

A little to one side and to the rear of Sheriff Reynolds came El-cahn and Say-es. Their dark glowing eyes craftily pierced the early morning light. Directly behind them trudged Has-ten-tu-du-jay and Bi-the-ja-be-tish-to-ce-an, murderers sentenced to life terms, who progressed with bowed heads and mumbled in Apache. Pash-ten-tah and Hale brought up the rear of the prisoners' line of march immediately in front of Holmes.

Suddenly there was a blood-curdling Apache yell and Pash-ten-tah and Hale turned upon Holmes with tiger-like speed. At the same instant, Sheriff Reynolds apparently realizing the convicts were too close to him, whirled around and was met by the impact of two solid bodies. In one fluid movement El-cahn and Say-es grabbed his arms with free hands, in a close-up frontal attack.

Back at the rear, Pash-ten-tah and Hale kicked and slugged Holmes until he dropped to the ground. When he landed, they literally mashed his head with vicious stomping. Pash-ten-tah seized his rifle and crushed, pounded, and, holding the weapon in one hand, sent a bullet through the battered head. The last earthly track of Hunkydory Holmes, Arizona pioneer and trail-blazer, was made by his life blood on the cold sand of the desert.

In the meantime, Avott, frozen with horror and terror, watched Holmes die and saw Reynolds struggling in the grip of his assailants. His impulse was to attempt to help Reynolds, but the move might be misinterpreted and Reynolds might shoot him as an accomplice. In any case he was terrified of the frenzied Apaches. The only alternative was to get up the grade as fast as possible and warn Middleton. He began to run.

Reynolds continued his desperate struggle. He held firmly to his shotgun with his left hand but the closeness of his attackers made it impossible to bring this gun into play. Blind with rage he fought hard to draw his six-shooter from under his buttoned overcoat. With a quick kick the sheriff sent El-cahn to his knees. A second kick landed on the shins of Say-es, who let out an Apache oath, but they did not loosen their grip on Reynolds. They wrapped themselves around him and held on tenaciously until Pash-ten-tah and Hale rushed to their aid.

Pash-ten-tah, carrying Holmes's rifle, stopped short, took accurate aim and fired. Shot through the body, the bloody, battered sheriff fell on the spot where he had so desperately fought for his life. Pash-ten-ah ran his free hand into Reynolds' overcoat pocket and found the keys to the handcuffs and tossed the keys to El-cahn and Say-es, who set about unlocking their manacles.

Suddenly Pash-ten-tah spotted young Avott running up the sandy grade. He let out a horrifying Apache yell and bounded after the fleeing Mexican, with Hale screaming at his heels. But Avott was just out of range. The yelling roused Reynolds and, making a final desperate effort to revive, he got to his knees. El-cahn tossed the manacles aside and, with the sheriff's own .45, fired point blank. The bullet caught Reynolds in the left shoulder and plowed downward. The lifeless form slumped to the ground in a grotesque heap. The next minute, Say-es grabbed the sheriff's shotgun and, holding it close to the dying man's head, pulled both triggers. The charge tore off part of the victim's face. Say-es and El-cahn, mad with lust for white man's blood, blazed into vicious fury. Accenting their slaughter with continuous spine-chilling yells, these blood-thirsty fiends dashed stones against the mangled head of their victim.

During these moments of ghastly carnage, the other two Apaches were actually awed by the fury of their tribesmen. They took no part in the slaying and, fearing for their own lives, had retreated to the side of the road, where they had remained silent and watchful.

Now, like fiends drunk with slaughter, Say-es and El-cahn reloaded the shotgun and checked the chambers of the six-shooter. The keys to the irons were in their possession, and they ran wildly up the grade, following Pash-ten-tah and Hale toward the stage.

During the ten or fifteen minutes that it took to dispose of the officers, the stagecoach had rounded several curves and made steady progress. Apache Kid and Hos-call-te sat sullen and moody while their fetters pressed deep on their copper-skinned bodies. Middleton thought he heard muffled reports of guns but believed the officers were merely target shooting. Again and again he glanced back, but not once did he see the figure of a man frantically running toward him. Finally convinced that he heard a voice, he stopped the stage and securely set the brakes. A moment later he saw a lone man approaching. Keenly watching the person who steadily came nearer, Middleton satisfied himself that it was the Mexican convict. Pointing his gun directly at Avott, he shouted in a loud, commanding voice, "Stop! Stop!"

"Help, amigo, help!" screamed the Mexican, ignoring the command and running with terror. Gasping for breath he reached the rear of the stage.

"Get in this stage or I'll blast you!" Middleton ordered.

"Por amor de Dios, don't shoot!" screamed the trembling Avott. "Apaches kill Sheriff and Hunky. They come kill me, hide me quick," he pleaded.

"K-killed! Impossible!" Exclaimed the stunned Middleton.

Apache Kid overheard the conversation and squirmed in his seat. Without doubt he was the key figure in plotting the escape, and his dream was about to materialize, if Middleton could be disposed of. He wanted to tantalize the already terrified Middleton as much as possible, so he let out a war cry and thrust his head out of the stage.

"Get yer damn head back in that stage or I'll shoot it off!" Middleton roared, looking down and pointing his gun at the Indian. "Try and get out and you'll be a dead Apache!"

"Don't shoot! Me sit down! Me lay down—anything! Apache Kid no run away! Me good Indian," he cried out, flopping back in his seat doing as he was bidden. As far as there is any evidence, official or otherwise, this was the last command that the Apache Kid took from a white man, and these were the last known words he ever spoke to a pale-face.

Meanwhile Avott, who had not relaxed for a moment, kept his eyes fixed on the trail behind him. He spotted Pash-ten-tah taking aim with the slain Holmes' rifle. "Look out Gene!" he screamed. "Apache shoot you!" Instantly the Mexican turned and dashed through the bushes. The dazed Middleton had barely heard Avott's warning when there was the crack of a rifle and a bullet cut through Middleton's neck and he toppled from the driver's seat to the ground. Near the right front yellow wheel of the new Concord, its owner lay in a pool of blood.

An instant later more shots were fired as Pashs-ten-tah cut down on the fleeing Mexican. Bullets whizzed past Avott, who rapidly put distance between himself and the frenzied Apache killer. Increasing his pace, he ran through the brush and over around rocks until he came to a clump of bushes, where he hid.

By the time Pash-ten-tah got over his anger for not hitting the fleet-footed Avott, Hale, El-cahn, and Say-es reached the stage. During the preceding tense moments Apache Kid and Hos-cal-te, inside the stagecoach, had maintained a neutral silence. The arrival of Hale, El-cahn, and Say-es confirmed the complete success of the coup, and Kid broke the silence with Apache yells. With exultant shouts, the murderers leaped into the stage and quickly liberated Apache Kid and Hos-cal-te. During all this commotion, the horses nervously stamped and twisted about, but their tight reins and set wagon-brakes prevented them from taking off.

With wild cries the Indians jumped from the stagecoach. El-cahn drew Reynolds' six-shooter from the belt he had strapped around himself and pointed the weapon toward the prostrate form of Middleton. Apache Kid saw the move and probably recognized the hated Reynolds gun, for he jerked the .45 from El-cahn's hand and stuck it in his own belt. It can only be supposed that he had considered Middleton already dead and was momentarily engrossed with the triumph of possessing his enemy's own weapon. At any rate, the incident saved Middleton's life.

Apache Kid, Hale, Say-es, Pash-ten-tah, and El-cahn set about robbing the bodies of their victims. Rolling Middleton's body over and over, they took his coats and personal effects. Racing down the road, they came to the mangled body of Sheriff Reynolds. Apache Kid's long, bony fingers reached into the dead man's vest pocket and found the gold watch and chain. He straightened up. Standing in the early morning light, his black eyes flashed with gratification as he gazed upon the sheep and cattle figures engraved upon the gold case. The crooked W tattooed upon the center of his bronze forehead turned to a dark crimson as deep in color as the blood-soaked sand upon which he stood.

Satisfied, now that he had in his possession the gold watch and chain that he had for so long desired, Apache Kid glanced anxiously at his partners, who, apparently, had paid no attention to their leader's loot. They were busy stuffing their booty into their own ragged pockets. Removing the overcoat from the body of the slain sheriff, he frantically searched each pocket until he grasped that which he was seeking. From an inner pocket, he took the money pouch containing about $350. He found the prisoners' commitment papers and took them.

Hale and Pash-ten-tah bent over the body of Holmes and systematically plundered it. With a cry of joy, Hale ran a few yards behind the dead man to where the deputy's cowboy hat lay. Jabbering excitedly, he threw his old straw hat into a cactus patch and donned the new headgear.

Apache Kid missed his Indian brothers and called out in a loud clear voice, "Has-ten-tu-du-jay, Be-the-ja-be-tish-to-ce-an!" Fearful for their lives, these convicts had kept out of the slaying. However, at the call of Apache Kid, they came from their hideout and joined their tribesmen without complaint, as did Hos-cal-te, who also did not participate. Apache Kid told his fellow criminals that he would lead them back to their homes on the reservation. Seeing the leader's calmness and confidence, and undoubtedly awed by the incredible turn of events, they willingly followed.

Middleton, although suffering untold agony, had not lost consciousness and had only feigned death during the ghastly affair. Convinced at last that the danger had passed, he opened his eyes. The wound in his neck bled profusely and he was getting cold, the escapees having robbed him of

The Indians who killed Glenn Reynolds on November 2, 1889.

his coats. Somehow he would have to get help. Suddenly he heard footsteps and hopefully forced his head an inch or two out of the bloodsoaked sand. To his horror he saw two of the Apaches directly in front of him and coming toward the stage. He had a shuddering sensation as if every hair on his head stood on end. Lying helpless on the ground, he realized the time had come for him to meet his Maker. He closed his eyes and waited for the end.

To his intense relief the killers passed by him and climbed into the stage. They had dropped the keys to the handcuffs when they freed Apache Kid and Hos-cal-te, and had returned for them in order to free the two Apaches who had retreated to the side when Holmes was attacked. After removing the handcuffs from the bony wrists of the last pair, the eight escapees, led by Apache Kid, scampered away and disappeared from sight into the desert waste.

EDITOR'S CONCLUSION

Middleton survived the attack and carried word of the murders to Riverside Station. Avott met a man driving a herd of horses from the Zellewager Ranch. He rode one of these to Florence to sound the alarm that the outlaws were on the loose. Word spread, but the Apache Kid escaped the dragnet and was never captured.

Hays gives the following information on the fate of the principal figures in this story:

Sheriff Glenn Reynolds, killed November 2, 1889.

Deputy W.A. (Hunkydory) Holmes, killed November 2, 1889.

Eugene Middleton, stagecoach driver, died at Globe,

Arizona, in 1929, of unknown natural causes.

Jesus Avott, no definite record, probably dead of this date (1954).

Pash-ten-tah, killed by the army at Ash Flat in May, 1890.

Hale, killed by the army at Ash Flat in May, 1890.

Has-ten-tu-du-jay, killed by the army at Ash Flat in May, 1890.

Bi-the-ja-be-tish-to-ce-an, killed by the army at Ash Flat in May, 1890.

El-cahn, killed by the army near San Carlos in September, 1890.

Say-es, died of consumption in cell 13, Yuma prison, March 29, 1894.

Hos-cal-te, died of consumption in cell 13, Yuma prison, April 1, 1894.

Apache Kid, whereabouts unknown.

THE HUNT FOR THE FUGITIVES AND RECOVERY OF THE GOLD WATCH AND PISTOL

by Bob Green

Of considerable interest is the fate of the pistol and watch that the Apache Kid took from Reynolds's body. These were found in Mexico years later and returned to Reynolds's widow. The following account by Albany rancher/writer Bob Green fills in some additional details:

Now the greatest organized manhunt in the history of Arizona territory began. Captain Bullis, commanding officer of the troops at the San Carlos Reservation and who had once been in command at Fort Griffin, Texas, where Reynolds had come from, sent his cavalry to all points where he thought the fugitives might be intercepted, but to no avail. So Reynolds's prized gold watch was now being coveted and carried by his killers as they ran for their lives in a chase to the death.

Sheriff Reynolds and Hunkydory Holmes were buried in the Globe cemetery, Glenn beside his little son, George T., who had died for lack of medicine at the Sierra Anchos Ranch.

On Glenn Reynolds's gravestone is a biblical inscription from Job Chapter 14: "Man that is born of woman is of few days and full of trouble. He cometh forth like a flower and is cut down." Hunkydory Holmes's grave was unmarked.

By 1894, of the eight Apaches who took part in the massacre at Kelvin Grade, all eventually were accounted for and were dead from various causes, with the exception of the Apache Kid.

He was never apprehended and entered into the mythology of Arizona and later, Hollywood, which produced three greatly glorified movies about him. Although the Apache Kid was never found, Sheriff Reynolds's gold watch did turn up.

In May 1890, south of the border, Colonel Kosterlitsky, a famous, hard-bitten Mexican soldier known as the "Eagle of Sonora," while leading his command of Mexican Rurales on a patrol, came upon three Apaches in Sonora, Mexico, and quickly killed them.

From one's body, an old man with white hair, and definitely not the Apache Kid, Kosterlitsky took Glenn Reynolds's gold watch and pistol, which he carefully forwarded to his superiors in Mexico City.

They, in turn, contacted the U.S. State Department in Washington, D.C., and the watch and pistol traveled up through the halls of protocol of both countries until on June 9, 1890, Arizona Governor Lewis Wolfley received both watch and gun and carefully returned them to Glenn Reynolds's widow, Gussie. Gussie never remarried and returned to live in Albany, where she died in 1943.

Glenn Reynolds' Grave Stone in Globe, Arizona.

Today, due to the generosity of her descendants, this still beautiful gold watch and chain are now on view for all to see in the Old Jail Art Center in Albany, Texas, a true surviving relic of the violence, romance, and drama that really did take place in the real American West. [Editors's Note: The pistol is in the possession of Robert G. Hollowell, a descendent of Glenn's wife.]

LETTERS RELATED TO REYNOLDS'S WATCH AND PISTOL

The following letters tell the story in the somewhat flamboyant style of the correspondence of the day. Unfortunately the writers erroneously thought that Reynolds was the sheriff of Tucson, not Globe:

Mexico, May 20th, 1890

Mr. Minister:

Glenn Reynolds' pocket watch, front side.

Glenn Reynolds' pocket watch, back side.

Glenn Reynolds' pistol.

I have the honor herewith to transmit to your Excellency copy of communications which the Secretary of the Treasury has addressed to me, that in an encounter had by some of the Customs Guards with Apache Indians the former recovered various articles, among which was a gold watch and its chain, the property of the Sheriff of Tucson, Arizona. Said watch is in the Department subject to Your Excellency's orders, so you may send for it whenever you desire.

I renew to Your Excellency the declaration of my eminent regard.

M. Asperoz

Secretary, Mexican Foreign Office
Legation of the United States
Mexico, May 23, 1890

Sir:

I am in receipt of Your Excellency's esteemed note of the 20th inst., informing me that a gold watch and its chain, the property of Sheriff of Tucson, Arizona, which was recovered in a recent encounter had by Mexican Customs Guards with some Apache Indians, is now in Your Department, subject to this Legation's orders.

I beg that Your Excellency will kindly cause said watch and chain to be delivered to bearer and that you will be pleased to accept this note as a receipt there of.

Thanking Your Excellency for the kindly courtesy shown in this matter, I take pleasure in reiterating the assurance of my highest considerations of friendly esteem.

Thos. Ryan

Legation of the United States
Mexico, May 23, 1890
To the Hon. James G. Baine
Washington, D.C.

Sir:

I have the honor to forward to the Department at Washington in today's mailpouch, a gold watch and chain delivered to this Legation by the Mexican Foreign Office, with the information that it is the property of the Sheriff of Tucson, Arizona, which was recovered in an encounter had by Mexican Customs guards with some Apache Indians. The Mexican Government with characteristic kindliness and courtesy has taken this method of returning this property to the owner. Upon the interior case is the inscription: Glenn

Reynolds, Albany, Texas, June 10th, 1884.

Copies of the correspondence relative thereto are herewith transmitted.

I am, Sir, very respectfully

Thos. Ryan

Department of State

Washington, June 2, 1890

The Hon. Lewis Wolfey

Governor of Arizona

Phoenix

Sir:

I have the honor to transmit a copy of a dispatch from our Minister in Mexico, regarding a gold watch, the property of Mr. Glenn Reynolds, late Sheriff of Tucson, Arizona, which has been recovered by Mexican Customs Guards from Apaches. The watch will be forwarded to you by express for delivery to the rightful owner.

As the Mexican Government would be glad, no doubt, to be apprised of its receipt, I trust that such acknowledgement may be made by the recipient through your office as seems proper. I will forward the same to our Minister.

I have the honor to be, Sir, your obedient servant,

James G. Blaine

Territory of Arizona

Executive Department
Phoenix, June 9th, 1890
E.H. Cook, Esq.
Atty. at Law
Globe, Ariz.
Sir:

I have the honor to advise you that I have this day received from the State Department, Washington, a watch and gun—property of the late Glenn Reynolds and the same will be forwarded by Express to your address tomorrow for delivery to the rightful owner. I also send to you (enclosed herewith) the correspondence between United States and Mexican Authorities—and letter from Secretary of State The Hon. James G. Blaine transmitting the same and advising of sending of the watch and gun. Please have the kindness to cause a proper receipt to be signed and executed and sent to me for transmission through the State Depot to the Mexican Government.

Yours Respy
Lewis Wolfey
Governor

CONTEMPORARY BIOGRAPHIES OF PRINCIPAL FIGURES

The following material comes from two books contemporary with George T. Reynolds, W.D. Reynolds, and J.B. Matthews. They repeat some of the information found elsewhere in the volume but are included because of the nature of the material and the overview of the men's lives.

Sec. I: from *Historical and Biographical Record*

George T. Reynolds

As a result of the Texan war for independence [from Mexico], the redeemed territory, in all its vast area, was thrown open for settlement, and there were many adventurous and aggressive spirits who were not slow to improve the opportunity afforded to them and press on across the boundaries of the new republic in search of its most favored regions. In the east and south, ranches, neighborhoods and communities began making their appearance in localities which a few years before had been guiltless of the marks of human presence, and gradually the frontier was pressed to the westward in spite of the resistance made by the savage tribes who claimed the prairies as their own. The period of disturbance coincidental with the Mexican War retarded the work of civilization for a time, but in the next decade it was recommenced with renewed vigor. In course of time settlements sprang up along the upper tributaries of the Trinity, and then the tide of pioneer life pressed on westward, and the curling smoke from the settlers' hearthstones began hanging in wreaths above the wooded hills of the Brazos.

B.W. Reynolds, the father of our subject, was one of the first white men to attempt a permanent settlement in the Palo Pinto hills. He was a Georgian by birth, descended from the sturdy Scotch stock which is so largely represented along the front of American civilization. He had fought in the Seminole War in Florida and Alabama, in 1836, and after that struggle had ended he married his wife being a Miss Ann M. Campbell, and, in 1847, moved to Texas, settling first in Shelby County, where he resided for thirteen years. His removal to Palo Pinto County was made in 1860, and the same year he moved still further westward, locating on the Clear Fork of the Brazos, in Stephens County, where he engaged in the cattle business, buying his cattle from J.R. Baylor, and paying in part with a colored girl, valued at $1,000, and the difference in gold. This was the first transaction in a long and successful career as a cattle grower and dealer, during which Mr. Reynolds received material aid and assistance from his sons, of whom our subject was the eldest.

George T. Reynolds was born in Montgomery County, Alabama, February 14, 1844, and was yet in his early childhood when his parents decided to cast their lot with the pioneers of the Lone Star State. Their subsequent move to the westward was made when he was but sixteen, and in facing the difficulties and dangers that confronted him in his new

The Reynolds brothers–Left to right, front–W. D. and George; back row–B. F. and Phinn.

home he had neither time or opportunity for completing the education of which he had received the rudiments in the schools of Shelby County. He assisted his father in the work of establishing himself on the ranch in Stephens County and in caring for his cattle, but was also watchful for an opportunity to make a start in life for himself, and made and saved his first money while conveying the mails for the government from Palo Pinto to Weatherford. The distance was between thirty and forty miles, and Mr. Reynolds made the trips on a pony, traveling by night in order to avoid the Indians, who were then very troublesome. In 1862 Mr. Reynolds entered the Confederate service, enlisting in Company E, of the 19th Texas Cavalry, Col. Nat. Bufford's regiment. His command was with General Marmaduke during his raids through Missouri and Arkansas, but Mr. Reynolds was wounded in 1863, and received an honorable discharge, re-

Sallie Reynolds Matthews, author of Interwoven.

turning to his home in Texas. His personal possessions at that time consisted of a pony and $300 in Confederate money, worth ten cents on the dollar.

He found the border in a blaze with Indian warfare and the few settlers contending against overwhelming numbers. The ranchmen in particular were suffering severely, for their herds were continually subjected to raids by thieving bands, who, not content with running off the cattle, would murder their owners and apply the torch to their dwellings. In January, 1864, shortly after his return from the army, Mr. Reynolds started south with his brother-in-law, Sam Newcomb, and five others, seeking a location where they would be free from the danger of the Indians. They went directly to McCamas' ranch, at the junction of the Colorado and Concho Rivers, where they secured a supply of provisions, which was very thankfully received, since they had been living for several days on buffalo and deer meat alone. They then followed the Concho along its upward course to Kickapoo Creek, their intention being to locate a ranch at Kickapoo Springs. On the day before they anticipated reaching their destination, they encountered several Indians driving a heard of horses, and decided to give chase, it being at that time the only safe plan to strive for the first blow when a conflict with redskins could not be easily avoided. On this occasion, however, the Indians were plainly outmarched and had no desire to show fight. Hastily rounding up their horses, each selected one, upon which they made good their escape, though the whites pressed them so close that they were forced to ride away barebacked, leaving their saddles on their jaded steeds. At this place Mr. Reynolds captured a fine Texas saddle, stained with the blood of its former owner, whom the savages had probably killed some days before. As the horse herd had undoubtedly been stolen, Mr. Reynolds and his companions determined to drive them to Fort Mason and attempt to find their owners, if possible, but in some way the report got out that the horses had been stolen from the Confederacy, and the State Rangers, who were then encamped at San Saba, arrested the party and threw them into prison, confining all seven in a little room, not over 8x10 feet square, and perfectly alive with vermin. Their story of how the horses fell into their hands was received with incredulity, and they were required to prove their identity, which, for a time they were unable to do; but after several days Mr. Reynolds was recognized by one of the Rangers who had previously worked for his father, and through his intercession the release of the party was secured. Mr. Reynolds could have escaped before this, but would not do so, since in saving himself he must have inevitably injured the chances of his friends. Given their freedom once more, the party made their way homeward, a long and tedious journey.

During this same year (1864) the noted war chief, Satanta, made a descent with 500 warriors upon the settlements of Elm Creek, in Young County, killing nineteen whites, men, women and children, and carrying away several prisoners and large herds of cattle. At the time of this raid Mr. Reynolds was in another encounter with the Indians, eighteen of them in all, while there were but seven of the whites, and but poorly armed. The Indians were repulsed after a short fight, in which three of them were killed, Mr. Reynolds killing the first, while the others were killed by a companion named Riley St. John. As Mr. Reynolds charged down upon the camp his horse gave out, and he shot an Indian from his pony, mounted it and joined his companions, but had a narrow escape from death by an arrow, and rode out of the fight at its close minus one pants leg. The horse captured by Mr. Reynolds on this occasion he retained and valued for many years. On this raid the Indians destroyed all the buildings at Ft. Bragg except George Braggs's house, and Satanta made good his escape with all his spoils. The subsequent history of this red warrior is known to all. He was made prisoner by the United States army in 1870 or '71, tried, and sentenced to imprisonment for life, but was paroled on good behavior after two or three years, and a few months afterward was captured with his son, Satonka, while on their way from the reservation to Texas on another raid. Satonka was killed while attempting to escape, and Satanta afterward committed suicide in prison.

In 1865 Mr. Reynolds made his first venture in the way of cattle speculation, buying 100 head of steers, which he afterward drove to New Mexico and sold at a good profit. In 1866 he rented the Old Stone Ranch, in Throckmorton County, to which he moved his father. During the absence of the father and sons from the ranch, in June of that same year, the Indians swooped down and drove away all the cattle, including even the milch cows, 500 head in all. Every horse on the ranch was taken as well, but this loss, though severe, was not allowed to discourage the Reynoldses from their determination to ultimately make a home in the wild region. Robbed of their cattle, they turned their attention to other pursuits and in the year following the Indian raid killed 1,000 buffalo and many deer. The Indians still made periodical descents upon the outlying ranches, and their encounters with the ranchmen were of frequent occurrence. In February, 1863, an incident occurred which caused Mr. Reynolds a great deal of trouble. He was out hunting cattle, accompanied by J.B. Matthews, afterward his father-in-law, and they had in their outfit a boy named Jack Marshall, but familiarly known by the nickname "Jacko." "Jacko" was not remarkable for his brightness, and the different members of the "outfit" were always "picking" at him, making his life a perpetual burden. Mr. Reynolds pitied the boy and favored him in every way possible, and thought that he had gained his friendship; but after-developments proved him mistaken. Left temporarily in charge of camp, "Jacko" stole the best horse in the outfit, which happened to be the property of Mr. Reynolds, and gathering up all the blankets and other articles of value, took his departure for regions unknown, leaving his late companions to suffer through the cold nights as best they could. Mr. Reynolds and Si Hough, a friend, followed him to Palo Pinto County, where they were joined by Tom Cranmer (Cranmer and Hough are now dead), and the trio pressed on to Parker County, where the fugitive was found on Morgan's ranch, near Weatherford. On the return, the party was met by J.C. Darnall, who suggested that it was a waste of time to take "Jacko" to jail when they might as well hang him themselves. The prisoner was led beneath a post oak tree, and a rawhide rope, part of the fruits of his theft, placed around his neck, while the end was thrown over a limb. His captors were very much in earnest, and Jacko felt the importance of the occasion and begged for time to pray. His request was granted, and the boy pleaded so pitifully for his life that he was released, after receiving a good flogging and promising to go east of the Brazos River and never return. Mr. Reynolds administered the whipping, and as to whip a man in this way was a penitentiary offense, he was at once liable to a criminal prosecution and the officers interested themselves in his capture. John Newcomb, the Deputy Sheriff of Palo Pinto County, started to Mr. Reynolds's home to arrest him, but met him on the way, accompanied by J.B. Matthews. Mr. Reynolds was not disarmed, as there was constant danger from Indians, and catching Newcomb off his guard, he drew his revolver and announced his intention of returning to his Stone Ranch, but instructed the sheriff not to follow. Later on, when Mr. Reynolds was going to be married, it was necessary to visit Palo Pinto to secure the license, and as the charges were still against him, he called on two friends, Tom Cranmer and another, to accompany him. They carried four revolvers and a shotgun each, and although their presence in town was noted, it is needless to say that they were not molested.

On the 3rd day of April, 1867, Mr. Reynolds, his brother, William D., and eight others, started on an Indian trail, but as it chanced, found more Indians than they had bargained for. They encountered the band at the mouth of the Double Mountain Fork, in what is now Haskell County. They were skinning a buffalo when the whites rode up on them, and at once showed fight, one of them, who could talk a little English, coming forward to meet them, cursing, and firing at them with two revolvers. Mr. Reynolds noticed that, although he leveled his arm properly in shooting, the revolver was invariably fired at an angle which threw the bullets far above their heads. Waiting until the Indian had emptied both weapons and unslung his bow, Mr. Reynolds fired, shooting him through the body, and as he turned to run, fired again with his revolver, breaking the Indian's neck. A running fight followed, and during its continuance Mr. Reynolds received a serious wound, an arrow passing through his body. He removed the wooden shaft from the wound, but the head of the arrow remained and he gave himself up for dead. As he lay on the ground, his friend, Si Hough, rode by and asked him if he knew which Indian shot him. "The one with the red shirt," replied Mr. Reynolds, feebly; and Hough answered with an oath that the would have that particular Indian's scalp in payment. He made his words good and upon his return to the wounded man shortly after exhibited the bleeding scalp in proof, and said, "Here's your man with the red shirt." Six Indians were killed in this fight and five of them scalped.

The head of the arrow which had wounded Mr.

Reynolds could not be removed, for it was firmly imbedded in the muscles of his back and there was no way in which it could be reached. He was conveyed to his home, a distance of sixty miles, on two pack horses, arriving there after twenty-four hours' travel. The nearest doctor was at Weatherford, a distance of 110 miles away, and he was sent for in all haste to dress the wound, though there were small hopes of Mr. Reynolds' recovery. Five days elapsed before his arrival, and by that time the wounded man was fairly on the way to recovery. Remarkable as it may appear, the elder Mr. Reynolds had dreamed of the fight and its results the night before it occurred, and had told of it at the breakfast table; but the dream failed to come true in all its points, for his son, instead of dying as he had foretold, rapidly recovered and was soon able to resume his saddle once more. The arrowhead remained in the wound for sixteen years, finally being removed by a quartette of surgeons in Kansas City. The sufferings endured by Mr. Reynolds in those long years can be better imagined than described, and it is hardly possible that the history of surgery can furnish a case parallel to this in all its particulars.

After he had recovered sufficiently to ride once more, Mr. Reynolds visited the scene of the fight. The Indians who were scalped were lying as they fell, except that the wolves had mutilated their bodies. The sixth Indian had been mortally wounded after his horse was shot from under him, but had managed to hide in a thicket and save his scalp. After the whites had left the battlefield, the Indians had returned and scalped the horse which had played its rider false, and had buried the Indian beneath a pile of logs and dirt, his shield and war bonnet with him. It seems to have been a custom of this tribe—the Comanches—to bury only those fallen warriors whose scalps were intact.

After his recovery, Mr. Reynolds was married to Miss L.E. Matthews, daughter of J.B. Matthews, whose biography is given elsewhere, and, in July, 1868, he started to Mexico with a herd of cattle, his wife accompanying him. Fortune was again against him on this trip. He was attacked by Indians and all of his horses were stolen, but he finally reached Mexico, where he disposed of his cattle, and going on to Colorado, settled on the Arkansas River, in Bent County.

A ranch was started at his location in Colorado, and in 1870 his brother, William, brought more cattle from Texas, and they drove them through to Salt Lake, where they expected to find buyers. Though cattle were in demand in Salt Lake City, the Reynolds brothers had a good deal of difficulty in disposing of their herd, for their extreme youth had aroused the suspicions of the buyer, who could not believe that the cattle were their own. They finally sold their cattle— 900 head—for $25 a head, and, going on to California, purchased there a herd of horses, which were afterward disposed of to advantage in Colorado.

After an absence of four years, G.T. Reynolds returned to Texas, and purchased a herd of cattle at Weatherford, from Charles Rivers. They were to be rounded up and delivered next day, but during the night the camp was attacked by Indians, who ran off the horses and mortally wounded Mr. Rivers, who lay sleeping by Mr. Reynolds' side. Though death-stricken, Mr. Rivers was mindful of his business obligations, and requested J.C. Loving, his brother-in-law, who was camped nearby, to fulfill his contract with Mr. Reynolds, a request which was carried out that same day. This herd was driven by the Reynolds Brothers to Utah and Nevada, and upon their return they brought a drove of horses again to Colorado. This drive was the last made by the Reynolds Brothers in which they came in actual contact with the Indians, but they have continued actively engaged in the business, though their varied interests in other lines now occupy a great deal of their time. The Reynolds boys, however, are known for their courage and resolution on the Western frontier, particularly Glenn Reynolds, a younger brother, who held for years the dangerous office of sheriff, in Arizona, and was killed by Indian outlaws while in the discharge of his official duties.

G.T. Reynolds is now fifty-one years old, but still retains the taste for adventure which has been one of the leading traits of his character through life. He has traveled extensively, and within the last few years has visited nearly all the Indian tribes from the tropical forests of Mexico to Alaska's ice-bound shores. In August, 1891, he was caught among the ice-floes in Glacier Bay, and later, was stranded in Peril Straits, but escaped all these dangers, and during his stay in Alaska visited all the mines and fisheries of the country and had many interesting adventures among the Esquimaux and their dogs.

Mr. Reynolds deservedly ranks as one of the wealthiest and most enterprising men of the state, and his wealth is invested in many ways. In company with his brother, W.D. Reynolds, he is very extensively interested in the cattle business, having large and well-stocked pastures in Throckmorton and Shackelford Counties, Texas, and also a large ranch in North Dakota, near the mouth of the Yellowstone River. G.T. Reynolds was at one time largely interested in oil mills in Mexico, but sold to parties in Monterey, in 1890. In local enterprises he has always held prominent part, and may be largely credited with the flattering growth of the town of Albany, Texas, in which he makes his home. He organized the First National Bank of Albany, of which he is now President, and is also President of the First National Bank of Oklahoma City, and Vice president of the Norman State Bank of Norman, Oklahoma Territory.

To the biography of such a man as our subject it is unnecessary to add anything in the way of comment or stereotyped peroration. His life speaks for itself, and the results of his efforts are patent to all. In building up his fortune, he has built, as well, a reputation of which he may well be proud, and has earned and holds the friendship and respect of his business associates and acquaintances.

W. D. Reynolds

In touching upon the early life of W.D. Reynolds, his school days will receive but the briefest mention. His history dates back to a time when schools in Western Texas were by no means common: and though he managed to secure the assistance of a teacher during a few short winter days, when his services were not needed at home, the lessons learned were neither numerous or profound. Mr. Reynolds' education has been gained in the school of actual experience, and his shrewd business ability is the outgrowth of observation and study, intensified by an enterprising spirit, and tempered by the wisdom that follows any daring business ventures.

His active life as a cattleman dates from the 22nd day of September, 1867, when he accepted a position with Messrs. Loving and Goodnight, and started with a herd of 3,200 cattle for Colorado. His salary was $50 a month, and he was expected to furnish his own horse and saddle. Mr. Reynolds was then the owner of forty-two head of cattle, which he had gotten together by dint of hard work and a good deal of trading. These he put in with his employers' herd, and disposed of when the stock was sold that winter. The price of cattle was running high at the time, and by saving the greater portion of his salary, Mr. Reynolds was enabled to produce, February 29, 1868, $700 in cash and a $125 mule as the result of the trip. Upon this trip to Colorado, Mr. Oliver Loving, one of the owners of the herd, was killed by the Indians, and Mr. Reynolds was one of the party who returned with the body, down the old Pecos trail to Weatherford. It was, indeed, a sad incident. Mr. Loving was a great favorite with all the cattlemen, and his loss was generally regretted.

Later in the spring of 1868, W.D. Reynolds and his brother George combined their cash capital and engaged in business together. Already known as shrewd, conservative men, they experienced no difficulty in purchasing several head of cattle on credit, and with the herd thus assembled, located in the southern part of Colorado. This was the beginning of the Reynolds Land and Cattle Company, which has since been incorporated and developed to such magnitude that his name is familiar throughout all the grazing regions of the West. The herd was held in Colorado until the fall of 1876, when a severe and long continued drouth compelled their removal, and they were driven to Roberts County, in the Texas Panhandle, and sold the ensuing spring, to Chas. Goodnight. A return to the ranch at Fort Griffin followed; and here, Mr. Reynolds was actively engaged in the cattle business until 1883, when he moved to Albany, invested heavily in town property, and secured an interest in the First National Bank of Albany, of which he is now vice-president. To mention, even in the briefest and most casual manner, the works he has accomplished and the business enterprises with which he has been identified in the last eleven years would be a task of no little magnitude; and instead it is only necessary to say that the Reynolds Land and Cattle Company has, in its operations, kept fully abreast of the times, and that its incorporators, jointly and severally, have been uniformly successful in their ventures. Among their more important moves has been the establishment of a herd in North Dakota, which they have been adding to and shipping from, yearly, since the first few hundred head were located there in 1885. The enterprise has proven a very profitable one, although there were heavy losses sustained through the winters of '86-'87.

W.D. Reynolds is a man whose figure and dignified bearing would attract attention in any company. His manner is modest and unassuming, and during his long, eventful career he has made only friends. No man stands better or has greater influence with the people of his section, and there are few more careless of the honor that might be gained for the asking. He has no political aspirations and has never allowed his name used in connection with a public office, always finding his greatest happiness in home surrounding and the companionship of his loving wife and merry group of little ones. He was married January 1, 1879, to Miss Susie Matthews, daughter of J.B. Matthews, of Albany, whose biography appears elsewhere. She is an accomplished lady of superior management, amiable and intelligent, a kind mother and genial companion, and has the love and respect of the community in which she was born and has spent her life. Eight children are the results of the marriage, all of whom are living: George Elton, Ella M., Willie D., Joseph, Annie Merle, Wendell Watkins, John, and Nathan B.

William D. and George Reynolds, as incorporators of the Reynolds Land and Cattle Company, are the owners of 100,000 acres of land, located principally in the counties of Shackelford, Throckmorton, and Haskell. They hold, at present, 20,000 head of cattle, making a specialty of breeding Herefords, and always having in their immense pastures some very fine specimens of this breed which has proven so valuable to modern breeders of Texas stock. W.D. Reynolds has some very large personal interests, including bank stock, ranch and city property. His residence is one of the most beautiful in Albany. Like the majority of old time Texans he values his wealth not for itself alone but for the good it can accomplish. He is always ready to do a kind and generous act; and at the time of the Cisco cyclone, in '93, he subscribed $250 for the benefit of the unfortunate ones.

The Reynolds family is of Scotch extraction. Barber Watkins Reynolds, father of W.D., was born in Geogia, married Anna Maria Campbell, the daughter of a prominent South Carolinian, and moved to Shelby County, Texas, bringing with him his wife and two sons, W.D. and George, an older son dying in infancy. Twelve years later when he removed to Fort Griffin, Shackelford County, the family had increased to five boys and two girls, all of whom are now living in or around Albany, with the exception of a son, Glenn, who was sheriff of Gila County, Arizona, and was killed November 2, 1890, by the notorious Apache Kid and his gang of eight Indians, while carrying them to the Arizona penitentiary. Mr. Reynolds' transactions in cattle dated from 1860, when he exchanged a Negro slave girl for a few head, and continue until his death, when the old family home was abandoned, and his widow took up her residence in Albany with her sons and daughters. Though seventy-eight years of age she is still hale and hearty, and enjoys life as thoroughly as many people one-third her years.

J.B. Matthews

J.B. Matthews is one of the oldest settlers of Shackelford

County. He located his ranch upon the Clear Fork of the Brazos when white residents in that region were few and far between, and Indians too abundant to be considered picturesque or otherwise interesting or desirable. Game was plentiful, and Mr. Matthews and his neighbors were never at a loss for a supply of venison or antelope steaks; but the trail leading to the nearest supply point was a long one, and in consequence there was a scarcity at times of the other necessaries of life. Thirty-five years have worked wonders in the development of this region. Railroads now surround Shackelford County on every side and pierce its very center. The Indians have all vanished and game is now little more than a memory, but many of the old time frontier dwellers still remain and among them the subject of this sketch.

John Matthews, the father of J.B., was a native of Georgia, as was also his wife, Elizabeth Harris. The greater portion of their married life was spent in Alabama, where they reared and educated a family of twelve children, a thirteenth dying in infancy. They were named according to age as follows: Nancy, Sallie, Winnie, Mary, Martha, Annie, Benjamin, John, Joseph B., James, Thomas, Andrew and Baker. Mr. Matthews died in Louisiana in 1859.

Born in Lowndes County, Alabama, August 24, 1824, Joseph B. Matthews was yet young when his father removed to Louisiana. He was married at Spearsville, in that state, to Miss Caroline Spears, and remained there for a few years, engaged in farming, with his father. Subsequently he crossed the Texas boundary and located for a time in Lusk County, then moved to Freestone County, and in 1859 located in Shackelford County, where he engaged actively in the cattle business. The Indians on the border were then quiet and peaceable, but in the first year of the Civil War they became very troublesome. Horse stealing was their principal and favorite pursuit, and they feasted upon stolen beef in preference to game. Making their raids during moonlight nights, and in the most unexpected quarters, they generally got away with the stock undetected. Mr. Matthews suffered as did also all of his neighbors, but never had any serious trouble with the Indians, though on occasions he was attacked by them while serving as scout. However, danger from Indians always threatened the settlers along the upper Brazos, and the need of protecting his home from their attack prevented Mr. Matthews from entering the army. The country was generally unsettled and perfect safety was a thing unknown. Tragedies were of frequent occurrence. In Palo Pinto County, about the time of Mr. Matthews' arrival, a man named Ko was killed while standing in his doorway. His assassin was never known. At Hubbard a man named

Joseph Beck Matthews ranch house down river from Fort Griffin.

Holden was killed by the Indians about 1859. About 1868 organized bands of cow thieves and desperadoes became such a nuisance that the citizens were compelled to take the law into their own hands, and a band of regulators around Fort Griffin took effective and positive methods to keep down crime. Wrong doers who fell in their hands were troublesome no longer. On one occasion they hung a lawyer, then the only one in the county, for defending a woman accused of poisoning her husband.

In 1863 or 1864, while Mr. Matthews was living on his ranch six miles below Fort Griffin, the Indians raided the settlement below him. The Lee ranch was attacked, Mr. and Mrs. Lee and one of their daughters massacred, and the rest of the family carried into captivity. Two years later they were rescued through the instrumentality of an old Negro, named Britt, who possessed considerable influence with the Indians, and often visited their camps. They usually held their captives for the hopes of obtaining ransom, and would take coffee and sugar or ponies in exchange.

They seemed to know how much ransom the friends of each prisoner could afford to pay, and always demanded as much as they could possibly hope to receive. Such is a brief description of Shackelford County twenty years ago, and of the hardships and dangers its citizens were then forced to contend with. But those troublous times soon ended, and with nothing to disturb him in the pursuit of his business of stock raising, Mr. Matthews soon became notedly successful. He is still busied in the cattle industry. Of the seven children that were born to him, six are still living, have married, and are living in and around Albany. His only son, J.A. Matthews, married Miss Sallie Reynolds, sister of G.T. and W.D. Reynolds, bankers and stockmen of the county. He is following his father's footsteps and devoting his time and energies to the cattle business. The five daughters have married well, and their husbands are counted among the most successful business men of the county. Bittie, the eldest, married G.T. Reynolds; Mary married John Larn; Martha, Mart Hoover; Susan, W.D. Reynolds, and Ella, F.E. Conrad. Mr. Matthews is justly proud of the family he has reared. They are worthy children of a worthy sire, and true types of that gentle, yet energetic, class of men and women to whom the new West is so largely indebted for its prosperity and social progress. Mr. Matthews has never shown any inclination for a political career, though his popularity would doubtless insure him recognition in case he should aspire to an office. So far his public services have been limited to holding the County Commissioner's office for a number of terms. He is a prominent Freemason and a strict member of the Presbyterian church.

Reprinted from *Historical and Biographical Records of the Cattle Industry and the Cattlemen of Texas and Adjacent Territories*. St. Louis: Woodward Tiernan Printing Co., 1895.

Sec. II: from *Prose and Poetry of the Livestock Industry*

William D. Reynolds

William D. Reynolds is one of the widely known cattlemen of the Southwest. As a native of the South, a citizen of Texas since his infancy, his earliest recollections are connected with the Lone Star State, and the principal efforts of his life have been directed in the development of one of the most promising regions of the globe. Starting in the cattle business on the open range, Mr. Reynolds has been a witness of mighty events in the progress of enlightened methods and subjugation of the wilderness to the uses of man. He has been an active participant in the evolution in America which will forever distinguish the last half of the nineteenth century as one of the most remarkable periods in the world's history. It is difficult or impossible in these times of affluence and peace to appreciate the conditions in West Texas for twenty years following 1860, when Mr. Reynolds first saw the plains. The most primitive conditions prevailed. The buffalo and the deer roamed over the vast stretches which were afterward occupied by the great herds of cattle; mustang horses grazed by thousands on the plains and the grassy valleys, and the creek bottoms abounded in wild turkeys and small game. The early settlers of Texas were poor in this world's goods—but they were rich in brotherly sentiment toward one another, and the most kind-hearted and hospitable people any country has ever known. The dugout or the log cabin may give shelter to peace and happiness, whose presence is not always felt in the elegantly appointed mansion. The early settlers of West Texas were essentially cowmen. No other occupation was thought possible, and upon these immense plains, with no advantages of education except those presented by contact with Nature and by the intense struggle for existence, were produced many of the most successful livestock men.

In the early days traveled roads were few and many miles apart, and settlers in their long journeys were guided by prominent land-marks or by the sun and the stars. Wagons were scarce, and markets were distant and difficult to reach. Travel was principally on horseback. The average cowman was a good rider and a good shot with the rifle, and was inured to long exertion, and acquainted with the habits and wily arts of the redskin, whose deadly enmity was a constant menace to the families and settlers for hundreds of miles along the Texas frontier. Indeed, Mr. Reynolds recalls the difficulty he himself experienced, after the Indian had finally been driven off the range, in avoiding the habit of constant watchfulness that became second nature to the frontiersman. This habit consisted in turning the head quickly from side to side while traveling in order to detect the presence of foe. Every rock, bush, and gully was possible shelter for lurking enemy, and constant vigilance was the price of safety. The only settlements in those days were on the banks of streams, as artificial earth "tanks," windmills, and artesian wells were unknown luxuries upon the plains. The settlers ground their grain for flour in handmills, and prices of commodities were so high that many families lived off the land and seldom visited a store. Yet the early settlers of Texas were happy, and set about cheerfully and with brave hearts clearing away the forest where necessary, plowing the ground, fencing the prairies, and preparing for the inevitable tide of immigration that set in from less favored states of the Union.

The region with which the fortunes of Mr. Reynolds were united was bordered on the west by the vast area known as the Staked Plains and the Trans-Pecos country, a portion of the sate almost wholly unknown. In remote parts of the Trans-Pecos country the [federal] government for years maintained military posts along the famous Butterfield Stage route, which followed a chain of forts far to the east of the Staked Plains, crossed the Pecos River at the noted pontoon bridge, now known as Horse Head Crossing, and for a distance of nearly 200 miles meandered through deep canyons and through rugged mountains, terminating at El Paso. But only a small part of the Staked Plains, even up to 1875, had been trodden by the foot of domestic animal or seen by the eye of white man. It was a great area of country, so little known that even the dauntless rangers, the fearless plainsman, or the well-supplied government troops had dared to traverse it only by following such well-defined routes as the Pecos River or the Butterfield Stage road. In this very region, at an altitude of five thousand feet, is now located one of the principal ranches of the Reynolds Brothers.

The veteran cowman in his reminiscent moods can tell a story that causes the heart to quicken its beat and carries the listener vividly back to the stirring scenes of pioneer days. The eye of the old cowman again sees the great black mass of buffaloes that once rolled and thundered along where yonder field of grain now waves; he lives again through the ceaseless vigilance he once kept around the bedded herd where the spires and domes of yonder town reflects against the horizon; or he feels once more the ominous uncertainty that precedes the approaching storm, that thundering, flashing monster that rides on the bosom of the night; he sees the lightning dancing on a thousand horns, and nerves himself for the explosion from the dream-like silence that pervades the herd, while, like a mother cooing her babe to sleep, he sings the song of the range night-watch to the object of his suspicions: then comes the wild flash, the deafening peal, and amidst a maelstrom of clattering hoofs and wild confusion, he rushes along in the blackness of night with the mighty stampede.

Can you imagine the transformation to be witnessed today?—where all was loneliness, uncertainty, and vastness of the prairie now reign contentment and bountifully provided homes.

The Reynolds family was one of the first families to locate permanently in Palo Pinto County. B.W. Reynolds, the father, was of Scotch descent, and inherited the sturdy characteristics that are recognized the world over as the foundation of the Scottish character. He came to Texas from Alabama, in 1847, and the outbreak of the Civil War found him with his family, consisting of a wife and seven children, at the border of civilization contesting with the Indian for a foot-hold. William D. was then a boy of fourteen years, but he was accustomed to outdoor life, and when the government troops were withdrawn from the frontier to take part in the war, he was enrolled with the Rangers, and during the war period he gained a practical experience in the field as an Indian fighter. The company of which he was a member consisted of forty men and was divided into four detachments of ten men each, one of the detachments being constantly in the field. The men not on duty looked after affairs at home, but were subject to call at any time. The Rangers wore no uniforms, as uniforms were luxuries not to be thought of. Each man provided his own horse and arms, and the most useful man was the one who had, as in the case of Mr. Reynolds, the qualitites of the scout—who could travel over a strange country and not become lost; whose instinct never failed to lead him in times of necessity to a water-hole; and who, securing a bead on an Indian, seldom failed to bring the enemy to the ground. The scouting parties patrolled the border constantly, for they were guarding defenseless women and children; and although the service led to many sanguinary encounters with Comanches, Kiowa, or the treacherous Apaches, Mr. Reynolds passed through the ordeal without bodily injury. The double-barrel shotgun was a favorite weapon with the early Rangers of West Texas, as it was a deadly instrument at close quarters. In one of the fights a soldier's blue overcoat which had been worn by one of the Indians was found upon the field. This coat had been pierced with twenty-nine buckshot in the course of the charge, and its former wearer was stretched out dead upon the prairie. The men who defended the border were as brave and coolheaded in times of the danger as any ever known in the annals of frontier life of America, otherwise the tide of civilization would have been swept far back to the established communities of the State. Once having gained a vantage-ground, these tireless heralds of a brighter day never relinquished their grasp except to advance another stride into the realm that had from time immemorial been claimed by the redman. The student of frontier life in West Texas is not surprised that men who gained recognized standing under these trying circumstances came to the front in the great movement of Texas cattle northward, which took place after the close of the Civil War. Many of the leading cattlemen discovered their ability while in conflict with the Indian.

In September, 1867, Mr. Reynolds went upon the trail. He engaged with Messrs. Loving & Goodnight at a salary of $50 a month, furnishing his own horse and saddle, as was customary in the earlier years of the trail. Mr. Reynolds was a cattle-owner himself, having acquired a modest holding of forty-two head of cattle. These cattle were driven north with the Loving & Goodnight herd and disposed of to J.W. Iliff at a fair price, so that early the following year the young cowman could claim $700 in cash and a mule worth $125 as a result of his first venture on the trail. As described elsewhere in this volume, Oliver Loving died on this trip from wounds received in conflict with the Indians. Mr. Reynolds was a member of the party that conducted the remains homeward over the trail to Weatherford. The body was placed in a metallic casket and conveyed in a wagon on the long journey to its final resting-place.

In the spring of 1868, Mr. Reynolds and his brother, George, began business for themselves, and the partnership has existed without interruption since that time. Although each of the brothers owns and operates independent ranches, the operations of the Reynolds Brothers in livestock for a third of a century past have been equaled in magnitude by only a few firms or individuals of the Southwest. The brothers each brought to the work certain qualities which led to success in almost everything they have undertaken, the field extending into banking, merchandise, real estate, cotton seed oil mills, and other enterprises connected with the growth of a newly settled region. From the start the operations of Mr. Reynolds have been based upon sound business principles, and the element of speculation has had practically nothing to do with the outcome. The Reynolds Land and Cattle Company is known as one of the best-managed corporations of Texas, and the financial standing of the brothers, as early as 1868, was such that they purchased cattle on credit for their first trail-herd to Colorado. This credit has never since been impaired.

The Texas headquarters of the Reynoldses were in Shackelford County of the Clear Fork of the Brazos River; but they early perceived the importance of a ranch further north, and in 1868 they established a ranch in the valley of the Arkansas, which was maintained for eight years. The headquarters of this ranch were on the north side of the Arkansas River, about a mile from the present town of La Junta. Thousands of Texas Longhorns were brought in from the south and distributed from this ranch. Mr. Reynolds went over the trail with a herd as far west as Salt Lake, Utah, and his trips led him north into Montana and North Dakota. He usually spent the winters in Texas, and as time passed and the Arkansas Valley ranch was encroached upon by newcomers, it was decided to change the base of operations again to Texas.

The power of the Indians had been largely broken, and a severe drouth in Southern Colorado caused short grass with its attendant inconveniences. The herd, which numbered

4,500 head of improved stock, was driven south eighty miles to winter and thence to the Canadian River. Early in the spring of 1878, the entire heard was sold to Charles Goodnight, and thus became the foundation of the celebrated "J.A." herd.

A goodly number of well-improved cattle had been retained by the Reynolds Brothers, and the ranch in Shackelford County now became a principal theater of operations, and has since been developed until it is one of the finest ranches in Texas.

Mr. Reynolds has, from his first experience as a cattle-owner, been a warm advocate of improving the herd and thus producing good form and quality. He early introduced bulls from the T.L. Miller farm at Beecher, Ills., and has been for thirty years a large patron of pedigreed stock. Operations have increased from year to year, until as many as 50,000 cattle are grazed at one time upon the Reynolds ranches, and the "Long X" brand was placed upon 17,000 calves in 1900. For fourteen years a ranch was maintained in North Dakota, but in 1902 the headquarters of the northern herd were changed to Milk River, Montana. Cattle of one, two, and three years old are sent to the Montana ranch to be finished for the market. At one time 20,000 sheep were handled on the Texas range, but the herd was gradually sold off. Under favorable grass conditions, Mr. Reynolds regards sheep as a desirable adjunct to cattle. He is an advocate of Hereford cattle as the best range stock, looking always to a moderate mixture of Short-horn blood in the herd to give it bone and body. Some of the handsomest specimens of Herefords in Texas are upon ranches controlled by the Reynoldses.

Mr. Reynolds has all his life been a practical man. Entertaining the broadest views as to the rights and opinions of others, he is a firm believer in the gospel of work, and he regards a willingness to labor as one of the most encouraging features in the character of any man. "Work," said he, "has been the salvation of many of man, and the greatest danger that can menace any country is the disinclination of young people to labor. There is always hope for the industrious man, and the most important part of education is to teach the young the dignity and the lasting utility of applying their energies in useful directions. Work is the greatest blessing we can imagine—far greater than mere good education, when the latter is applied to one who has no vital interest and cannot absorb it.

"Texas," said he, "is destined to be the leading producing State of the Union, and the prophecy of Judge John H. Reagan that the state will some day have a population of 25,000,000 people, is no exaggeration. Consider the immense area, the diversified climates of the state, the variety and fertility of the soils, the livestock interests, the vegetables that can be raised, the sugar, rice, cotton, corn, and wheat and forage plants, and the great area yet available for cultivation. People of Texas who have lived in the state all their lives do not appreciate its resources. The possibilities are simply beyond our imagination. Manufacturing has not yet started in the state, and Texas is just as capable of maintaining large factories and supplying the raw material as any state in the Union.

"As to West Texas," said he, "the changes of the last thirty years surpass belief. We have many of the advantages of the North and the Northwest. It is always cool in the shade: in West Texas the air is pure and dry, and there is no malaria. West Texas is going to be a great cotton country. Cotton is not a wet-weather plant, and it can be grown even in the dry years.

"When I first went upon the range we never thought of

land being worth anything. Afterwards the great pastures were fenced, and we were assured that West Texas and the Panhandle would always be a range country, as Providence had so ordained it. Along came the farmer, and we found we had a farming country. Now it is known that a man with a family can live well and make money on four sections of land. The result is that land is selling at $5.00 an acre and upwards, and values are advancing. Ultimately all of that part of the State as far west as the Pecos River will be divided up into small farms and ranches, and hundreds of thousands of people will occupy the region formerly roamed over by the buffalo and the Indian."

One of the sorrows of the life of Mr. Reynolds was the violent death of his brother, Glenn, Sheriff of Gila County, Arizona, November 2, 1890. Glenn Reynolds was for many years prominently identified with the Texas Rangers in ridding the State of the most desperate class of cattle rustlers any state has known. These reckless characters threatened extermination to the stock business upon the border ranges, and as the cattle thieves were armed with the most improved weapons that money could buy and were thoroughly acquainted with their use, the rustlers were much more dangerous enemies than were the Indians. Glenn Reynolds was one of the leaders who cleared Texas of these desperadoes. He first showed the mettle that was in him, when a lad, defending his home on the Clear Fork of the Brazos from an attack of Indians. This was in 1865. Later he became recognized throughout West Texas as a dead-shot and one of the most fearless men ever known in the state. In 1885 he moved to Arizona, and it was while conducting Apache Kid and eight of his followers to the penitentiary that Glenn Reynolds lost his life. The Indians were chained together in threes, and the sheriff was assisted by only one deputy. On account of the difficult nature of the road, the sheriff and his prisoners descended from the vehicle in which they were riding. At a preconcerted signal the prisoners attacked the sheriff and deputy and instantly killed them. The circumstances of the tragedy were never fully disclosed, but it is believed that during one fatal moment the ever-watchful Glenn Reynolds was off his guard. Apache Kid and his followers escaped across the line into the mountains of Mexico. Troops of the United States and Mexican governments made every effort to avenge the deed, and the Reynolds Brothers offered a reward of $5,000 for the capture of Apache Kid. Several months later the watch of Glenn Reynolds was found on the body of an Apache who was killed in Mexico. The watch was sent to Washington, and Secretary James G. Blaine, of the Department of State, restored it to the Reynolds family at Albany, Texas. A revolver belonging to Sheriff Reynolds was also recovered. It is believed that the entire party of Apaches met their merited punishment in conflict with Federal troops in Mexico, but the fate of Apache Kid has never been officially reported.

In management of his extensive ranch interests, Mr. Reynolds has adhered to the principle of advancing capable employees, and many of the men upon the Reynolds ranches have spent the most of their active career in the service of one employer. A faithful employee thus receives merited recognition, and a feeling as of one large family is a pleasing characteristic of these ranches. Mr. Reynolds is the gentlest of masters, and is so quiet and unostentatious in manner that he is in marked contrast to many men in charge of much smaller affairs. A simple "yes" or "no" from him has more meaning in an important business transaction than a half-hour's talk from many men of less impressive character.

Mr. Reynolds is a man of handsome form and countenance, and has an air of self-possession and a personal magnetism that have assisted him greatly in influencing others throughout his long business career. His is one who possesses within himself the resources capable of clearing a way through any obstacle, or removing the obstacle itself. He is recognized as one of the leading men of Texas, not on account of large wealth, but on account of natural ability, sound judgment, and financial acumen possessed by few men, even of the great State of Texas. He is a member of the Presbyterian Church, a Mason of high standing, and belongs to the class of men who give strength and dignity to a state and durability to a nation.

Mr. Reynolds was married January 1, 1879, to Miss Susie Matthews, daughter of J.B. Matthews, of Albany, Texas, where the family made its home until 1903, when Fort Worth was selected as the place of residence.

The following children have been the result of the married: George Elton, Ella M., Willie D., Joseph, Annie Merle, Wendell Watkins, John, and Nathan B.

Mr. Reynolds began in the cattle business when there was no market for cattle, and the only outlet of the Texas live-stock man was to trade his cattle in East Texas for horses or barter them in small lots for the necessities of life. As an early trailman, Mr. Reynolds became acquainted with the possibilities and the natural resources of the country east of the Rocky Mountains—the greatest natural cattle country to be found on the globe. This information has been to him of inestimable value in the many transactions he has been required to pass upon.

The valley of the Arkansas, where once he ranched, is now a smiling garden, threaded with railroads and teeming with a vigorous population. The slow-moving trail-herd has given way to the special-scheduled livestock train, and the

Texas Longhorn is superseded by some of the most beautiful types of animals to be seen in the world. The hand of destiny points to still greater achievements in years to come, and it is the ambition of Mr. Reynolds that his sons may perform their share in the mighty work yet to be accomplished.

George T. Reynolds

The lives of some men are immensely inspiring. The simple presentation, without any attempt at ornament, fixes the attention, arouses the interest, and instills a lesson which is never forgotten. The Bible is a striking illustration of the power of biography, and it is probable that the Bible will stand as long as the history of the human race survives as the greatest collection of lives in the world.

The lesson of biography is to show what man has accomplished, and therefore what those who follow may accomplish. The lives of men of action are a constant encouragement whose value it is impossible to estimate. As has been aptly said: "The career of a useful man remains an enduring monument of human energy." It is a legacy to the world, more to be prized than mere wealth, the possessor of which is often quickly forgotten. Life in the final analysis is simply a great school of experience, in which the highest object is the development of noble character.

These few words of introduction lead to the remark that among the livestock men of America are to be found many of the most inspiring characters history has produced. The pioneer livestock men were, in a number of instances, great men—men of unshaken resolution, undaunted courage, great strength of character, and power of foresight. They were men who commanded because of natural fitness for the position, and their judgement on important questions connected with the industry was almost unerring. The early Texas cowman is recognized the world over as a master of his calling. The man who gained acknowledged standing on the open range and on the trail in the decade following the Civil War, and who has held his position through all the changes the industry has witnessed, belongs to a type justly held in highest esteem. It is a type now rapidly passing from the stage. In a few years the last of the pioneer cowmen will have departed, and a new generation with new ideas, new methods, will be at the helm.

On the 14th of February, 1844, in Montgomery County, Alabama, George T. Reynolds first saw the light of day. Could his parents have been given a correct horoscope of the life of their son, they would have rejected it as wholly impossible. It would have seemed stranger than a tale from the Arabian

George T. Reynolds house built in 1875 in Reynolds Bend on the Clear Fork

Nights; it would have revealed a path beset by dangers of the most startling-nature—the trials of the rough frontier—the tragedies of the Civil War—innumerable conflicts with blood-thirsty Indians—vicissitudes and perils of the cattle-trail—startling changes of fortune, and finally a position of ease and affluence which the brightest imagination of the pioneer, half a century ago, could hardly have pictured. The life of Mr. Reynolds presents all the phases necessary for a drama of surpassing human interest, and the mind is led to the conclusion that surely in this instance a divine Providence exercised a special prerogative in protecting the life of a favorite child. Mr. Reynolds, himself at the age of three-score, does not hesitate to ascribe his preservation in times of extreme danger, to the prayers of his mother, a woman of distinguishing traits of character, strong mental qualities, and of profound religious convictions. The world is a sphinx, and human life is often a riddle, but in this instance there is evidence of a power unseen, whose preserving influence has enabled Mr. Reynolds to live and enjoy the fruits of many years of toil and self-denial.

The father of Mr. Reynolds, B.W. Reynolds, was a genuine frontiersman. He was of Scotch descent, a native of Georgia, and in 1836 engaged as a soldier in the Seminole War. He was united in marriage to Miss Anna M. Campbell, and attracted westward by opportunity of providing for his growing family, he emigrated to Texas in 1847. George T. was then three years of age, and Texas has been his home during a larger part of the time that has elapsed. The family settled in Shelby County, and there remained for thirteen years. In 1860, just before the outbreak of the Civil War, another move was decided upon, as East Texas had become almost as thickly inhabited as the older states towards the East. After stopping in Weatherford, the family located for a time in Palo Pinto County, a few months later settling in a beautiful spot on the Clear Fork of the Brazos River in the northern part of Stephens County. Weatherford was then the advance post of civilization in West Texas. Beyond Weatherford, as far west as El Paso, 600 miles of rolling prairie was in almost undisturbed possession of the Indian and buffalo. Any man prophesying its settlement within fifty years would have been classed as a dreamer. It was an immense open range, destined by nature as the years passed to become one of the greatest cattle-breeding regions the world ever knew: not, however, until after many great obstacles had been overcome and at the cost of immense hardships and suffering.

"The history of the trials and suffering of the early settlers of West Texas will never be written," said Mr. Reynolds, in referring to experiences of life upon the frontier. "The most of the actors have passed away, and a line of graves extending from Weatherford as far west as the Rio Grande River tells a story more impressive than words. I doubt if any region of similar area in the United States ever witnessed so many tragedies as the result of encounters with the red man. The settlers were subject for many years to excursions of the Comanches, Kiowas, Kickapoos, and other plains tribes, and a man traveled with his gun in his hand, and was obliged to be as wary as the Indian himself if he reached the end of his journey to safety. Every frontiersman was a good horseman, a good shot, and the successful man was also an athlete, and ran great risks in protecting his property from the thieving and murderous foes that infested the country. Picket houses for the protection of families were erected at convenient points, and there the women and children gathered while the men scoured the surrounding country to rid it of the inveterate foe. Under these circumstances, little opportunity was offered for education in the rude log schoolhouses, and the boys and girls grew up without the advantages of education now offered even in the back districts."

Mr. Reynolds calls attention to the fact that there is scarcely an instance on record in the State of Texas of the marriage of a white man to an Indian squaw. In extensive travels which he has made among Indian tribes of North America he found squaw-men in all the States as far north as Alaska, except in Texas. In Texas the continual hostility that prevailed between the whites and the Indians was an effective bar to the formation of family ties between the two races. Nowhere else did the Indian make such desperate efforts to retain the hunting-grounds of his fathers, and the prolonged contest cost thousands of lives and immense sacrifices in time, exertion, and money. The line of the frontier, extending back into the settlements for a hundred miles or more, was a battle-line, where any day of the year an encounter to the death might be witnessed. Surely here is material for the most sensational yellow-back novel.

Although settlers on the Indian border were exempt from conscription during the Civil War, having quite enough fighting on their hands to hold back the Indians, Mr. Reynolds enlisted in the Confederate service, and at eighteen years of age was enrolled in Company E, 19th Texas Cavalry, Colonel Nat Buford in command. The regiment took part in the raids of Marmaduke in Missouri and Arkansas. Mr. Reynolds was so severely wounded in 1863 that he received an honorable discharge from the service, and he returned to his home in Texas to enter upon a most exciting career.

At twenty years of age Mr. Reynolds began to think seriously of locating himself and making a permanent start in the cattle business. He was well equipped to meet the exigencies of the frontier. Soon after arriving in West Texas, as a boy, he had engaged in carrying the mail between

Weatherford and Palo Pinto, often riding by night to avoid encounter with Indians. The war experience was most impressive and gave him a confidence in himself and his own resources which assisted greatly in his ultimate success in directing large enterprises. He was versed by actual experience of several years in the saddle, knew nothing of fear, and was a born Indian fighter.

In January, 1864, Mr. Reynolds set out with six companions in search of a new location farther south, where the Indians might not be so troublesome. The party was obliged to subsist entirely on buffalo and deer meat for several days, and finally on the Concho River, in the region of Kickapoo Springs, they came upon a band of Indians driving a herd of stolen horses. The Indians leaped upon the backs of fresh horses and escaped, the herd falling into the hands of the white men. Mr. Reynolds came into possession of a Texas saddle, which bore the blood stains of its former owner. The party started to drive the horse herd to Fort Mason and turn the horses over to the military, but at San Saba, fell into the hands of a company of Texas Rangers. Here Mr. Reynolds and his friends were thrown into a room as prisoners and horse-thieves, and were in great danger of losing their lives, as the Rangers dealt out only one penalty to gentlemen of that persuasion. The good fortune of Mr. Reynolds prevailed; he was recognized by a member of the Rangers who had formerly worked for his father, and the release of the whole party was effected. This was a narrow escape, and led to the abandonment of the project of establishing a new home.

The next adventure of interest was a fight with a band of eighteen Indians belonging to the noted Satanta's followers. Satanta was the terror of West Texas settlers, and had swooped upon them at the head of 500 warriors, who distributed themselves over a wide expanse of thinly populated country, killing settlers, burning their houses, and driving off the livestock. The Indians killed nineteen men, women, and children on this raid, and created general distress along the frontier. The Civil War was still in progress, government troops were withdrawn, and the settlers were obliged to depend upon themselves for defense and retaliation. Under these circumstances, when seven white men, Mr. Reynolds among the number, encountered a party of eighteen Indians in camp, there was instant battle. As the whites dashed upon the foe, the horse of Mr. Reynolds gave out and sank to the ground, but the rider shot an Indian from his pony, snatched the reins of the pony, and assisted in putting the Indians to flight, losing a leg of his pantaloons in close encounter, and escaping narrowly with his life from an arrow. Three of the Indians were killed. Satanta afterwards committed suicide in the government prison [in Huntsville, Texas].

At the close of the Civil War Mr. Reynolds drove a small heard of 100 steers to [New?] Mexico, and disposed of them at a fair profit. This was one of his first trail experiences, and led to extensive operations in which the Reynolds brothers gained a wide reputation as trail-men. Their name became known as far west as California and north to the line of British America. Previous to this, however, there were many trying experiences to pass through. One of these experiences was caused in 1866 by a raid of the Indians, in which they ran off 500 head of cattle belonging to the Reynoldses. This included even the milk cows, and as the horses of the ranch were lost in the same raid, operations were for several months almost brought to a standstill. The Reynolds family had a lease upon the Stone Ranch in Throckmorton County, but bravely decided to remain on the ranch, gradually gathering in cattle of their own brand, which had not been driven entirely out of the country. Many encounters took place with the Indians, who twice attacked the home of the elder Reynolds.

One day an incident occurred which led to quite a serious complication, not with Indians, but with regularly authorized officers of the law. A boy named Jack Marshall, nicknamed "Jacko," was in the employ of the outfit. Mr. Reynolds had befriended him on occasions when attempts to impose upon him were made by other members of the party, but the kindly spirit was poorly recognized. "Jacko" rode out of camp on the back of one of the best horses owned by Mr. Reynolds. As soon as the theft was known, pursuit was inaugurated, and the boy was captured on Morgan's Ranch near Weatherford. He was conveyed into Palo Pinto County, where a council was held, and in a few minutes a rawhide rope was hanging over the limb of a postoak, one end of the rope around the neck of the horse-thief. He pleaded so earnestly for life that the sentence was commuted to a sound flogging, the boy promising to go east of the Brazos River and never return. Flogging under such circumstances was a criminal offense in Texas, and as Mr. Reynolds performed the act, he soon met John Newcomb, Deputy Sheriff of Palo Pinto County, who had a warrant for his arrest. The meeting took place in the roadway, but the young Texas cowboy proved too quick for the officer of the law. He threw his revolver down on the deputy and announced that he was on his way to the Stone Ranch and expected to proceed without any further interruption. Warning the deputy not to follow, Mr. Reynolds rode on to the ranch unmolested. A short time afterwards, however, a new difficulty presented itself. Mr. Reynolds was engaged to be married to a daughter of J.B. Matthews, and it was necessary, as the time for the ceremony approached, that the prospective bridegroom should visit Palo Pinto to secure a marriage license. He invited two of his cowboy friends to accompany him. It was not an ordinary procession that rode into the town of Palo Pinto that

The State of Texas, }
County of Shackelford. }   Albany, Texas, November 3, 1952

    My name is Ben G. Reynolds. I have resided in Albany, and an adjoining county for over fifty years. I have been City Marshall and Chief of Police of Albany continuously for the past twenty years. I am a nephew of George T. Reynolds and William D. Reynolds both deceased.

    In relating some of his early experiences to me my uncle, George T. Reynolds, told me that after he returned from his Service in the Confederate Army he had in 1866 a cowboy working for him called Jaco who stole his personal cowhorse and a fine overcoat belonging to William D. Reynolds.

    Jaco was overtaken and captured near Palo Pinto with the horse and overcoat. It was then an unwritten law and custom to hang a horse thief when captured. The men with George T. Reynolds voted to hang Jaco, but George T. Reynolds felt sorry for the boy and prevented his being hung but in their presence gave him a good whipping with a quirt and let him go giving him both a horse and the overcoat he had stolen as the weather was cold.

    Jaco went to Weatherford which was dominated by Carpetbaggers and filed a complaint, and it was noised abroad that George T. Reynolds would be arrested if he could be caught by the Carpetbaggers.

    My uncle George T. Reynolds told me that when he went to the Courthouse in Palo Pinto after his marriage license in July, 1867 armed cowboys went with him to protect him from Carpetbaggers, and they stood guard around the Courthouse when he went in after his marriage license, and that he was never arrested but when the facts were known he was exonerated from any wrongdoing.

                               Ben G. Reynolds

    Sworn to and subscribed by Ben G. Reynolds, before me, the undersigned authority, on this 3rd day of November, A.D. 1952.

    Given under my hand and seal of office at Albany, Texas.

                          Ann Coker
    SEAL   Notary Public in and for Shackelford County, Texas.

An affidavit signed by Ben G. Reynolds concerning the altercation with Jacko.

day. Each man carried a shotgun heavily loaded, and four revolvers. The trio had only one mission to perform, proceeded about it leisurely in broad daylight and without any apparent nervousness, and, although the Sheriff's office received notice of the visit, there was no attempt to stop the proceedings. Mr. Newcomb, formerly deputy sheriff, has been for years upon one of the ranches of Mr. Reynolds as a trusted employee.

One of the remarkable adventures in the life of Mr. Reynolds—an experience that stands perhaps without a parallel in the history of border Indian warfare—took place on the 3rd day of April, 1867. Mr. Reynolds was then twenty-three years of age, fully inured to hardships of the dangerous life he had been leading from the time he first reached West Texas, and had an acknowledged reputation among the frontiersmen of West Texas as an Indian fighter. In company with his brother, William, and eight others, he started upon an Indian trail which led to the mouth of the Double Mountain Fork, in what is now known as Haskell County. The Indians were skinning a buffalo when the white men caught sight of them, but one of the savages started immediately in the direction of the unexpected visitors, a revolver in each hand, firing as he advanced. The bullets flew wide of the mark, and, waiting until the foe had emptied his revolvers, Mr. Reynolds fired, shooting the Indian through the body. When the Indian turned to run, a second shot broke his neck. In the fight which followed an arrow passed into the body of Mr. Reynolds. He drew the wooden shaft from the wound, but the iron arrow-head remained, fixed in the muscles of the back. The blood gushed forth in a volume, and apparently the end was at hand.

"While I was lying on the ground," said Mr. Reynolds, "my friend, Si Hough, rode up and asked: 'Which Indian was it shot you?' 'The one in the red shirt,' was my reply. 'I will have the scalp of that Indian!' exclaimed Hough, with an oath, as he put spurs to his horse and plunged forward. In a few minutes Hough returned, waving a scalp-lock in the air. 'Here's your man with the red shirt,' said he."

Mr. Reynolds was in a desperate condition. More than 100 miles from the nearest physician at Weatherford, with no means of transportation homeward except on horseback, and his home sixty miles away—death seemed absolutely certain. There was one a hope, however, that sustained him. He was engaged to be married to a charming young lady, and he determined that death should not interfere with the program. It was his nerve that saved him. He had assisted many wounded men in the Civil War, and now his experience on the battle-field came into practical use. It was necessary to reach home as quickly as possible, and he had strength to direct that he should be placed across the backs of two steady pack-horses. The constant jar caused the blood to collect in the cavity of the body, and at frequent intervals the wounded man was taken from his position and laid upon the ground so as to allow the blood opportunity of escaping. The journey was a terrific experience, but Mr. Reynolds reached home alive, and five days later, when the physician appeared, the patient had passed the critical stage, and in a few weeks he was again in the saddle.

A feature of special interest connected with the event, as told by Mr. Reynolds, is that his father saw the battle with the Indians in a dream the night before. He saw the arrow sticking through the body of his son, and in the morning he related the vision to his family. He felt that his son was dead, but in this respect the psychic impression was not true. The son lived to marry the girl of his choice, Miss L.E. Matthews, who is by his side at this writing, and has been to him a devoted wife and wise adviser.

The arrow-head, which was the cause of a vast amount of suffering, remained in its place for sixteen years. At last Mr. Reynolds decided to submit to a surgical operation for its removal. He went to Kansas city, and for three days the surgeons consulted as to the possibility of his surviving the proposed operation. Years of suffering had convinced Mr. Reynolds that the head of the arrow was in his body, although the surgeons would not agree that this could be possible. When the operation was finally performed, an iron arrow-head two and a half inches long was found, which had almost worked its way through the muscles of the back. The arrow had, sixteen years before, passed between the folds of the stomach and the intestines without injuring either seriously. Fortunately the stomach was empty at the time. Mr. Reynolds submitted to the operation without the use of anaesthetics. A. E. Pierce, known in the live-stock world as "Shanghai" Pierce, was present when the arrow-head was removed. The relic is now in possession of Mr. Reynolds.[i]

The following is the certificate of the surgeon performing the operation:

"Kansas City, MO, August 1, 1882.

"This is to certify that on Tuesday, July 17, 1882, at the St. James Hotel, Kansas City, Missouri, with the assistance of Dr. Griffith, of Kansas City, and Dr. Powell of New York City, I successfully removed a steel or iron arrow-head from the back of George T. Reynolds, of Fort Griffin, Texas, and that the said arrow-head entered the body in front and passed directly through his abdominal cavity and lodged in the muscles of his back on the 3d day of April 1867. M.D. Lewis, M.D."

In the summer of 1868, Mr. Reynolds drove a herd of

cattle through to Mexico. His young wife accompanied him on the trip but the Indians proved too numerous and crafty. They stole all the horses of the party, and the venture did not prove as successful as Mr. Reynolds expected. He accordingly decided to locate a ranch in the North, outside the Indian country, near the cattle-trail, and accordingly established himself in Bent County, Colorado, where now the flourishing town of La Junta is situated. This ranch he and his brother, William, conducted for a number of years engaging also during the same time in many livestock enterprises. In 1870 cattle were brought over the trail from Texas, and the brothers drove them north to Cheyenne and west to Salt Lake, where the cattle were sold at $25.00 a head. Pushing still further west, the Reynolds brothers purchased a herd of California horses, which were delivered to them at Reno, Nevada, and drove the horses back to Colorado, where they were disposed of at a handsome profit. Four years later the brothers drove a second large herd of Texas cattle to Utah and Nevada. This herd was bought of Charles Rivers, near Weatherford, Texas. This transaction nearly cost Mr. Reynolds and Mr. Rivers their lives. They were sleeping side by side under the same blanket upon the ground. A party of Indians dashed into the camp, filling the air with bullets, one of which passed through the body of Mr. Rivers. The whirlwind passed over the camp, and the stricken man knew that he must die.

"Oh, my poor wife and children!" exclaimed he. "What will become of them?"

Mr. Reynolds had gone into camp two miles away, but visited the camp of Mr. Rivers early in the evening, and was prevailed upon to remain for the night. His own outfit of sixty horses was not discovered by the Indians, but all the horses of Mr. Rivers were stampeded and lost. In the neighborhood was camped J.C. Loving, a brother-in-law of Mr. Rivers. Mr. Loving was summoned to the side of the dying man, whose sense of business responsibility was so great that he requested him to see that the contact with the Reynolds brothers was fully complied with. The wishes of Mr. Rivers were respected, and the cattle were delivered at the appointed time. Mr. Reynolds conducted herds for years to North Dakota and Montana and as far north as the British possessions. He established a ranch in North Dakota, which was maintained for fourteen years, where he delivered over 50,000 head of cattle from Texas. Later, a large ranch was located by the brothers on Milk River, Montana, where many of their Texas steers have been fattened for the market.

A number of times in the course of his history Mr. Reynolds was obliged to take refuge in the thickets from Indians; but one of his narrow escapes was from a heavy whip handle at the hands of an angry German ranchman, whose range was on the plains east of Denver, Colorado. The ranchman's name was Herman. As Mr. Reynolds was passing with a herd of cattle the German appeared and demanded, in authoritative tones, that the cattle should be stopped and rounded up. He desired to look the herd over, claiming that some of his cattle were in it. Although Mr. Reynolds knew the assertion was not true, he acquiesced, and soon the German was at work. The first animal cut out was a black cow with the brand of the elder Reynolds upon her. Ten or eleven more cattle were rapidly separated from the main herd. Mr. Reynolds protested, which aroused the German to a furious degree, and he rushed at Mr. Reynolds to strike him with a heavy whip handle. A moment later the assailant was lying on the ground with a bleeding skull. The skull had come into contact with the white-handled revolver of Mr. Reynolds, and a cowboy who came forward at an opportune moment, completed the work of subduing the irate ranchman.

War was now declared. The German swore out a warrant for the arrest of Mr. Reynolds, and for several years Denver was debatable ground for Mr. Reynolds to visit. As the sheriff, his deputies, and the cowmen generally, were friends of the Reynoldses, Mr. Reynolds always succeeded in receiving the "tip" before the officers of the law arrived at the hotel where he was stopping when necessarily in the city.

Mr. Reynolds has been personally acquainted with nearly all the leading cattlemen of the southwest since the industry assumed any importance in that region. He was upon the trail with John S. Chisum, John Sparks, Richard King, "Shanghai" Pierce, Seth Mabry, Charles Goodnight, J.C. Loving, C.C. Slaughter, and a score of scarcely less noted names of those exciting times. Kit Carson and Dick Wooton were warm friends of Mr. Reynolds. Si Hough, heretofore named in this article, was one of the peculiar characters of the plains. "Hough," said Mr. Reynolds, "was an ideal plainsman, and was most at home when in the excitement of a fight with the Indians. He lifted the scalp of many a red skin. One day three of us, Hough among the number, were traveling on the Pecos. A war party of 500 Navajo was in the immediate vicinity, and we were on the lookout. Our horses were almost exhausted, and we knew we were in very bad condition for a fight. Suddenly we saw three men on horseback coming towards us. We were in a peculiar condition, and we expected fight with the chances all against us, for after the fight started the whole 500 red devils would be upon us. Then it was that Hough showed his metal. 'Boys' said he, 'don't shoot until they come within range of my shotgun. I'm good for two of them.'

"When we had approached a little nearer we threw our

glass down on them, and discovered that it was a little party of United States soldiers. It was one of the greatest reliefs of my life. Great drops of perspiration were upon our faces, showing the strain that was upon us."

It is said the bravest men turn pale at the approach of battle, and the acknowledgment of Mr. Reynolds is an evidence of the truth of the statement. It is impossible for a generation living under the blessings of peace and general prosperity to appreciate fully the dangers and struggles which the early cowmen were obliged to endure.

"The plains Indians," said Mr. Reynolds, "had peculiar ideas concerning the future life. In one of our fights in Shackelford County we scalped several of the Indians, but one of the wounded Indians got away and died in a thicket. We returned to the battlefield a few days after the fight. The Indians had paid no attention to those of their comrades who had lost their scalps. Their bodies were left lying upon the ground, as it is a belief among them that the warrior who loses his scalp goes to the bad hunting-ground. We found the grave of the warrior who died with his scalp on. His shield was buried with him with its face to the sand and in the shield cover was a looking-glass and also a plug of tobacco, wrapped up in a newspaper know as *Brick Pomeroy's Democrat*, bearing the date of June 1, 1886. The fight took place in April, 1887. The horse of the dead warrior had failed to carry its rider safely and therefore was not entitled to go to the good hunting ground, so his foretop was cut off.

"Traveling north on the trail to Kit Carson, in West Kansas, we one night met I.W. Allen now of Kansas City, and a party of cowmen, bound for the Arkansas valley. They gave an alarming story of the depredations of the Cheyennes upon grading camps along the Kansas Pacific Railroad. We proceeded to Kit Carson, where we arrived at daybreak, and for hours dead bodies were being brought into camp. It was the greatest killing I ever knew the Indians to accomplish, and before night there were forty or fifty bodies laid out at Kit Carson. The Indians had literally cleaned up the grading camps for fifty miles along the railway.

"The Indian is often a good judge of human nature, and he knows the difference between a tenderfoot and a real fighter. One evening on the Yellowstone I sent several men out to establish a camp at the mouth of the river. A band of twenty Indians under Chief Crow-Fly-High rode into the camp as if aching for a fight. 'One more sleep, you go!' commanded the chief, pointing sternly in the direction he wished the campers to take. The men were panic-stricken, and nearly killed their horses getting back to our camp, fully believing they had narrowly escaped with their lives. In reality it was all a bluff."

Mr. Reynolds and his brother, Benjamin, killed the first white buffalo of which there is any record in Texas. The animal was a two-year-old bull, and the skin of this buffalo is in the Smithsonian Institute at Washington. Several white buffaloes were killed in Texas during the period of 1873 to 1878, when extermination of the great herds was in progress upon the plains.

Although Mr. Reynolds has been obliged, far beyond the ordinary, to mourn the death of friends and relatives on account of Indian atrocities, the death of his brother, Glenn, was one of the heaviest blows he has known. Glenn Reynolds gained a high reputation in Texas as a cowman, ranger, and officer of the law. He moved to Arizona, where, while serving as Sheriff of Gila County conveying Apache Kid and seven of his followers to the Federal penitentiary, he was murdered.

When quite a young man Mr. Reynolds chained the county line of Shackelford County. He was at his father's house when Captain Sul Ross of the Texas Rangers, late governor of Texas, arrived there in charge of Cynthia Ann Parker, who had been rescued from captivity among the Indians.

Mrs. Reynolds, the mother of the family, is still living at the age of eighty-six years, in possession of health and remarkably clear mental faculties. Of her children, the following are alive: George T.; W.D., partner of George T. since 1868; B.F., County Judge of Throckmorton County; P.W., in charge of an oil mill at Cisco, Texas; Mrs. J.A. Matthews and Mrs. N.L. Bartholomew, both of Albany, Texas.

Mr. Reynolds has witnessed many great changes in the cattle industry. One of the most disastrous was in 1886, when the firm lost 10,000 cattle from drouth on the plains of Texas. The surviving cattle were driven over the trail to the Yellowstone River, arriving late in the fall, to encounter one of the severest winters ever known on the northern ranges. Nearly all the herd perished in the snow. Through good judgment and active business management, the losses were recouped, and the firm is one of the largest in Texas today. Their holdings include large ranches owned or leased in Shackelford, Pecos, and Davis Counties, Texas; in the Black River range, New Mexico; and on Milk River, Montana. Upon these ranges more than 50,000 cattle are grazed yearly. Mr. Reynolds has been for many years extensively interested also in organizing and managing banks, in cotton seed oil mills, and in large enterprises incident to the growth of a growing country. Albany, Shackelford County, was his home until 1901, when he took up his residence in Fort Worth, filling the position of president of the Forth Worth Live Stock Commission Company. He has found time, notwithstanding his numerous business engagements, to travel extensively, and has developed into an enthusiastic fisherman. One of his recent catches was a fish of 350 pounds off Catalina Island.

The life of Mr. Reynolds has been governed by the following principles: To do the best he could in everything he undertook, never to yield to discouragement or to apparent defeat; to deal justly with all men. It is his abiding conviction that the person who lives up to these principles cannot fail of true success.

EDITOR'S NOTE

[i] The arrow head, the pistol used in killing the Indian, and the bridle from the Indian's horse are in the National Cowboy Hall of Fame in Oklahoma City.

A Parting Word

The history of the Fort Griffin and Clear Fork area is among the richest in Texas. It lacks the aura of the shrines of the battle for Texas independence in South Texas, and it has no support group such as the Daughters of the Texas Revolution. It does, however, have dedicated fans and supporters. The now-remote stretch along the Clear Fork has a history that epitomizes the frontier experience—Indians, soldiers, buffalo hunters, cowboys, and trail driving. Here is indeed a rich legacy for Texas life that gives Albany part of its focus. *The Fort Griffin Fandangle* is their effort to bring some of these characters and events to an appreciative audience each June. We thank Bob Nail, Alice Reynolds, and others who created this show, and those who continue it.

FURTHER READING

Biggers, Don H. *Buffalo Guns and Barbed Wire*. Ca. 1902. Rpt. Lubbock: Texas Tech University Press, 1991.

———. *Shackelford County Sketches*. Ed. Joan Farmer. 1908. Rpt. Albany, Texas: The Clear Fork Press, 1974.

Caldwell, Clifton. *Fort Davis: A Family Frontier Fort.* Albany, Texas: Clear Fork Press 1986.

Cashion, Ty. *A Texas Frontier: The Clear Fork Country and Fort Griffin, 1849-1887.* Norman: University of Oklahoma Press, 1996.

Fehrenback, T.R. *Comanches: Destruction of a People.* New York: Knopf, 1979.

Gard, Wayne. *The Great Buffalo Hunt.* Lincoln: University of Nebraska Press, 1959.

Hunter, J. Marvin. *The Trail Drivers of Texas.* 1925; Rpt. New York: Argosy-Antiquarian Ltd., 1963.

_____. *Lottie Deno: Her Life and Times.* Bandera, Texas: The 4 Hunters, 1959.

Metz, Leon Clair. *John Selman: Texas Gunfighter.* New York: Hastings House, 1966.

Richardson, Rupert N. *The Comanche Barrier to South Plains Settlement: A Century and a Half of Savage Resistance to the Advancing White Frontier.* 1933. 2nd ed. Ed. Kenneth Jacobs. Abilene: 4-O-Imprint, HSU Press, 1996; Rpt. Austin: Eakin, 1996.

Rister, Carl Coke. *Fort Griffin on the Texas Frontier.* Norman:

University of Oklahoma Press, 1956.

_____. *Robert E. Lee in Texas.* Norman: University of Oklahoma Press, 1946.

Robinson, Charles, III. *The Frontier World of Fort Griffin: The Life and Death of a Western Town.* Spokane, Wash: The Arthur H. Clark Company, 1992.

Rye, Edgar. *The Quirt and the Spur: Vanishing Shadows of the Texas Frontier.* 1909; Rpt. Austin: Steck-Vaughn Co., 1967.

Wallace, Ernest, and E. Adamson Hoebel. *The Comanches: Lords of the South Plains.* Norman: University of Oklahoma Press, 1986.

Webb, Walter Prescott. *The Great Plains.* New York: Grossett & Dunlap, 1931.

THE AUTHORS

Lawrence Clayton has written extensively about the life and lore of this region, especially the cowboys who ride the ranges. His *Watkins Reynolds Matthews: Biography of a Texas Rancher* is a study of one of the principal modern figures important to life along the Clear Fork.

Col. M. L. Crimmins was a Rough Rider with Theodore Roosevelt and a veteran officer of World War I. He was also a leader in the treatment of snake bites. Crimmins published more than 200 articles in historical journals.

Joan Halford Farmer was for many years archivist for the Robert Nail Collection at the Old Jail Art Center in Albany and a prolific writer on the life and lore of the region. Her "Remember When" column in the *Albany News* is a gold mine of area history, much of it never before published. She has delved deeply into the historical resources of the region.

Ben O. Grant was a history teacher and principal in the Albany public schools and later taught at Hardin-Simmons University. He produced an impressive volume of work about this area.

Bob Green, an area rancher and writer, knows the history and lore of this area as well as anyone else ever will and is dedicated to bringing it to the attention of audiences through video tapes and his writing, much of which has appeared in the *Albany News* and in the printed programs for the *Fort Griffin Fandangle*.

Marilynne Howsley was a student of life in the area as well as a successful professional person from Albany. She was strongly influenced by Ben O. Grant.

Morris Ledbetter was a local historian whose knowledge of this area is remarkable. His family goes back to the days of earliest settlement, and the picket house from their ranch on the Clear Fork of the Brazos River now sits in a park setting in downtown Albany.

W. B. Parker was a civilian attached to the campaign of Capt. R. B. Marcy, a well-known explorer and map maker of much of the West, especially Texas.

Rupert N. Richardson was a distinguished Texas historian and a prolific writer of history of Texas and Comanche Indians. He also served Hardin-Simmons University as president as well as professor.

Carl Coke Rister was a distinguished historian first at Hardin-Simmons University and later at the University of Oklahoma. He wrote extensively about the area of concern here, especially in *Robert E. Lee in Texas* and *Fort Griffin on the Texas Frontier*.

J. R. Webb, not a trained historian, nonetheless made a remarkable contribution by interviewing and then writing down the stories of pioneers in the area. Without his work, much of this record would be lost.

A Parting Word

INDEX

Note to the reader: Because this collection presents writings from numerous authors and from different eras, spellings-especially those of proper names-differ from author to author. Much of this can be attributed to oral histories and phonetic spellings. Also, most of the writing featured in this collection was rendered without a technical understanding of Indian languages. Indian names were generally spelled phonetically, and one name could be spelled any number of ways. For example, the Comanche leader Ketumseh's name is spelled five different ways in this collection alone. For indexing purposes the publisher has posted the most widely accepted or reliable form of a name and listed any variants in parentheses.

101 Outfit, 251

Abilene, Kansas, 247, 267
Abilene, Texas, 128, 243
Adams (man), 166
Adobe Walls, 242, 246, 257
Adobe Walls Ranch, 246
Albany, Texas, 17, 60, 106, 123, 137, 138, 148, 149, 156, 165-169, 173, 184, 195, 197, 199, 202, 204-209, 214-217, 230, 235, 256-260, 293, 294, 311-315, 318, 329, 330, 348
Albany News, 202
Alexandria Gazette, The, 72
Allen, I.W.,
Amarillo, Texas, 266
Anadarkos (Ah-nan-da-kas), 19, 24, 74, 105
Anderson, A., 230
Anderson, Andy, 161

Anderson, Bill, 161
Anderson, H., 137
Anderson, Henry, 161
Anderson, John, 161, 237
Anderson, Lottie, 161
Anderson, Mich, 230, 237
Anderson, Rich, 137
Apache Kid, 209, 256, 279, 280, 282, 285-290, 293, 315, 328, 329, 347
Apaches, 209, 323
Aqua Quash (Waco), 131
Arkansas River, 81, 83, 239, 240, 242, 252, 257, 266, 267, 310, 325, 330, 346
Arlington, Virginia, 52
Asperoz, M., 296
Atlanta, Georgia, 205
Augur, Gen. Christopher C., 12
Austin, Stephen F., 127
Austin, Texas, 60
Avery, Bill, 257, 258
Avott, Jesus, 269, 278, 282-287, 290, 291

Baird, Dr., 203
Baldwin, Archie, 237
Band of Hope (Fort Griffin), 118
Bar CC Outfit, 241
Barber, Lee, 196
Barron, Dan, 244
Barry, Capt. J.B. "Buck," 37, 137, 158, 169, 233
Bartholemew, N.L., house of, pictured 122, 172
Bartholemew, Mrs. N.L, 348
Baxter, N.J., 64
Baylor, John R., 23, 34, 35, 37, 39, 40, 52, 67, 81, 82, 135, 228, 301
Baylor County, Texas, 227, 243
Bear River, 267
Beard (cattle inspector), 166
Bee Hive Saloon, 195, 244, 245
Beecher, Illinois, 326
Belknap, Texas, 41, 140
Bell County, Texas, 40
Bennett, John, pictured 254
Bennett Girls, 196
Bent County, Colorado, 310, 343
Best, Steve, 255
Biggs, Marshall, 208

Big Bend, 3, 4
Big Dry Creek, 262
Big Hubbard Bridge, 138
Big Missouri River, 261, 262
Big Sandy Creek, 150
Big Spring, Texas, 182
Big Spring, 182, 128
Big Stinking Creek, 243
Big Wichita River, 64, 85, 131
Biggers, Don H., 223
Billings, Montana, 259-262
Bitter Creek, 266
"Bivouac of the Dead" (poem), 49, 71
Black Ford, Utah, 267
Black Hills, 252, 253
Blaine, James G., 297-299, 329
Blanco Canyon, 242, 243
Bland, Bill, 244, 245
Blevins, Deputy, 270
Blevins Boys, 256
Blount, Charlie, pictured 254
Boggs, James, 138
Boggs, John, 138
Boggs, Tom, 138
Bosque County, Texas, 37
Boswell, N.K., 263, 264
Boswell Family, 161
Bowman, James, 64
Bowers, Joe "Tol," 9, 238, 239
Bozeman (man), 161
Bragg, Billy, 187
Bragg, Mrs. Billy, 187
Bragg, George, 305
Bragg's Fort, 188
Brazos Reservation, 19, 22, 38, 39, 40, 53, 74, 132
Brazos River (see also the various forks), 19, 50, 50, 51, 74, 85, 105, 126, 128, 132, 163, 175, 226, 247, 307, 317, 338
Breckenridge, Texas, 161, 171, 201, 204, 229
Bronte, Texas, 156
Brownfield, T.B., 140
Browning, Angelina McCarty, 230
Browning, Joe, 173, 230
Browning Boys, 228
Bryan, Ohio, 219
Buchanan County (see Stephens County)
Buell, Lt. Col. George P., 8, 9, 12, 175
Buffalo Gap, Texas, 232

Buffalo Hump (Comanche), 23-25, 79, 81, 131, 133
Buford, Col. Nathaniel, 303, 335
Bugbee, Tom, 242
Bull Run, Second Battle of (1862), 58
Bullis, Lt. John, 292
Burleson, E.N., 36
Bushnob (Throckmorton County), 166
Butler, Pvt. John F., 6, 8, 61
Butler, Tobe, 254
Butte Creek, Colorado, 240-243, 246
Butterfield Stage, 151, 159, 161, 170, 190, 200, 230, 321, 322

Cabello, Domingo, 126
Cable, C.M., 137
Caddos, 19, 21, 24, 49, 74, 105
Caldwell, Capt. J.N., 51
Caldwell, Kansas, 168, 173, 247, 248, 251
Calhoun, Capt. P., 22, 81
Callahan County, Texas, 148, 203
Calvert, Texas, 10, 172, 207
Camp Belknap, 48
Camp Cobb, Indian Territory, 53
Camp Colorado, 56, 72
Camp Cooper, 2, 17, 23, 26-29, 35, 48-56, 67, 72, 74, 76, 81, 82, 129, 133-138, 141, 150, 151, 156-160, 167, 169, 170, 188, 198, 199, 230-234
Camp Johnston (Johnson), 73
Camp Wilson, 4, 57, 163
Campbell, Berry, pictured 112
Campbell, Lt., 165
Canadian River, 25, 53, 88, 127, 242, 246, 249, 251, 257, 326
Cantrell Ranch, 201
Cap Rock, 85
Capron, Horace, 73
Carpenter, Capt. Stephen D., 55, 136
Carrizo Creek, 241
Carson, Christopher "Kit," 345
Carter (men), 166
Carter, Brights, 253, 254
Carter, Capt. Robert G., 62
Casa Grande, Arizona, 278
Catumseh (see Ketumseh)

Chaffee, Capt. Adna R., 6, 60, 61, 65
Champion Creek, 180
Charlotte, North Carolina, 49
"Cheap" John, 114
Cherokee Strip, 251
Cheyenne, Wyoming, 264, 266, 267, 343
Cheyenne River, 252
Cheyennes, 248-251, 346
Chicago, Illinois, 168, 204
China Relief Expedition, 60
Chisholm Trail, 168, 172, 174, 207, 247, 248, 267
Chisum, John S., 345
Chivington, Colorado, 257
Choctaw Tom (and party of), 36, 37
Christenson (Christianson), Edgar, 137, 161
Christenson, Elgy, family of, 230
Christenson, Walter, 261
Cimarron Expedition, 53
Cimarron Cutoff, 241
Cimarron River, 53, 241, 247, 251, 252
Cincinnati, Ohio, 219
Cisco, Texas, 315, 348
Civil War, 2, 3, 56, 58, 60, 146, 158-165, 188, 196, 199, 205, 209, 220, 230, 233, 234, 316, 323, 324, 331, 333, 335, 337, 341
Clark, A.A., 167
Clark, Alex, family of, 230
Clark's Fort, 229
Clarke, R.A., 137
Clayton, Ellen, 196
Clayton, W.T. 196
Clear Fork of the Brazos River, 2, 4, 9, 17, 19, 21, 48, 49, 57, 59, 60, 73, 74, 79, 81, 82, 85, 86, 99, 101, 105, 121, 127-132, 137, 138, 145, 156-162, 167, 173, 174, 176, 178, 188, 195, 198, 199, 218, 226, 229, 233-235, 238, 240, 301, 316, 325, 328, 334
Clear Fork Station, 170, 230
Clifton, Mrs., 187
Coatzacoalcos, 55
Cockrell (citizen), 9, 238, 239
Coe, Capt., 241, 242
Coffee, Glenn, pictured 254
Coke County, Texas, 199
Colbert's Ferry, 240
Cole, Dale, 259

Collins, Mr., 163
Collins Creek, 59, 163, 196
Colorado City, Texas, 128, 180, 181
Colorado River, 50, 51, 54, 74, 126, 128, 304
Comanches, 2, 6, 8, 18-42, 48-50, 54, 60, 61, 67, 68, 72-83, 85, 86, 126, 131-134, 146, 214, 217, 218, 220, 221, 231, 233, 247, 309, 323, 334
Comanche Reservation (Texas), 17-42, 48, 49, 53, 73, 74, 81, 82, 129, 132-135, 158, 160-162, 168, 199, 231
Concho River, 51, 54, 73, 80, 176, 177, 304, 336
Confederate States of America, army of, 49, 56, 156,199, 235
Conner (German settler), 88, 89, 95, 104
Conrad, Ella Matthews, 319
Conrad, Frank E., 166, 179, 238, 319
Conrad, John, 261
Cook, E.H., 299
Cook, Mahalia, pictured 7,
Cooper, Andy, 255
Cooper, C.C., 138
Cooper, Gen. Samuel, 49
Couch, Bob, 243
Couch, Mose, 265
Corinne, Utah, 267
Coronado, Francisco, 125, 126
Crain, Harry E., 263, 264
Crane County, Texas, 127
Cranmer, Tom, 307, 308
Cratton, Mr. (cattle man), 267
Cresswell, Hank, 241
Crow, E.C., 202
Crow, George W., 202
Crow, William, 202, 203
Crow-fly-high (Indian), 347
Crowley, Sam, 219, 220, 222
Crowson, Fos, pictured 254
Cruger (Kruger) Bill, 166, 208, 244
Crystal Falls, Texas, 170
Culberson, D.R., 205
Curtis, Tom, 165

Dale Creek, Wyoming, 266
Dalhart, Texas, 260
Dallas, Texas, 57, 166, 183, 222
Dalrymple, Col. W.C., 55, 136, 196

Darnell, J.C., 307
Davis County, Texas, 348
Davis Mountains, 259, 260
Dawson, John, 228
Dawson, Texas, 226, 227
Deadman's Creek, 6, 60
Deep Creek, 159, 203, 217, 235
Delaware Creek, 127
Delawares, 100
Delaware Scouts, 76, 84, 85, 95, 99
Denison, Texas, 58, 128, 240
Denver, Colorado, 258, 266, 344, 345
Department of Texas (see Texas, Military Department of)
Desdemona, Texas, 172
Dickens County, Texas, 227
Dickinson, North Dakota, 251
Doan's Store, 247, 248
Dodge City, Kansas, 115, 247
Dodge Trail, 247, 251, 261
Dona Ana, New Mexico, 127
Double Mountain Fork of the Brazos River, 8, 51, 85, 146, 161, 237, 243, 308, 340
Double Mountains, 8, 51, 128, 176
Drake, Jim, 161
Dripping Springs Valley (Arizona), 275
Dumas, Allison Edgar, Cebron, 173, 174, 176
Durgan, Lottie, 160, 187
Durgan, Minnie, 160, 171, 187
Dutch Nance Store, pictured 109

Eagle Pass, Texas, 2
Eastland County, Texas, 172, 173, 207, 147, 148
El-cahn (Apache prisoner), 283-285, 287, 288, 291
Eliasville, Texas, 226
Elliott, James, 64
Elliott, Samuel, 64
Elk Creek (Indian Territory), 254
Elm Creek (Young County; raid on), 54, 160, 185,188, 228, 233, 235, 305
Elm Creek (Taylor County), 243
El Paso, Texas, 56, 72, 143, 144, 305
Erath, G.B., 40
Erath County, Texas, 37, 148, 172
Erwin, B.J., 263
Evans, Mr., 206

Farmer, Joan, pictured 142
Federal Guaranty Company, 222-224
First National Bank of Albany, 173, 311, 313
First National Bank of Oklahoma City, 312
Five Forks, Battle of (1865), 58
Flat, the, 9, 10, 164, 166, 173, 238
Folwell, Jimmie, 241, 242
Ford, Col. John S. "Rip," 36
Forsythe, Dick, 248
Fort Belknap, 3, 4, 27, 35, 51, 72, 74, 79, 80, 82, 85, 101, 104, 105, 128, 132, 175, 176, 188
Fort Bliss, 4, 57
Fort Bragg (civilian), 305
Fort Brown, 4, 72
Fort Chadbourne, 2, 3, 21, 22, 50, 72, 80, 81, 85, 104, 128, 133, 151, 156, 170, 199
Fort Clark, 2, 4
Fort Concho, 3, 10, 12, 57, 59, 60
Fort Croghan, 72
Fort Davis (civilian), 137-139, 150, 158-162, 163, 165, 173, 176, 188, pictured 189, 192, 193, 199, 201, 229-235
Fort Davis (US), 4, 57, 72
Fort Duncan, 2, 4
Fort Gates, 72
Fort Graham, 72
Fort Griffin (and town of), 3-12, 48, 56-65, 106- 123, 145, 146, 150, 162-169, 173-184, 195- 201, 207-208, 210, 214, 217, 219, 221, 223, 226, 238-244, 248, 249, 292, 315, 318, 342
Fort Griffin-Dodge Cattle Trail, 208
Fort Griffin Echo, 111-113, 118, 195-197, 200
Fort Griffin Masonic Lodge, pictured 108
Fort Griffin on the Texas Frontier, 224
Fort Griffin State Park, 196
Fort Hubbard (civilian), 138, 217, 229
Fort Laramie, Wyoming, 252
Fort Lyon, Colorado, 242
Fort McIntosh, 4, 72
Fort McKavett, 2, 3, 4, 12, 72

Fort Mason, 50, 69, 72, 304, 336
Fort Phantom Hill, 2, 3, 72, 128, 177-180, 183
Fort Preston (see Preston)
Fort Quitman, 4, 57
Fort Richardson, 3, 4, 56, 57, 62, 64
Fort Sill, Indian Territory, 64, 248
Fort Smith, Arkansas, 10, 59, 84, 127, 128
Fort Stockton, 4, 12, 57
Fort Terrett, 2
Fort Towson, Indian Territory, 128
Fort Washita, Indian Territory, 48
Fort Worth (military post), 72
Fort Worth, Texas, City of, 111, 148, 166, 174, 241, 247, 264, 267, 348
Fort Worth & Denver Railroad, 266
Fort Worth Livestock Commission Company, 348
Fox (Indian), 39
Frankel, E., 111, 112
Franz (France, Frans), Jim, 137, 161, 190, 192
Franz, Matt, 229, 235
Franz, Steve, 237
Freestone County, Texas, 316

Galveston, Texas, 172
Garland, Peter, 37
Garza County, Texas, 85
Gentry, Mart, 240, 246, pictured 254
George, Jim, 137
George, Phil, 137
Gila County, Arizona, 256, 315, 328, 347
Gila River, 275-277
Gilbert Russell Young, pictured 7
Givens, Capt. Newton C., 28, 141, 143, 146, 160, 234
Glacier Bay, Alaska, 311
Globe, Arizona, 208, 271, 272, 277, 290, 292, 294
Gonsolus, Florence, 204
Gonsolus, Peter, 144, 204
Gonsolus Creek, 204,
Goodnight, Charles, 231, 232, 241, 242, pictured 246, 247, 256, 264-266, 312, 313, 324, 326, 345
Goodnight, Texas, 256, 257, 266
Goodnight-Loving Trail, 231
Gossett Family, 199

Gould, Jay, 258
Graham, Texas, 169
Gray, Zane, 255
Great Plains,125
Great Salt Lake, 267
Greeley, Colorado, 266
Green River, 266
Greer, Cal, 146, 147, 202
Greer, George, 146, 158, 159, 173, 202, 203, 235
Greer, G.W., 202
Greer, Jackson W. 202
Greer, J.H., 203
Greer, John R., 203
Greer, S.A., 202
Greer Community, 146
Greer Ranch, 188
Grenada, Colorado, 240, 241
Griffin, Georgia, 205
Griffin, Gen. Charles, 4, 57, 163
Griffith, Dr., 342
Guadalupe Mountains, 265
Guymon, Oklahoma, 241

Hale (Apache prisoner), 284-289, 291
Ham's Ford, Utah, 267
Hamner, H.A., 136
Hardee, Maj. William J., 49, 67, 69
Hardin, John Wesley, 165, 230
Harper (sutler), 158
Hart, James, 202, 203
Hashknife Outfit, 243, 255
Hashknife Ranch, 243, 245
Hashknife Trail, 252
Haskell, Texas, 176
Haskell County, Texas, 146, 177, 178, 210, 227, 235, 240, 308, 314, 340
Has-ten-tu-du-jay (Apache prisoner), 283, 289, 291
Havana, Cuba, 55
Hayes, Bill, 166
Hayes, John, 166
Hawkins, Thomas T., 31, 32, 35
Hazelwood, George, 138
Hazlett, John, 166
Hepe Creek, 243
Herman (rancher), 344, 345
Herron, Alice Rucker, 206
Herron, Henry C., 206, 207

Hervey Family, 198
Hicks (man), 166
Hill (Indian agent), 81
Hill County, Texas, 184, 207
Hillsboro, Texas, 172
Hittson, Bill, 140, 160-162, 192, 233, 234
Hittson, John, 137, 141, 150, 160-162, 192, 229, 233, 234
Hoffman, Pvt. Charles, 6, 8, 61
Holbrook, Arizona, 208, 255
Holden (man), 318
Hollowell, Robert G., 294
Holmes, W.A. "Hunkydory," 256, 269, 270, 273, 275, 279-287, 290, 292, 293
Holt, C.W., 176
Honeycutt, John, 260
Hood, Gen. John B., 134
Hoover, Bill, 160
Hoover, M.V., 138
Hoover, Mart, 160, 174, 319
Hoover, Martha Matthews, 319
Hoover, William, 138
Horsehead Crossing, 221, 232, 321
Hos-cal-te (Apache prisoner), 279, 280, 282, 285, 287, 289, 290, 291
Hough, Si, 161, 232, 237, 307, 308, 340, 341, 345
Hourigan Girls, 196
House, Jim, pictured 254
Houston & Texas Central Railroad, 172, 176
Howard, T., 75
Hubbard Creek, 138, 144, 146, 149, 159, 173, 202-204, 207, 217, 235, 317
Hughes (rancher), 245
Hugo, Colorado, 252, 257
Hunnywell, Kansas, 247, 248
Hunter, Jack, 104
Hurricane Bill, 164, 165
Hurricane Minnie, 164
Hutton, Mr., 267

Ibex, Texas, 138
Iliff, John Wesley, 266, 267, 324
Indianola, Texas, 55

Indian Territory, 38, 40, 41, 53, 80, 135, 158, 160, 187, 249, 254, 255
Interwoven, 191, 230, 303
Irwin, Annie Harris, 199
Irwin, Atlee E., 199
Irwin, Emily E., 199, 200
Irwin, Ennis, 171
Irwin, J.C., 150, 151, 156, pictured 157, 158-171, 198, 199
Irwin, J.G., 137, 139, 151, 156, 199, 230, 235
Irwin Family, 199

Jack County, Texas, 39
Jack County Rangers, 39
Jackett, Mr., 171
Jacksboro, Texas, 39, 56, 57, 59
Jackson, Joseph, 206
Jackson, T.E., house of pictured 122, 137, 139, 161, family of 230, 237, 238
Jacobs, Henry, 255
Jacobs, John, 104, 177, 178, 182
January Family, 161, 230
Jefferson Barracks, Missouri, 67
Jeffries, Jim, 244
Johnson, Britt, 160, 187, 318
Johnston, Col. Albert Sidney, 52, 134
Johnston, Gen. J.E., 193
Jones County, Texas, 6, 9, 148, 227, 230
Jose Maria (Anadarko), 24, 37
Johnson (man), 35
Johnson, Capt. Richard, 54

Kansas City, Missouri, 161, 237, 245, 309, 342, 346
Kansas Pacific Railroad, 346
Kelly, Lt. U., 6
Kendrick, J.B., 267
Kennedy (rancher), 9
Kennedy's Ranch, 9
Kent, Texas, 259, 260
Ketumseh (Comanche; also spelled Catumseh, Katumse, Ke-tum-e-see, Ka-tem-e-see), 19- 24, 26, 27, 32, 33, 49, 50, 67-69, 73-83, 86-89, 94, 95, 97, 101-103, 131, 133

Key West, Florida, 55
Kichais (Wichitas), 19
Kickapoo Creek, 304
Kickapoo Springs, 304, 336
Kickapoos, 93, 100, 334
King (hanged man), 163
King, Capt. J.H., 51
King, Richard, 345
King, William, 147, 202
Kiowa Creek, 54
Kiowas, 25, 62, 72, 171, 188, 323, 334
Kismet, Montana, 262
Kit Carson, Colorado, 240, 346, 347
Knox & Gardner (cattle outfit), 234
Ko (man), 317
Kosterlitzky, Col., 293
Kotsoteka Comanches (see also Comanches), 25
Koweaka (Wichita), 130
Kruger (see Cruger)
Kwahadis (see Quahadi Comanches)

La Grange, Texas, 81
La Junta, Colorado, 240, 266, 325, 343
Lamar, Colorado, 257
Lambshead Creek, 200
Lambshead Ranch, marker on pictured 142, 210
Lambshead (Lamb's Head) Valley, 174
Lane, Tom, 161
Laramie, Wyoming, 252, 266
Larn, J., 198
Larn, John, 165, 166, 171, 174, 198, 230, 319
Larn, Joseph B., 198
Larn, Mary Matthews, 319
Larn, S.W., 198
Larn, Will, pictured 254
Ledbetter, John Calvin "Johnnie," 149, 214, pictured 215, 217-219, 223, 224
Ledbetter, Harve, 217, 218
Ledbetter, W.H., house of pictured 121, 148, 174, 216, 217, 221, 235
Ledbetter, Mrs. W.H., 218, 219, 223, 224
Ledbetter Family, 216-218, 220, 222
Ledbetter Ranch, 6, 60
Ledbetter Salt Works, 147-149, 202, 217, 235

Lee, 2d Lt. Fitzhugh, 54
Lee, J.B.C., 4
Lee, Lt. Col. Robert E., 17, 49-52, 56, 60, 64, 67-73, 82, 83, 134, 141, 156, 157, 170, 193, 199
Lee, Mr., 137, 318
Lee, Mrs., 318
Lee Family (Spephens County), 170-171
Lee Ranch, 318
Leeper, Mathew, 25-28, 34, 39
Lewis, M.D., 342
Lewis, Mr. (principal), 118
Leyendecker (trader), 21
Lindley, Sam, 138
Lipan Apaches (see also Apaches), 32
Little Buffalo (Kiowa), 171
Little Missouri River, 251, 252
Little Wichita River, 64
Llano River, 126
Long, S., 64
Long X Brand, 255, 326
Los Adaes (Spanish settlement), 126
Los Angeles, California, 219
Los Animas, Colorado, 240
Louisiana Pascagoula Military Academy, 70
Loving, J.C., 310, 344, 345
Loving, Oliver, 231, 232, 265, 266, 312, 313, 324
Lowe, William W., 53
Lowndes County, Alabama, 316
Lueders, Texas, 129
Lynch, F.J., 204
Lynch, Icebenda C., 204
Lynch, J.C., 138, 143-145, 149, 158, 173, 204, 217, 223, 235
Lynch, J.G., 204
Lynch Ranch, 138, 188, 217, 229

M O Outfit, 247
McAnulty, R.E., 241
McCarty, Marion, family of, 230
McCarty, Mich, family of, 230
McCarty, N., 137, 140
McCarty, Pres, 162, 189, 192, 233
McClintock & Woods (ranchers), 168
McCluskey, Henry, 159
McCulloch, Col. Henry E., 56, 136, 137
McCombs, Joe S., 106-107173-184, 207
McFaddin, Tom, 254

McGough, Billy, 147
McGough Springs, 147
McKamy, Texas, 243, 244
McLennan County, Texas, 40
Mabry, Seth, 345
Mackenzie, Col. Ranald S., 62, 64, 166-169, 174-176
Mackenzie Trail, 174, 243
Malta, Montana, 259, 261, 262
Manning, Bill, 198
Mansfield, Col. J.K.F., 51
Manypenny, George W.,133
Marcus v. Wright, 167
Marcy, Capt. Randolph B., 19, 20, 73-80, 84-86, 92, 95-97, 99-103, 127, 128, 132
Mares, Jose, 127
Marfa, Texas, 257
Marmaduke, Gen. John S., 303, 335
Marshall, Jack "Jacko," 306, 307, 338, 339
Martin's Ranch, 53
Ma-si (Apache), 273, 274
Mason, A.B., 54
Matthews, Andrew, 316
Matthews, Annie, 316
Matthews, Annie G., 200
Matthews, Baker
Matthews, Benjamin, 316
Matthews, Caroline Spears, 209, 316
Matthews, Elizabeth Harris, 316
Matthews, J.A., 145, 146, 200, 209, 210, 318
Matthews, James, 316
Matthews, John (father of J.B.), 316
Matthews, John Jr., 316
Matthews, Joseph B., 145, 146, 173, 174, 176, 209, 306, 307, 310, 315-319, 330, 338
Matthews, Martha, 316
Matthews, Nancy, 316
Matthews, Sallie, 316
Matthews, Sallie Reynolds, 145, 191, 200, 209, 210, 230, 238, pictured 303, 318, 348
Matthews, Thomas, 316
Matthews, Tom, 257, 259
Matthews, Will, 257
Matthews, Winnie, 316
Matthews Ranch, 6
Mauldin, Mrs. C.B., 207

Maxwell, Mr., 163
Maxwell, Mrs., 163
Maxwell Creek, 163
Maxwell's Ranch, 57
May, Jonathan, 138
Memphis, Tennessee, 51
Menard, Texas, 126
Mercer, Mr., 138
Mexican War (US war with Mexico), 58, 67, 70, 71, 301
Metcalf Gap, 173
Meyer, Charlie, 111, 112
Meyers, Lt., 244
Mezierres, Athanase de, 126
Middle Concho River, 232
Middleton, Eugene, 269, 271-290
Midland, Texas, 183
Milk River, 326, 344, 348
Miller, George, 251
Miller, T.L., 326
Miller's Creek 176, 243
Millett, Cap, 245
Millett Outfit, 174, 243-245
Minter, Lt., 156, 158, 199
Mississippi River, 220
Missouri, Kansas & Texas Railway, 58, 240
Missouri Pacific Railroad, 257
Mitchell, Beverly, pictured 254
Mockingbird Springs, 178
Mokochope (Comanche), 77, 96
Moore, Will, 255
Moran, Texas, 205
Morgan Creek, 181
Morgan's Ranch, 307, 338
Mormon Battalion, 70
Mossy Rock Springs, 182
Mountain Pass, 54, 177
Mugginsville, Texas (civilian fort at), 188, 229
Mullen, John, 64
Murphy, Tim, 276
Murphy, William, 276
Murray's Fort, 188
Musgrave, J.C., 137, 161
Musselshell River, 261
Mustang Pond, 183

Nacogdoches, Texas,126
Nah-diez-az (Apache), 270, 281
Nance, Dutch, 238
Naroni (Comanche), 89-91, 102, 103
Navajos, 345
Navasota, Texas, 219
Neighbors, Robert S., 19-23, 34-39, 41, 48, 73, 74, 79, 80, 81, 85, 86, 104, 129, 132, 133, 143
Nelson, Allison, 36
Newcastle, Texas, 128, 160
Newcomb, Art, 195
Newcomb, John, 307, 338, 340
Newcomb, Sam, 137,161, 189, 190, 192, 230, 238, 304
Newcomb, S.S., 138, 139, 141
Newcomb, Susan Reynolds, 204
Newcomb, Tull, pictured 112
Newcomb's Grove, 167
New Mexico-Colorado Trail, 252
New Orleans, Louisiana, 58, 172
New York, New York, 55
Nokoni (Nakoni) Comanches (see also Comanches), 25, 26, 28, 87, 131
Norman (Oklahoma) State Bank, 312
North Concho River, 232
North Platte River, 252
Northern Trail, 257
Nye, Bill, 266

O X Outfit, 241
Oak Creek, 128
Ogallala, Nebraska, 245, 267
O'hara, Capt. Theodore, 49, 70
Old Jail Art Center, 294
Old Law Mob, 163
Old Sod Ranch, 167
Old Stone Ranch, 143, 146, 160, 174, 178, 201, 204, 234, 240, 306, 307, 337, 338
Olney, Texas, 257
One Mile Hill, 205, 206
Otero, Colorado, 208
Otey's Creek, 49
Oti (Comanche), 86, 87, 89
Owl's Head (Fort Owl's Head), Texas, 188, 189, 229

Pace, Sol, 180
Pahayuco (Comanche; also spelled Pah-a-yu-ka), 131
Paint Creek, 6, 202, 175, 177, 178
Palestine, Texas, 222, 223
Palmer, Capt. Innis, 35, 55
Palo Duro Canyon, 218, 233, 242
Palo Pinto, Texas, 36, 169, 336, 338
Palo Pinto County, Texas, 11, 37, 173, 301, 302, 307, 322, 333, 338
Parker, Cynthia Ann, 54, 55, 169, 170, 214, 348
Parker, Isaac, 54
Parker, John, 55
Parker, Quanah, 214, 247
Parker, W.B., 74-79, 85
Parker County, Texas, 116, 117, 161, 239, 240, 307
Parker's Fort, 55
Pash-ten-tah (Apache), 283-289, 291
Pease River, 54, 169
Pecan Bayou, 51
Pecos, Texas, 260
Pecos County, Texas, 348
Pecos River, 127, 221, 223, 232, 264, 265, 321, 322, 328, 345
Peeler, Tom, 245
Peking, China, 60
Penateka Comanches (see also Comanches), 20, 25, 73-81
Penn, Maj., 222
Penniston, Glenn, pictured 254
Peril Straits, Alaska, 311
Peta Nocona (Comanche), 170
Phantom Hill, 60
Philadelphia, Pennsylvania, 85
Pickettville, Texas (civilian fort at), 188, 204, 229
Pierce, A.E. "Shanghai," 247, 261, 342, 345
Pitcock, Bob, 180
Planter's Hotel, 195
Platte River, 1
Pleasant Valley War, 208, 255
Poer, Will, 257
Pollard, R.W., 37
Porter, Lt. A. Parker, 54
Porter, Jack (Comanche), 32
Powell, Dr., 203, 342
Pratt, Lt. R.H., 8
Prescott, Arizona, 239

Preston (Fort Preston), Texas, 2, 128
Pueblo, Colorado, 242

Quahadi (Quahada, Kwahadi)
    Comanches (see also Comanches),
    25, 60, 214
Qua-ha-we-tah (Qua-ha-we-ti)
    (Comanche), 86, 89
Quisquate (Tawakoni village), 126

Randolph County, Alabama, 172, 207
Ranger Creek, 240
Rath, George, 179
Ratliff, Arch, 137, 161, 230
Ratliff, Rom, 161
Raton, New Mexico, 228
Ray, W.W., 138
Raymonds, B.W., 137
Reagan, John H., 327
Red Fork, Indian Territory, 247
Red Mud Creek, 243
Red River, 2, 25, 53, 54, 64, 71, 99, 127, 128, 131, 240, 247, 248
Red River Crossing, 174, 247
Reed, Charly, 244
Regan, Pvt. James, 61
Regiments (CS):
    19th Texas Cavalry, 303, 335
Regiments (US):
    2d Cavalry, 49-56, 67, 69-72, 82, 134
    4th Cavalry, 62
    6th Cavalry, 4, 6, 60-62
    10th Cavalry, 6, 8, 9
    2d Dragoons, 28, 141, 151, 156, 199
    1st Infantry, 51, 55, 56
    5th Infantry, 48
Reno, Nevada, 343
Republican River, 257
Reynolds, Anna Marie, 201, 301, 315, 333, 348
Reynolds, Annie Merle, 314, 330
Reynolds, Augusta, 200, 208, 209, 269, 272, 280, 293
Reynolds, B.F., 200, 227, 228, 238, 260, pictured 302, 347, 348

Reynolds, Barber Watkins, house of pictured 120, 146, 160, 161, 200, 201, 239, 240, 301, 315, 322, 333, 341
Reynolds, Eaton, 260, 261
Reynolds, Ella M., 314, 330
Reynolds, Elmer, pictured 254
Reynolds, George (son of Glenn), 209, 260, 292
Reynolds, George Elton, 314, 330
Reynolds, George T., 146, 161, 227, 232, 237, 238, 240, 258, 259, 262, 300, 301, pictured 302, 303-315, 324, 331-349
Reynolds, Glenn, 167, 200, 208, 209, 227, 238, 256, 269, 270, pictured 271, 272-299, 311, 315, 328, 329, 347
Reynolds, Joe, 260
Reynolds, John, 314, 330
Reynolds, Joseph, 314, 330
Reynolds, L.E. Matthews, 310, 319, 341, 343
Reynolds, Nathan B., 314, 330
Reynolds, Phin W., 226, 226, 227, 238-262, pictured 302, 348
Reynolds, Susan Matthews, 314, 319, 330
Reynolds, Watt, pictured 254
Reynolds, Wendell Watkins, 314, 330
Reynolds, Will, 260
Reynolds, William D., 146, 161, 226, 226, 227, 232, 237-240, 244, 245, pictured 246, 263-267, pictured 302, 308-315, 318-332, 343, 348
Reynolds, Willie D., 314, 330
Reynolds Bend, 200
Reynolds Branch, 238
Reynolds Land and Cattle Company, 146, 240, 241, 246, cowboys of pictured 254, 255-260, 313, 325
Reynolds & Matthews Cattle Company, 247, 248
Richards, Tot, 257, 259
Ringgold Barracks, 72
Rio Grande, 1, 2, 4, 48, 52, 71, 72, 127, 334
Rister, Carl Coke, 224
Rivers, Charles, 310, 343, 344
Riverside Station, Arizona, 256, 269, 275, 277- 279

"Robbers Roost," 241, 242
Roberts County, Texas, 313
Rock Creek, Texas, 116
Rock Island Railroad, 247
Rocky Ford, Colorado, 240
Rogers, E.W., 137
Roman Nose (Cheyenne), 249-251
Ross, Capt. L.S. "Sul," 54, 169, 348
Ross, S.P., 24, 39
Rotan, Texas, 178
Rucker, Ettie Estellah, 206
Rucker, Georgia, 206
Rucker Minnie M., 206
Rucker, Theodore, 206
Rucker, Weldon, 205, 206
Rucker, Weldon Leander, 206
Rulin, Mr., 221
Rush, Col., 260
Russell, Pearl, 200
Ryan, Jerry, 270, 273
Ryan, Pvt., 6
Ryan, Thomas, 297, 298

Salt Creek Prairie, 62
Salt Fork of the Brazos River (see also Brazos River), 54, 176
Salt Lake City, 266, 310, 325, 343
Salt Prong Creek, 235
Sanaco (see Senaco)
San Antonio, Texas, 4, 10, 23, 41, 51, 52, 56-59, 79, 104, 126, 127, 149,157, 174, 176, 197, 215, 224
San Carlos Reservation, 292
San Francisco, California, 151, 159
San Francisco County, Missouri, 220
San Pedro River, 277
San Saba, Texas, 305, 336
San Saba, Mission and Presidio of, 126
San Saba River, 75
Santa Anna (Indian), 26
Santa Fe, New Mexico, 126, 127, 144, 204, 232
Santa Fe Trail, 228, 241
San-ta-na (widow of), 89-90
Santiago, Cuba, 60
Satanta (Kiowa), 62, 305, 306, 336, 337
Satonka (Kiowa), 306
Say-es (Apache prisoner), 282-289, 291
Saylor, S.C., 277

Scarborough, George, 230
Scott, Gen. Winfield, 72
Sebastian, Charlie, pictured 254
Secession Convention (Texas), 56, 136
Selman, John, 137, 161, 165, 166, 230
Selman, Lucinda, 140
Selman, Sam, 260
Seminole Scouts, 175
Seminole War, 70, 301
Senaco (Comanche; also spelled Sanaco, Se-na-ca), 20-24, 73, 75-81, 86-89, 96, 97, 99, 131, 133
Seymour, Texas, 247
Shackelford County, Texas, 11, 19, 164, 167, 171, 178, 188, 202, 204, 207, 208, 117, 125-151, 217, 227, 235, 255, 256, 311, 314-316, 318, 325, 326, 346, 348
Shaw, Jim, 24
Shelby County, Texas, 301, 302, 315, 333
Sherman, Texas, 165
Sherman, Gen. William T., 62
Shipwell Ranch, 252
Shoffitt, Louis, 257
Sibley, Capt. H.H., 130
Sieber, Al, 267, 281
Sierra Anchos Ranch, 293
Signal Mountain, 182
Simonds, Vol, 147
Simpson, Green, 208
Simpson, John, 245
Slaughter, W.B., 190
Sloan, Bob, 159, 235
Smith, Capt. E. Kirby, 56
Smith, Hank, 242, 243
Smith, Frank, 165
Snalum Creek, 159
Snow, George, 166
South Concho River, 232
South Platte River, 252
Souther, Mr., 137
Southerland, Billy, 161
Southern Overland Mail (see Butterfield Stage)
Southern Trail (see Chisholm Trail)
Spanish-American War, 60
Spangler, Sgt. John W., 54
Spears, Nelse, 237
Spearsville, Louisiana, 316
Spiller, E.B., 266

Stage Line Creek, 159
State Department (US), 293, 298, 299, 329
Staked Plains, 321
Steele, J.G., 137
Steele Family, 161
Steen, E., 80
Stem, Jesse, 129-132, 141
Stephens County, Texas, 11, 137, 148, 150, 170, 188, 201, 209, 227-229, 253, 301, 302, 334
Stephenville, Texas, 172
Stevens, Bob, pictured 254
Stewart, Strawn & Bartholemew, 172
St. James Hotel, 342
St. John, Riley, 228, 232, 305
St. Louis, Missouri, 10, 58, 59, 151, 159
Stockton, Tom, 228
Stoneman, Capt. George, 28, 49, 51, 70
Straight Fellow (Indian), 89, 91
Strawn, Belliol, 172
Strawn, Texas, 172
Stribling, Callie, 196
Stribling, C.K., house of pictured 119, 159, 174
Sturgis, Col. Samuel D., 4, 62, 163
Sutherlin Family, 230
Suvench, Vol, 202
Sweetwater Creek, 53

Tanima Comanches (see also Comanches), 25, 81
Tarter, Wesley, 180
Tasker, Charles, 243
Tawakonis (To-wac-ko-nies), 19, 21, 74, 105
Taylor, John, pictured 254
Taylor County, Texas, 177, 227, 232
Tecumseh Creek, 162, 167, 174, 192, 233
Tenawa (Ta-na-wa) Comanches, 131
Tepe City, Texas, 243, 244
Texas, Military Department of (US), 4, 12
Texas Rangers, 36, 54, 233, 328, 336, 347
Thomas, Maj. George H., 53, 54
Thornton, Nancy, 218

Thorp (Thorpe) Jim, 137, 161, 196, 229, 235
Thorp, Susan, 196
Throckmorton, Texas, 160, 161, 169, 171, 196, 197, 257, 260
Throckmorton County, Texas, 9, 11, 19, 133, 148, 158, 162, 166, 167, 169, 175, 178, 192, 202, 208, 210, 227, 233, 234, 240, 247, 248, 251, 311, 314, 337, 348
Tiger Jim, 218
To The Last Man, 255
Tonkawas (Tonkaways, Ton-kah-was),105, 175, 196
Tonkawa Scouts, 8, 9, 60, 74, 86
Trammell, Francis, 205
Trammell, William M., 205
Treadwell, James M., 199
Treadwell Family, 199
Treadwell Survey, 198
Trinity River, 19
Tucker, Tom, 255, 260
Tucson, Arizona, 277, 294, 296-298
Turkey Track Outfit, 241
Tuton, Lee, pictured 112, 222, 224
Tuton, Susie Ledbetter, 222
Twiggs, Gen. David E., 55, 56

Unexplored Texas, 74
Union Pacific Railroad, 258, 267
United States Military Academy (West Point), 67, 70, 71

Van Camp, Lt. Cornelius, 26
Van Dorn, Maj. Earl, 49, 50, 70
Vial, Pedro, 126-127
Vigilance (Vigilante) Committees:
    Fort Griffin, 114-117, 163, 165, 166, 230
    Pueblo, 242

W O O Outfit, 255
Waco, Texas, 140, 226
Waco Register, 2
Wacos, 21
Walker, Breck, 171
Walker, Judge, 171
Walnut Creek, 160, 174, 234

Ward, Samuel J., 196, 197
Warren, Henry, 62
Warren Wagontrain Massacre (see also Elm Creek), 62, marker pictured 63, 64
Washington, DC, 10, 32, 35, 38, 52, 55, 60, 76, 77, 83, 95, 222, 223, 293, 329, 347
Washita River, 40, 247, 255
Washita Valley, 135
Waxahachie, Texas, 222, 224
Weatherford, Texas, 59, 140, 148, 166, 173, 176, 232, 238, 239, 244, 266, 302, 307, 309, 310, 313, 324, 333, 334, 336, 338, 341
Webb, W.H., 183
Webb & Hill Outfit, 256
Weldon Railroad, Battle of (1864; spelled Welden in text), 58
Wesley, Robert, 220
Wesley, S.W. (John Weatley; see also Ledbetter, John Calvin), 150, 214, 215, pictured 216, 219-224
Western Trail, 106, 116
West Point (see United States Military Academy)
Wheeler, J., 137
Whitall, John A., 48
White, Tonkawa, 226
Whiting, Lt. Col. Charles J., 49, 51, 70
Wichita, Kansas, 267
Wichita River, 53, 74, 85
Wichitas, 79, 99, 104, 105
Wilderness, Battle of the (1864), 58
Williams, Maria, 230
Williams, James, 64
Wilson, Billy, 265
Wilson, Lt. Henry H., 4
Wilson, Mr., 140
Witby, Tom, pictured 254
Wolfley, Lewis, 293, 298, 299
Wool, Gen. John, 70
Wooton, Dick, 345
Wright, Min, 228
Wyoming Stock Growers Association, 263

X I T Outfit, 257-259

Yamparika (Yamarika) Comanches, 25, 83, 131
Yellow Horse Canyon, 167, 174, 175
Yellowstone River, 311, 347, 348
Young County, Texas, 11, 19, 35, 128, 171, 185, 188, 228, 305
York & Company Store, 108, 195
Yuma, Arizona, and prison at, 209, 256, 278, 279, 282

Zellewager Ranch, 290

www.ingramcontent.com/pod-product-compliance
Lightning Source LLC
Chambersburg PA
CBHW030301080526
44584CB00012B/391